PAGANINI

by
RENÉE DE SAUSSINE

foreword by
JACQUES THIBAUD

translated by
MARJORIE LAURIE

GREENWOOD PRESS, PUBLISHERS
WESTPORT, CONNECTICUT

PAGANINI

PREFACE

"I can find no base for this column of flame and cloud," wrote Goethe, when he had heard Paganini for the first time in Weimar in 1829, "I can only say that I was aware of some meteoric sounds, which I have not yet succeeded in interpreting. . . ."

To us, a century after his death, that romantic column remains a mystery. Those trails of fire from a meteoric career are now seized upon by critics, authors, and historians. A haze of legend surrounds the great violinist, whom all Europe believed to be possessed of the devil.

There was no other explanation possible, they declared, for his infernal skill, the long procession of adoring women, the infatuation of entire nations. Actuated by vanity or credulity, Paganini bore on his lean shoulders the double inheritance of Orpheus and Don Juan. The legend of Faust, which was beginning to spread through Italy, contributed to the Mephistophelian aspect of the virtuoso, without actually defining the details of a possible pact.

From the æsthetic point of view, Paganini's music has, in general, been severely criticized. Like Liszt, the composer is penalized for the triumphs of the executant. And as a composer Paganini was by no means the equal of Liszt or Chopin. But without him there might never have been a Liszt, a Chopin.

Let us leave the "meteoric" gift, which galvanized those young musicians and influenced their careers, and, in the case of Liszt, inspired compositions that have become classics. We will seek in Paganini that mysterious thing, which, in a poet, constitutes the creative value of a work of art: his "Line." What is meant by that term? Jean Cocteau supplies the answer:

"It is life itself. By 'line' I understand the permanence of personality. It is expressed in the glance of the eyes, the quality of the voice, the gestures, the gait, the entire physical structure of the creative artist. It implies a force which directs a man's whole nature."

(Oh that silhouette of Paganini's which baffled a whole generation of portrait painters!)

"In the case of a composer," the author of *Orpheus* continues, "thanks to a somewhat rare phenomenon, it is possible now and then to catch a glimpse of this phantom line. It becomes incarnate in a melody, when the melody is so closely wedded to the movement of the line that it becomes an integral part of it."

Such, in brief, was Paganini's mode of expression. Like a thunderstorm, it was both visible and audible. His *Moto Perpetuo* resembled forked lightning, while his *Sonata Napoleon*, his *Campanella*, had the freshness, the brilliant hues of a rainbow. Virtuosity is born of these rich but conflicting elements, which it has to reconcile and illuminate. The rest can be left to the genius of the art, the sense of rhythm and harmony, that is to say, to the impressive handling of a typically romantic product: the artist who is both virtuoso and composer.

There remains the purely instrumental problem. This has never been solved. The famous secret, which according to Schottky, none of the Conservatoires of Music succeeded in divining, is buried in Paganini's grave. He had intended, when he was weary of journeys and concerts, to explain his method to the world. "It would enable a young man to achieve in three years the same degree of perfection which, by ordinary methods, would entail ten years of drudgery."

The promise was never fulfilled. The enigma has survived its propounder; the detective story is left unfinished. The clue to the mystery is lacking: his manuscripts are scattered all over the world, and lost. Only the testimony of his contemporaries remains to us, together with a voluminous correspondence, in which technical details are mingled with the wildest poetical rhapsodies. It is with the help of such materials, in which fact and legend are mingled, that I have endeavoured to revive the "flames," the "clouds," popularly supposed to have had their origin either in heaven or hell, which surrounded the figure of the maestro and perhaps nurtured his genius. The correspondence already alluded to, which has been collected in a masterly work (*Paganini Intimo*) by Professor Arturo Codignola, has proved a vital source of information. I have to acknowledge gratefully information contributed by the Countess Pecci-Blunt, owner of the Villa Bacciochi at Marlia; Professor E. P. Curtius of the Roman Seminary at the University of Bonn; Count Bérenger de Miramon Fitz-James, of the Academy of Marseilles,* and the invaluable advice afforded by Monsieur Jacques Prodhomme, former director of our libraries of the Conservatoire and the Opera.

For the illustrations, I have to express once more my gratitude to Professor Arturo Codignola. Through his kind offices, I was able to obtain contributions from the Museum of Genoa (in the house of Paganini's birth), and that of Parma (portrait of Elisa Bacciochi, Grand Duchess of Tuscany), etc. I owe the charming silhouette of the child Nicolò to the kindness of the learned Professor Indrich Kott of Prague, the distinguished author of the Czecho-Slovac version, *Paganini carodêj*.

RENÉE DE SAUSSINE

* *Paginini in Marseilles*, Fuéri, Marseilles.

CONTENTS

LIST OF ILLUSTRATIONS

FOREWORD IN THE FORM OF A LETTER

My Dear Friend,

My aim is to present the illustrious figure of Nicolò Paganini in all simplicity. Novelists, historians, imaginative writers with a leaning to the fantastic, are free to interpret him according to their bias. The legend of Paganini, like the river of life in spate, has risen beyond the confines of probability and reason, and the flood has carried his name across two continents, from the sun-baked south to the frozen north. For my part, I recognize that the astounding art of technique, invented by this great man, who amazed all Europe and the whole civilized world, might well seem to have its root in the supernatural, where magic and witchcraft meet. Yet I confess that I am not sufficiently superstitious to invoke the devil on his behalf. It is enough for me to conjure up the man himself, who was an incomparable master of the language of art.

One cannot but recognize the genius of this man, who not only created a new style of playing, but showed the way to boundless developments in the sphere of violin technique. His genius was seconded by incredible virtuosity, which anticipated all the musical art of the future. His fame, which was endorsed by the enthusiasm of the multitude, often astonishingly discerning, has never ceased to dazzle our eyes. His compositions, which are of such infinite variety, such vital originality, will, I trust, always receive their meed of respect and admiration. Not only from the instrumental point of view, but also from that of the thematic, they appear to me to bear the imprint of that quality, which so often earned for them the epithet "divine."

In instrumental art, Paganini forms a double link between the classical-romantic and the modern style. He was a century ahead of contemporary writers of violin music. I am convinced that his inventions, his discoveries, his happy creations, influenced the technical possibilities of universal orchestration. Illustrious composers, such as Robert Schumann, Johann Brahms, Berlioz, Franz Liszt, not only admired him but often drew from him their inspiration. They did not hesitate to transform certain of his violin compositions into masterpieces for the piano. No man, no artist, was ever worthier of the attention of biographers. If he appeared to draw his inspiration from the realm of the supernatural, it is all the more essential, all the more instructive, to analyze the potency of his purely human gifts. That, dear friend, is why this study of Paganini, so suggestive, so full of colour, which you, yourself a magnificent violinist, have consecrated to his memory, deserves a warm welcome and every success. I congratulate you whole-heartedly. I am convinced that, besides the pleasure your work will give your readers, it will advance the glory, the vital grace of art . . . art, which is perhaps the only truth in the Universe.

JACQUES THIBAUD

"This man with the long black hair and the pale countenance, opens to us with his violin a world which we had never imagined, except perhaps in dreams. There is in his appearance something so supernatural that one looks for a glimpse of a cloven hoof or an angel's wing."

Leipziger musikalische Zeitung. No. 38. 1829

PART I ITALY

THE DREAM

IT WAS about this time," Paganini used to say, repeating his words emphatically, "it was about this time that the Saviour appeared to my mother in a dream."

What did the vision signify? A birth and a destiny, which were to be ordered and governed under the auspices of that mysterious sign? Not one of Paganini's biographers has ventured to pass over the incident in silence.

But even in earlier days there had been much in this region to attract lovers of the mysterious. Of all the countries rich in fascinating legends, it was Northern Italy that bore the palm— superstitious Italy with its maledictions, its raptures, its carnivals, its violins, its romances, its angels, its singers, its villas, its princes. No one in Italy, from the most illustrious prince to the humblest fisherman, would have deemed it strange, that He, the Spellbinder, whose name they were loath to utter, should have been born in the *Passo di Gatta Mora*, the Close of the Black Cat.

Genoa is a city of contrasts. It has its famous gaily coloured palaces, but in the heart of the quarter which lies between the port and the Cathedral, there is a narrow squalid street, with steps running down the middle. Here all day long the seafaring sounds from the harbour mingle with the homely bustle from the market square. All this region from the *Casa di Colombo*, the house of Christopher Columbus, which is only a stone's throw away, teems with life—a life that is full of colour and rich in odours. But if, after nightfall, the traveller revisits these

3

cutthroat alleys, this relic of the violent Middle Ages, all is deserted. There is nothing to guide him, except a gleam of white from the wash flapping at the windows, or the glimmer of a light behind the grating of a tiny shrine, or a drainpipe disgorging its filth. Overhead, the tall houses, with the plaster peeling off them, seem to threaten the sky. The crumbling steps are strewn with refuse of every description. The whole place reeks of filth, fear, and devilry.

But even between the years 1782–1790, the period to which Paganini, in a brief autobiography, ascribed his early childhood, the Paganinis, although they lived in this squalid quarter, were by no means destitute. According to their genealogy, which they could trace back until about 1700, they might have been described as decent humble folk belonging to the lower middle classes. They were, however, somewhat eccentric in their tastes. Antonio, the head of the family, actually owned at Polcevera, a suburb of Genoa situated on the river of that name, a small house called *Ramajona*, which must certainly have been a pleasanter abode than the hovel in the *Passo*. Polcevera possessed a quarry which provided the choicest marble for the handsomest altars in Italy's finest cathedrals. Below it lay the coastline with Pegli, Sanpierdarena, and Genoa itself. The Corniche Road embraced a panorama, enveloped in a bluish haze, of Genoa the Superb, spread out like sumptuous tapestry. But Antonio preferred the odours and noises of the port, where he was employed as a *ligaballe*, a packer who corded up bales of merchandise for ships of every nation. They arrived with news of the outer world, and presently, heavily laden, proceeded on their voyage to America or the East. Each departure was accompanied by the same commotion: the endless manœuvring, the clanking of anchor chains, the cries of raucous voices shouting farewell. After their work was done, the packers, bathed in sweat, would go off to quench their thirst in one of those semi-subterranean taverns which, in the past, had served as refuges during the raids of the Saracens. There, in these later days, Chianti and fried octopuses awaited them, and they could pick up surreptitious tips about likely numbers in the forthcoming lottery. Antonio, with his brown face and low forehead, would lean on the counter, gaily thrumming an accompaniment on his mandolin to his comrades' singing. In the town register he was entered as a professional mandolin player, which in the census taken during Napoleon's régime, was translated as "keeper of amandolines."

Like her husband Antonio, Teresa, *née* Bocciardi, and often referred to as la Bocciardi, had her head full of music, but it was music of a different kind. Although Genoa, once the rival of Venice, could not compete with the operas of San Samuele, San Benedetto, and the still more celebrated operas of Milan, Rome, Florence, and Naples, it managed to remain in the swim. Teresa met in the market and in friends' houses, people who travelled a little and who all returned home dazzled by the splendour of the great new Scala in Milan, all white and red and gold, which poured forth music of the same brilliant hues. They would stroll along the streets, lustily singing, in unison or in parts, airs from Paisiello's *Barber of Seville* or snatches from Cimarosa's sparkling burlesques. Other enthusiasts preferred purer forms of music. As soon as they had finished their business in the fish market, they would hurry away to scrape the violin or viola in a quartet by Boccherini, and engage in endless discussions about bows and virtuosi. At the court of Turin there was said to be a brilliant violinist, Gaetano Pugnani by name, who was famous throughout Europe but made himself ridiculous by his inordinate vanity. He was always dressed in a little frock coat of blue silk, with a bouquet of flowers pinned to his chest. He had assumed the title of "The Caesar of the Violin." Was he really the equal of Tartini, his illustrious master, who, thanks to a dream, had no less a person than the devil himself at his beck and call? Such is the story as Tartini himself told it to the astronomer Lalande:

"One night, in the year 1713, I dreamt that I had made a pact with the devil, who took service with me. Everything went swimmingly. My new servitor anticipated every one of my wishes. I amused myself one day by lending him my violin to see if he could play me some attractive tunes. To my amazement I heard a sonata so strange, so exquisitely beautiful, played with such consummate skill that it transcended all I had ever imagined. Such was my rapture that my breath failed me. The feeling of suffocation was so intense that it awoke me. I snatched up my violin to try to recapture at least a part of that which I had heard. But in vain. Certainly the piece I then composed was the finest of all my works and ever afterwards I called it the 'Devil's Sonata.' But it fell so far short of the one I had heard in my dream that, had it been possible, I would have broken my violin and abandoned music forever."

A pact with the devil! Teresa had to tear herself away from such tales, which held for her an ever present temptation.

The Palazzo Durazzo, where visiting musicians gave concerts, which were known as *Accademias*, was another source of temptation to Teresa. She had to force herself away from its seductive posters. There was the soup to be prepared for Antonio and the children. Her head was ringing with snatches of tunes, while wonderful tales, all white and red and gold, mingled with her dreams.

But no one would ever hear that music, for la Bocciardi, poor soul, had no talent. For his part, Antonio sang out of tune and had no idea of time. Carlo, their elder boy, had been taught the violin, but at nine years old he was nothing more than a satisfactory pupil and a fair musician. There remained the baby, Nicoletta, aged one, and finally their younger son, Nicolò.

Nicolò! Ah, Nicolò! At the thought of him Teresa crossed herself, so deep was her feeling for this child of hers. Would she ever succeed in rearing him? Although he was not yet six, he had often been at death's door. He was so fragile, so terribly fragile. His reaction to the least emotion, especially that caused by music, was so violent that he was threatened with convulsions. His eyes would sparkle feverishly in his pale face framed with dark curls. The slightest mistake on the part of Antonio, who was teaching him the mandolin in the evenings, roused him to fury. At the sound of bells he would burst into a prolonged fit of sobbing. When he was taken to the Cathedral he would tremble violently all over with rapture at the sound of the organ, while his skin, which was remarkably delicate in texture, would break into a profuse perspiration, exposing him to chills, colds, and bronchitis, which he had not the strength to resist.

Just a year ago, as he was playing on Carlo's little fiddle to the delight of all the urchins in the street, he was suddenly stricken with catalepsy, the after effects, the doctors considered, of an attack of measles. He remained for nearly forty-eight hours as rigid as if he were dead. In fact his parents, dissolved in tears, had gone so far as to prepare his shroud.

As Teresa went about her household tasks, she trembled lest that unknown world from which her child had barely escaped with his life, should yet spirit him away. Doubtless it was a world of mystery, darkness, and fear. Yet perhaps it had its own peculiar joys. It might well be that those swelling organ notes to which Nicolò listened, wide-eyed with wonder, were the language of that country. Yet earthly life, too, was fair, with its sunshine and its spring. How intoxicating it must be to inspire universal admiration and devotion like the great artists of whom her friends had told her! Surely it would be worth while, even if, like Tartini, one made a pact. . . .

Thus musing, she would continue her work mechanically, or fix her unseeing gaze on some trifling object.

"She is in one of her trances," the neighbours would say.

❧ There were many different versions of the dream that visited Teresa. The details, which the neighbours repeated, originated with her, but had been passed from one to the other, distorted and elaborated by many commentators. Perhaps Teresa herself had unconsciously varied her story with each new listener, until her own recollections became confused. But it was generally agreed that Nicolò was five years old at the time of the dream.

According to some versions a winged creature, a genie, had appeared to la Bocciardi in her sleep, and had hovered above the head of her son. According to others (and this was the story that, later, Paganini himself vouched for) the Saviour Himself had visited her in a dream and had bidden her ask of Him a boon.

The final version was a medley of many rumours and surmises. Teresa was wafted in a trance to a great gloomy theatre which was filled with mysterious music. The soloist was Nicolò himself, grown tall and strong, and his music had a triumphant rhythm.

But who was that other figure, that venerable maestro who was conducting the orchestra? At first she had taken him for Tartini, but gradually—and surely it was not merely the footlights—he became surrounded by a shining halo, which sent out rays of splendour. His gestures guided a chorus of voices, so exquisitely tender that it brought tears to the eyes. But yonder on the stage, a hostile figure with a guitar in his hand stood behind Nicolò, and fought the Master for him, note by note.

This personage was slim, dark, and lame. He was dressed in red from head to foot and there were horns upon his brow.

"*Santa Maria!*" exclaimed Teresa. At her cry everyone vanished: the maestro, her son, and the Devil himself—for the Devil it certainly was. The theatre was filled with dense smoke, which was dispersed now and then by witches in headlong flight, who brushed against la Bocciardi and collided with the clanging chandeliers. How long had the theatre been burning? An hour? An eternity? Where the guitarist had stood, she saw a monster with sharp-edged scales, who might well have been responsible for the conflagration, for he was belching forth foam and fire. She could see his fiery breath, and the leaping flames, and the particles of charred wood floating about in the air. Then the roof burst with the heat, and through the wide cracks she could see the sky, faintly luminous.

Suffocated by the smoke, she was losing consciousness when suddenly the reddish mist that had filled the theatre took shape and assumed a face and form, such as she had sometimes seen in the clouds. And this radiant being lifted her on balmy wings and wafted her upwards. His face was that of an angel.

Per Bacco! If there were sceptics who sneered and went away, there were others who remained to hear the end of Teresa's vision. She had, they learned, addressed that dazzling countenance. She had pleaded for the future of her son while she was still borne upwards in the angel's arms. And his flight and her own prayer were sustained by the singing of that divine choir. They reached the great roof, which was supported by four winged genii each with a golden trumpet. Within the blackened walls, the choir burst into a hymn, in which the words, "song, glory, love, and gold," were woven into a perfect harmony.

Overwhelmed with emotion, she stretched out her hands. But at that moment the air began to quiver as in an earthquake. She was snatched from the arms of her rescuer and hurled to the ground like a stone. She saw the cracks in the ceiling widen until it was split right across from the gallery to the upper boxes, and through this gap the angel escaped with his cloud of music. High in the air, hovering above the tottering theatre, she could see the balconies crashing down into the darkness.

The next morning Teresa awoke with her head on the flagstones of the floor. She was haunted by confused memories of her dream.

"An angel," she said to her younger son, "appeared to me last night in all his splendour, and he said to me that whatever I prayed for should be granted. So I prayed that you might become the greatest violinist in the world, and he promised that my prayer should be heard."

THE PASSO DI GATTA MORA

Nicolò's earliest memories dated from that Annunciation. Teresa herself drew new strength from this story of hers, which she told so often, while to the child it embodied all the magic of music. Music was to become his own language, developing with Nicolò himself, absorbing his experiences. It was like his own slangy vocabulary, containing both good and evil, that which was permitted and that which was forbidden. It was part of him, like the circulation of his blood. Like his mother, he loved to wander about the streets, picking up tunes and rhythms, which mingled with his childish thoughts and were woven into enchanting harmonies, in a setting of sunshine, songs, oranges, and boyish escapades.

He was to be found playing in the tarry harbour with boys of his own age, his feet bare, and the hairs of his violin bow quivering in the wind—a ragged little urchin, still with the same frail limbs, the onyx eyes, large nose, and girlish complexion.

But now Antonio took him in hand. Nicolò was subjected to a course of methodical training. He would hear a heavy tread on the steps of the *Passo*, and his father would come in twirling a leather strap. There was to be no more larking about with his merry playmates. Nicolò was shut up in his room and made to work.

"When I was seven," wrote Paganini, "I received my first violin lessons from my father. He had no ear, but was passion-

11

ately fond of music. Within a month or two I was able to play some pieces of music by sight."

Antonio, too, had conceived the idea of making his son a virtuoso, and Nicolò was soon undergoing the classic training of an infant prodigy. If he did not practise, he was beaten and starved. But there were occasions when Antonio showed him off to his friends. Then he was petted and perched on the table at dessert, where he stood like a statue, surrounded with cakes and sweets. When there were musicians present, they were astonished at the boy's ability. But Nicolò missed his audience of street urchins. After the performance, he went back to his scales, to raps with the bow, and scoldings.

Before long he had outstripped Antonio, who handed him over to a master of the name of Cervetto, who was a sound violinist and played in the theatre orchestra. Cervetto had a weakness for exercises in which the fingers remained on the strings, and he was always exclaiming: "Don't lift the third finger. Don't lift the third finger!"

Normal difficulties hardly existed for this boy. He was obliged to invent new ones for himself. Disregarding ordinary rules, he coaxed from the upper register of the violin tender sounds like the twittering of a nest full of young birds. The silver G string seemed to link him like a shining thread of gossamer to Teresa's dream, and he composed a solemn hymn for it. He would spend hour after hour studying and mastering new problems until he was exhausted, partly, perhaps, because he had been beaten or starved. Then a shudder, which was strangely voluptuous, would creep over his skin.

Presently the black and white Duomo, the Cathedral of San Lorenzo, standing aloft on its hill, became a part of his life. "At eight and a half I played a Concerto by Pleyel in a church. I received thirty lessons in six months from Master Costa, the first violin."

But in addition to his work under Costa, who was choir-

master at the Duomo and at Sant' Ambrogio, he steeped himself in all the ceremonies of the Cathedral: the pomp, the
processions, the lilies, and the mystic language of the organ,
until at times he swooned with fervour. He played at least
three times a week at church festivals, and when his repertoire
was exhausted, he delighted in giving definite form to the
vague music that was floating about inside his head. Had not
Mozart, when he was scarcely older than himself, written a
concerto for piano with an accompaniment of trumpets and
trombones, which was so difficult that the executants protested? He, too, would express himself in his own idiom.

Under Francesco Gnecco of Genoa, who was a good musician, he studied harmony, and his first Sonata was written
when he was eight years old (1790).

In San Lorenzo all was peace: Advent and Lent, Lent and
Advent followed each other in due rotation. By way of contrast,
news of tumultuous events came pouring across the frontier.
The French Revolution was at its height, and was a much
discussed topic in Genoa. Even little Nicolò, returning home
from his pious duties in the church, his *funzioni* as he called
them, amused himself by writing variations on *La Carmagnole*,
a revolutionary song which had a great vogue in Genoa.

The Duchy of Genoa, the Republic of the Doges, was,
however, still to enjoy a few years' grace before it was super-
seded by Bonaparte's new and more democratic republic.
Five years after Paganini had written his first Sonata it was
still possible for Marchesi, one of the greatest of male sopranos,
to disembark at Genoa and to give a concert—an unequalled
treat for all lovers of *bel canto*. Italy, always passionately devoted to music, continued to sing and dance on the revolutionary volcano. And in that gay aviary the favourite kind of
singing, the timbre of voice that was specially appreciated was
that of *soprani castrati*, such as Marchesi.

Until the eighteenth century, women had been forbidden

by the Pope to appear on the stage, and in consequence the male sopranos had reigned supreme. Now they had to accept the new conditions and share the principal roles with women singers.

Often enough, however, the real *prime donne* were ousted in favour of their equivocal male rivals, with their melodious and penetrating voices, who had become indispensable to their admirers. The Sistine Chapel continued to employ castrati, with their boyish voices, while at the theatre the public did not hesitate to hiss any *prima donna* who had taken the place of a favourite male soprano. Their patrons fought for their services. Princes coveted them for their private chapels, impresarios for their concerts, and even foreign courts put in a claim. In the old days, Charlemagne was given a mechanical clock as an act of homage, but Christina of Sweden, who was a great *connoisseuse*, was actually supposed to have demanded one of these wondrous freaks of nature as a condition of granting a treaty. At the beginning of the eighteenth century the most celebrated castrato of all, Carlo Broschi, known as Farinello or Farinelli, made such a complete conquest of Puritan and prejudiced England that for a long time no other singer could hold his own with him. The first time Farinelli appeared on the London stage, his rival, another soprano of the name of Senesino, forgot that he was playing the part of the cruel tyrant, and, bursting into tears of emotion, threw himself into Farinelli's arms.

As a climax to all these triumphs, Philip V, in the hope that that heavenly voice might assuage his neurasthenia, had carried off the "divine Farinelli" and attached him to the court of Spain. From being the King's confidant he rose to the rank of minister, and long after the death of Philip, the royal favour was continued to him by his successor Ferdinand V.

It is not so many years since those days when Italy lavished the most doting care on rearing those rare songsters. Nothing was too good for them, not the most spacious, the most efficient training school in the world.

"In the college of Naples," whote Dr. Burney, "there are sixteen young castrati, whose apartments are kept warmer than those of the other boys for fear they should catch cold.

"They are allowed only a few days' holiday once a year, in the autumn. In the winter these children rise two hours before daybreak and begin their exercises, which continue till eight o'clock at night, with the sole interruption of an hour and a half for dinner."

At the school in Rome, where the training was completed, general culture formed part of the curriculum. The day began with an hour which was devoted to practising specially difficult and complicated passages. This was followed by a literature lesson. After this came vocalizing under a master's eye, in front of a mirror, for training body, forehead, eyelids, mouth in the most appropriate gestures. Next came harmony, composition, counterpoint, and plain-song. Then they had to accompany each other on the harp, write a motet, go out to practise singing in the open air, and to listen critically to the echo of their own voices "outside the Porte Angélique, near Monte Mario." Finally they had to sing in church, and to listen attentively to the greatest virtuosi of the day, so that they could imitate their technique to the satisfaction of their exacting master.

But once the Draconian training was completed and the finished product appeared on the stage, they were allowed every conceivable liberty. They would indulge in incredible ribaldry. With amazing facility they would read off and sing a new composition, adding improvisations of their own, and substitute the trills of a nightingale for what the outraged composer had written.

In the brilliantly lighted hall, filled to overflowing in their honour, under the approving eyes of their protectors (often a

Cardinal of Rome, whose bountiful gifts of palaces, villas, and the like were too numerous to be reckoned), intoxicated by the ovations of the enraptured public, they would be guilty of the most glaring eccentricities, the most flagrant absurdities.

When the sopranos played the role of *prima donna*, they had necessarily to be dressed as women. They would flaunt their jewels, their satins, their feathers, their chubby arms, and roll their languishing, made-up eyes. They would talk to the prompter, make signs to the audience, and beat time to the music with fan or sceptre. Sometimes they would take snuff and unfasten the collars of their gowns "to sing more at their ease." Indeed "some of these ladies," it was said, "were half undressed by the time they left the stage."

Sometimes they took male parts. Julius Caesar elected to roll at the base of Pompey's statue in patent-leather shoes with red heels and diamond buckles. He wore emerald clasps and false hips, and his face was framed in flowing, powdered curls. The famous Marchesi, who was more virile than the others, made his appearance, standing at the top of a sloping stage, clad in all the pomp and panoply of war. He was arrayed in "a plumed helmet, carried a spear and buckler and was announced by a fanfare of trumpets. After this he would embark upon one of his favourite arias, generally one borrowed from another opera." *

◀ But Marchesi was not in his war-paint nor was he accompanied by a fanfare of trumpets when, correctly dressed in an embroidered waistcoat, he entered the Duomo, the Sunday after his arrival in Genoa. The usual sacred concert was proceeding, but what was that strange liquid music that flooded the Cathedral and held all the faithful spellbound? Surely he was familiar with every voice and every instrument. He attempted to make a gesture and to break the compelling charm.

* Lord Derwent. Rossini.

The house of Paganini's birth

Paganini as a boy

But from a raised stand, two burning eyes glared down at him and bound him to the spot. He could see a hand, with hardly a change of position, running its fingers up and down the strings of a violin as if tracing the signs of a cabalistic algebra. Who could it be? The superstitious singer took a step forward, crossed himself and hurried from the Cathedral. The smell of incense, he said, had turned him faint.

Marchesi made inquiries. He had no difficulty in finding Antonio and obtaining his consent to his proposal. A concert was to be arranged and to be advertised in the *Avvisi di Genoa* for July 31, 1795. The star performers would be himself and Madame Albertinotti of Bologna, who were both on tour in Genoa, while the Genoese would have the opportunity of hearing their infant prodigy, young Paganini, of whom the whole town was talking eight years ago, make his *début* in a concert of the utmost distinction.

Nicolò sat with drawn face huddled up in a corner of the shabby, dusty, green-room. He was more emaciated, more transparent than ever. Teresa was so overcome with emotion that she had hidden herself, while Antonio prowled about between the box-office and the hall, keeping his eye on the receipts. Marchesi and Madame Albertinotti, who were first on the programme, were at the clavecin trying a few roulades. Nicolò was left alone.

At last they came for him. He took his violin bow and music. The raised platform was scrubbed white, like the deck of a ship, and at the edge, like a rim of fire, was the glare of the footlights. Standing there alone, with pinched nostrils, he thought he would die before he could make a sound. But the tiny impact of his first note broke the flaming nimbus that surrounded him. His variations fell like a shower of sparks into the darkened hall. The audience stirred. The unknown force that possessed him was multiplied by innumerable eyes that gazed, innumerable hands that clapped, innumerable hearts that beat—the plaudits of a great ovation. His mother! His mother's dream! At last he understood.

"But, Lord!" he murmured. "How terrifying is thine Angel!"

Drenched with sweat, he returned to the green-room, where he came to himself. What a crowd! What an uproar! And Teresa, where was Teresa? Marchesi had disappeared leaving a trail of perfume. But that tall gesticulating figure over there, near Antonio, was none other than the Marchese Gian Carlo Di Negro. Nicolò had played several times in the Marchese's *villeta*, which was already famous for the performances of the great Kreutzer. Its drawing-rooms were always crowded with celebrities, foreigners, and great ladies. At that moment Nicolò's whole future was at stake. Di Negro was arguing and becoming heated.

"That boy," he declared, "shall have the best masters that can be found."

PAGANINI'S FIRST TOURS; HIS "CAPRICES" *

THE proceeds of the concert enabled Paganini to travel in the interests of his musical training. Antonio accompanied him. His father's tutelage was becoming irksome to the boy, but Antonio would stand no nonsense. Two places were booked in the stage coach. Possibly Di Negro, who was enchanted with Nicolò's talent, would accompany them. Father and son set out for Florence.

In Florence, Salvatore Tinti, the composer, was astonished at the boy's Variations on *La Carmagnole*. But he was neither a professor nor head of a school of music and could do nothing for them. Almost immediately the Paganinis left Florence for Parma, where Rolla, a highly gifted violinist and composer, resided. Subsequently he became conductor and leader of the Scala orchestra in Milan. Besides Rolla, there was Paër, a German born in Parma, who had his own Conservatoire of Music. They thought that they might settle in this town.

When they called on him, Rolla was ill in bed. Those importunate strangers in the next room disturbed him. He was about to send them his excuses. . . .

* Op. 1. By their melodic inspiration and harmonic and technical boldness, these Caprices were to influence all virtuosi, not only of the violin, but of the piano.

In 1833 Schumann published in two volumes, twelve transcriptions of Paganini's Caprices, and later Six Concert Etudes, after Paganini's Caprices, Op. 10. Studies in Bravura, after Paganini's Caprices, arranged for the piano by Liszt, appeared in 1842.

At that moment the solo of his new Concerto, of which the manuscript, with the ink hardly dry, was lying on his desk, sounded through the adjoining room. The rendering was so fresh, so spontaneous, so true to the composer's own ideas, that the maestro jumped out of bed in amazement.

"I was reading the Concerto at sight," Nicolò recorded. "Rolla was greatly impressed. But instead of teaching me the violin, he advised me to study counterpoint with Maître Ghiretti, the Neapolitan, who was violoncellist to the Court, and had been master of Maître Paër himself. Ghiretti gave me three lessons a week and taught me counterpoint, using the pen alone, and keeping away from the instrument. He took such a fancy to me that he plied me with lessons. Under his auspices, I composed vast quantities of instrumental music. Two of my Concertos were performed at the Teàtro Grande, after I had played at Colorno and Sala to the King and Queen, who were staying on their country estates. They rewarded me handsomely. The owner of a Guarnerius violin said to me: 'If you can play this Concerto at sight, you shall have my Guarnerius.' I won it."

In this strange way, he was equipped for the battle, and stage by stage he continued his victorious career. The Paganinis remained two years in Parma, the town of Correggio. After this they spent many months travelling from place to place. By this time the boy's musical baggage was heavy—far outweighing the little bundle of personal possessions which he clutched so anxiously as he sat in the diligence. At each new halting place, Parma, Milan, Bologna, Florence, Pisa, Leghorn, there was one experience that he longed for, yet dreaded. It was to feel again upon his brow the breath of the angel of Genoa, to be transformed once more into the fiery medium that could kindle multitudes.

In this superheated atmosphere the childish mould was gradually cracking. He emerged from his concerts perspiring and exhausted, with a pulse that was hardly perceptible. This talent which he could feel growing within him to such colossal proportions, this talisman (for such it was) no longer opened the heavens to him as of old in San Lorenzo. He knew no more ecstasies, no more delicious tears. His childhood was dead. But now under those ornate theatre ceilings with their lavish decorations of lyres, hearts, fauns, and nymphs, where his life was spent, what use was he making of his liberty and his youth?

He was losing weight. He wished he had all the gold in the world, so that he might purchase his freedom from the paternal yoke. He longed for leisure, relaxation, pleasure, distractions. His thoughts turned to women. After his concerts they clustered around him petting him, embracing him, maternal tenderness mingling with their admiration.

A snore from Antonio banished these feverish dreams. Dawn was filtering through the window. In another hour they would take coach again. The motion of the diligence helped him to think clearly. He brooded on plans only to discard them with the passing scenes. One scheme, however, persisted. He was resolved to make a bid for freedom. Soon the annual musical fête would be celebrated at Lucca on St. Martin's Day. Lovers of music, Italians and foreigners, would be flocking thither. This famous festival attracted vast crowds. There would be celebrations, competitions, concerts. Should he take the opportunity to break away, to become his own master and find a place in the sun? But at the first hint, Antonio was up in arms.

❦ More formidable obstacles arose. When they returned to Genoa after an absence of three years, they found it in the grip of war. It was 1799. Time was marching on and with it the Napoleonic conquest. The new Ligurian Republic, by which Bonaparte replaced the ancient Duchy of Genoa, was fighting on his side against Austria. Masséna was holding out in the citadel and conducting a defence, which lasted till

1800 and became famous in history. The population of the city were suffering privations. Food was running short. Panic seized them as the spectre of famine and the nightmare threat of bombardment loomed before them.

The Paganinis moved to *Ramajona*, the "casino," the little house, owned by Antonio in the suburb of Polcevera. The family consisted of Teresa, as stout-hearted as ever, Antonio and his mandolins, Carlo, Nicolò's elder brother, who had become an accomplished violinist, the two little sisters, Nicoletta and Domenica, the latest born, and Nicolò himself, now in his seventeenth year. With their curly hair, their musical instruments, their squabbles, their dark eyes, they looked like a troop of gipsies arriving at Polcevera. They were to remain in this temporary abode for two years.

Balked of his escape, Nicolò threw himself heart and soul into his work. He allowed nothing to interrupt it, except an occasional expedition to Genoa, which siege conditions rendered difficult. His art was to console him for his frustrated plans.

"At this time I composed some very intricate music," he remarked. "I was constantly practising technical difficulties of my own invention, which I succeeded in mastering."

Antonio disapproved of his son's new tendencies and his increasing predilection for musical acrobatics. Nicolò had refused to join any of the schools and conservatoires which counted for so much in the cities of Italy. His eccentricities threatened to lose for him all the ground that he had gained. Why could he not follow the classical tradition? Antonio was continually punishing him.

But what was the loss of a favourite dish, or even a full meal, compared with the iron discipline which the young man imposed upon himself? Shut up in his room for eleven hours a day he grappled with adversaries, which hitherto no virtuoso had attempted to tackle.

What were these enemies? One was ponderousness, a problem on which he concentrated, mastering it by the extreme rapidity of his technique, achieving a supple balance, which became almost automatic. He set himself to capture the minds of his listeners before they had time to think. Natural laws were attacked with every weapon in his armoury: his *legato*, his *staccato*, his *spiccato*, his *sautillé*, until the victory was won. Then there was the factor of human resistance. Nicolò trained his muscles, as if they were soldiers, until they were proof against fatigue. His whole physique gradually adapted itself to his violin, which became part of him, co-operating with the organs of his body and finally dominating all of them. He strained his joints and overtaxed his brain, determining the physiological conditions of his whole future life, while he tracked down his quarry, the Impossible, to its last stronghold. Dawn would find him still on his feet, pale as a ghost, with bow or pen in his hand.

He was now better acquainted than Antonio with the whole realm of the violin and its dynasties, which embraced the last two centuries. He had the run of Di Negro's library and studied the old masters during these years of retirement. It was this library that was the object of his surreptitious visits to Genoa, which he made by night, with all the precautions of a *franctireur*. He brought back with him strange booty: manuscripts and documents which were the titles to fame of his illustrious predecessors, who had pitted their instruments against the human voice. He could now refer authoritatively to the great founder of his art: Arcangelo Corelli, beloved of Handel; to Corelli, whose honoured bones rest with those of Raphael in the Pantheon in Rome; to Corelli's pupil, Geminiani Veracini, whose style was as ardent and pure as a painting of Veronese; to Vivaldi the Venetian, surnamed *il prete rosso*, the red priest, who was said to have interrupted his mass to write down the theme of a concerto; to Vitali, Fiorillo,

Nardini, and Somis. Among more recent masters there were Tartini, the "builder" of the violin, Pugnani and his wonderful pupil Viotti, who had a school of his own in the North. In France there were Leclair, a pupil of Somis; Gavinisè; Kreutzer; in Germany Stamiz, who was Kreutzer's master. Among them there was only one ghostly father, Pietro Locatelli, with his *Arte di nuova modulazione,* called in the French edition *Caprices énigmatiques.*

He pondered on this new kind of modulation, which was suggestive and emotional. The tones were as varied as the expressions on a human countenance, and on this pivot turned the whole of the new technique. It was not a mere *tour de force,* but an intrinsically musical achievement, vital and stimulating.

In the works of the old masters the harmonic value was often of secondary importance, while the unexpected was of rare occurrence. Whether they appealed to the emotions or to the intellect, their works were as formal as the geometrically planned gardens in what is now known as the "French style." On the other hand he was aware that composers, who, like Haydn, Mozart, and Beethoven, belonged to no definite school, were free to follow their own impulses, especially in the *soli.* He would prove that an artist could identify himself with his instrument, and combine within himself every kind of reaction: muscular, melodic, harmonic, and poetic. In his modulations, he would soar to heights of virtuosity—like a bird of prey about to swoop on its quarry. The acrobatic suppleness of his frame, all that he had learnt from old Ghiretti, together with an imagination which had been set free by the asceticism of his family life, combined to achieve this result.

His Twenty-four Caprices flowed like visions from his pen. He was nineteen, and each of these Caprices symbolized a conquest of the world. He poured forth his treasure with open hands.

These Caprices of Paganini were the spring itself, stirring in the fibres of a violin, fauns with silver flutes in forest glades, hunting horns that replied, and startled the wild denizens of the wood; they were the footsteps of the year; the ponderous rhythm of horses' hoofs, mirthful villagers dancing to the airs of a hurdy-gurdy; a marriage feast; duets of lovers, voicing their bliss in passionate thirds.

But in the tenderest passages, there was always a strange undertone of cynicism.

❲ And now for life! It was high time. He would escape to Tuscany, to Lucca. He had done with childish fears. He would be off. October was already here in bright array. If he were not to be the last arrival at the fête of St. Martin's, there was no time to be lost. One evening, when he heard his brother Carlo's footsteps in the hall, he called him into his room. Far into the night, the neighbours could see the shadows of two heads, close together, bending over a map.

PRINCESSES

IN March 1805, Marie Elisa Bonaparte, Napoleon's eldest sister, had been crowned Princess of Lucca and Piombo. But in spite of her exalted rank Marie Elisa was bored.

No doubt in 1797, when she had married him and brought him to Paris, Captain Felix Bacciochi, with his classic features and wavy hair, had been more of an Adonis than he was now, while she herself had been only a girl of twenty. She was not beautiful like Pauline, Napoleon's youngest sister, whose features Canova had borrowed for his Venus Victrix, which was now in the Borghese Gallery in Rome. Still, she was attractive; she had fine shoulders, a sensual mouth, and a lively expression. Before long she had established a *salon*, which was eagerly frequented by men of intelligence and statesmen of the day, such as Châteaubriand, who came to her house to meet each other and to talk. This contented her for two years. Then Napoleon was crowned; the imperial fireworks began, and she aimed at higher things. A *salon* was all very well, but a court was even better.

But now that she was reigning in the little capital of Lucca, with its proud history, its jewels of churches adorned with exquisite mosaics, its great girdle of ramparts, she was homesick for Paris. Although she queened it over the fine flower of Tuscan nobility, it cannot be denied that Marie Elisa was bored.

Sometimes in the ducal palace, when she passed from the hall of mirrors to the balcony, where she stood leaning against the balustrade, the voices of her ladies-in-waiting would reach her ears. One day she listened idly to their prattle.

"The evening concert took place at the Capuchins," said one of the voices, "and when he had finished playing, the enthusiasm of the audience was so frantic that even the monks rushed from their stalls. . . ."

The speaker was Dida, a Florentine princess, who bore a name known to all the court. Elisa's attention was roused.

"Four years ago," Dida continued, "he ran away from home and went to Lucca, and competed at the fête of St. Martin. The republic of Lucca appointed him to be first virtuoso at the Theatre. But although he had the brain of a genius, he was still a mere child, who could not resist temptation. In spite of his official position, he was sometimes found in a swoon, as the result of too much love-making. At other times he would lose everything he possessed at the gaming tables, including his violin—just two hours before a concert. . . ."

"At Parma," broke in one of the other ladies, "he won a Stradivarius from Pasini the painter, who had challenged him to play at sight an appallingly difficult manuscript. . . . Much the same thing happened at Leghorn where he won from a French merchant, Monsieur Livron, a Guarnerius, the instrument he plays on at his concerts. On that occasion he had to play a Concerto of Viotti's by sight."

"A Swedish amateur," said a third, "who played the bassoon, complained that there was no music difficult enough for that instrument and commissioned Paganini to write some compositions for him. Paganini supplied his need."

"At the concerts at Santa Croce in 1801," said another, "people at first made fun of his long bow, his thick strings, and his excessively pale face. . . . But when he had finished playing, all the other competitors had fled in panic."

"Is he handsome?" asked one of the ladies.

"There are times," Dida replied, "when heaven is in his

eyes, and there are times when hell is there. He has curly hair like a woman's, his cadaverous form reminds one of certain insects. His skin is sometimes dry as if it were electrified; sometimes it is moist with pleasure, and its touch makes every other contact dull. There was once a woman who was so passionately in love with him that she carried him off to her castle. In her arms he forgot everything else in the world, Lucca, his post, and even his violin.

"He took up the guitar. Even agriculture seemed to have a charm for the pair, as they wandered through the Tuscan landscape with its bluish haze. He came back from these rambles with a Duetto Amoroso for guitar and violin humming in his head. This he dedicated to 'a lady of noble birth.' It was a duet between the two lovers and consisted of nine parts: *Beginning, Entreaties, Consent, Timidity, Satisfaction, Quarrel, Peace, Pledge, Leave-taking.** Its alternative title was 'Minuet for the French Guitar.' As his dedication confessed, he was for this woman 'her *implacabilissimo,* her most exacting friend, and her most obedient slave.' In any case," Dida said emphatically, "he is the Napoleon of violinists!"

Listening on her balcony Elisa was crimson with rage. The idea of comparing her brother to a mountebank! She slammed down the window behind her, and the voices were silenced.

Before long the Princess saw Paganini for herself and heard him play. She commanded him to conduct the Opera orchestra and to perform his own compositions. At the end of August 1805, the court had moved to Marlia, a favourite resort in the autumn months, in the neighbourhood of Lucca. Already Paganini was invited to all the court functions. The days passed swiftly for Elisa. She was now the envy of her ladies, as they sat gossiping in their boxes at the open-air theatre. The setting

---

* Now Op. 63. Op. 4 and 5, each consisting of Three Quartettes for violin, viola, cello, and guitar date from the same epoch (1804) and were probably composed at Genoa.

had a dreamlike beauty, and there were plays and concerts nearly every night. It was for her sake that he appeared, violin in hand, among the statues at the Comédie Italienne, with a face that was even paler than the marble. The moonlight sometimes betrayed him gliding ghostlike along the terrace towards her bedroom, where as scandal had it, Elisa awaited him, "quivering with love."

Elisa threw herself whole-heartedly into this wonderful new interest. She vowed to protect this strange lover from himself and to help him to achieve a glorious future. She had her reward. The realm of music was revealed to her, as his magic hands translated the language of love into that of art. She never ceased to stimulate both these passions.

"In my official capacity," Paganini recorded, "I had to play in both the weekly concerts. I always improvised. I would write a base for the piano and on this I would develop my theme. Once, about noon, the court demanded a Concerto for violin and English horn, to be performed that evening. The director of music protested that there was not sufficient time, so the task devolved on me. In two hours I wrote the orchestral score, and Professor Galli and myself improvised the solo parts. It was a tremendous success. . . ."

With a new star in the ascendant, music set the tone and virtuosity became the fashion. It was said that Prince Felix himself, who had been banished from both state and private apartments, was practising scales on the violin.

"For three years," said Paganini airily, "I gave lessons to Bacciochi."

From Elisa's lips the terms *pizzicato, staccato, flautini*, came as glibly as so many Corsican imprecations. But, being in love, she began to torture herself with doubts. Could she hope to keep this comet whom everyone desired? She had heard about a former liaison of his, which had intrigued all Florence; its echoes had reached even the palace at Lucca. Was the heroine Dida? The mere mention of that name made her tremble. Could it be that he still loved her?

"Princess Elisa," Paganini continued, "would sometimes swoon away when listening to my playing. She would occasionally absent herself so as not to deprive others of the pleasure of hearing me. . . .

"A lady to whom I was much attached was a constant attendant at my recitals. Insensibly our mutual passion grew. But there were strong reasons in favour of discretion and concealment. This merely served to increase our love. One day I promised I would write for her a musical fantasy, which would contain allusions to our love; it was to be performed at the next concert. I announced it to the court as a new composition, under the title of *Scène Amoureuse*. Their curiosity was aroused, but what was their surprise when they saw me appear on the stage with a violin from which two of the strings had been removed. I had retained only the G and the E. The E was to express the lady's sentiments, the G the passionate language of her lover. The tenderest tones were followed by the ravings of jealousy; melodies, plaintive and cajoling, alternated with phrases, expressing rage or happiness. The climax was the reconciliation of the lovers, which was embodied in a *pas de deux*, ending in a delirious coda. The piece had a favourable reception. After praising me up to the skies, the Princess said, graciously: 'You have just performed impossibilities on two strings. Would not a single string suffice for your talent?' I promised to make the attempt. Some weeks later I composed my Military Sonata for the G string, entitled *Napoleon*, which I performed on August 25 before a numerous and brilliant court. People were never tired of hearing this composition on one string. At Lucca I led a whole opera with a violin with two strings only. This won for me a wager consisting of a luncheon for twenty-five people."

Decorations and appointments were showered on him.

Nicolò was already first violin of the Court and leader of the Opera orchestra. What else could Elisa think of for him? She could not make him either a duke, a marshal, or a cardinal, so she conferred on him the rank of Captain of the Royal Body Guard.

The sister of the Emperor of the French knew how to handle men.

❨ In the summer of 1806, however, the Princess changed her tactics and loosened the reins. She gave him leave of absence, together with a letter of introduction to the British Consul at Leghorn.

"Though I remained attached to her court," wrote Paganini, "I travelled in Tuscany. At a concert in Leghorn, I ran a nail into my heel and came limping on to the stage. This made the audience laugh. As I began to play, both candles fell out of my music desk. More laughter. After the first few bars of my solo my E string broke, causing more hilarity. But when my audience saw me continuing to play the Concerto on three strings, their mirth was soon changed into wild applause. I made three more tours in Lower Italy, at intervals of five years, and on each occasion I played a different programme."

But this was not the only change. The Borghesi, the Emperor's younger sister and her consort, were now the ruling family at Turin. They extended their patronage to Paganini. Blangini, the director of music, wrote to a friend in Paris describing each of his concerts as a triumph. Pauline herself hinted to him that it might be blissful . . . for him . . . and for her . . . if. . . .

But this idyll came to nothing. He had a sudden attack of extreme exhaustion, such as he had been subject to in his adolescence, accompanied by violent pain in the lower region of the stomach. Utterly worn out, he lay some days in bed thinking of the only peaceful years of his existence, that time of fragrant memories, when he had lived with Dida, who was older than himself.

He saw again at twilight the walls of her castle where the heat of the sun still lingered. He recalled those idyllic days of idleness when everything served as a pretext for waiting on Dida, for caressing her guitar, her hands, the folds of her gown. Now he realized that in the end the violin would destroy him.

In the meantime Princess Elisa had become Grand Duchess of Tuscany and had separated from Prince Bacciochi. In 1809 she was organizing festivals in honour of the Peace Treaty between France and Spain. She sent at once for Paganini, begging him to hurry back since he was the chief attraction of her court. Bartoloni, the great sculptor, was waiting to make a marble bust of him.

When he received her letter he was still writhing with agony, but he seized a piece of paper and drew up three programmes. A bust of himself! In marble! Music! Florence!

He left the next day.

❰ In the last five years he had become the victim of an outcry of opprobrious epithets, such as "sorcerer," "charlatan," "*carbonaro*." They had originated at Lucca and spread to Florence, where they penetrated even through the massive walls of the Pitti Palace. People were jealous of Nicolò, who had returned to Florence all-powerful. But the Princess, who had at first laughed at all the rumours about him, now began to resent them. His traducers had carried their impertinence so far that they had sent the Grand Duchess a privately circulated pamphlet entitled *The Five Encounters*. It was attributed to the writer, Alessandro Amati. The pamphlet was in the worst possible taste and shed a fantastic light upon her leading virtuoso.

"Beyond the Pitti Gate of Florence," it read, "there is a hill, which is crowned by the ancient town of Fiesole, once

the rival of the Tuscan capital. There on the crest of the hill
the air is pure and the view has a dreamlike beauty. One bright
May morning as I was climbing the hill, a stranger who was
walking ahead of me drew my attention by his extraordinary
behaviour. He was talking and laughing to himself, until suddenly his demoniac gaze was attracted by a young peasant
girl of ravishing beauty who came tripping along towards us
carrying a basket of flowers. Scarcely had she caught sight of
this eccentric figure, than she took fright, stumbled, and ran
away to hide behind some rocks, while a curious smile hovered
upon the stranger's lips."

The next meeting, which took place on the following day,
occurred in a raging tempest. Dark clouds, like waves of the
sea, were rolling across the sky, when Amati, after crossing the
Bridge of the Graces, took refuge in a ruined castle. There,
adding his groans to the wailing of the storm, he saw the
stranger lying on a bed of moss.

The next evening he met him on the banks of the Arno in
soft moonlight, which was the signal for all the riverside birds
to burst into song. The stranger's whistling rivalled even the
sweet voice of the nightingale.

Their next encounter took place on the following day. He
was surrounded by a crowd of young people, who were passing
by the Uffizzi under the eyes of their illustrious Tuscan fore-
fathers. The stranger snatched a guitar from one of the young
men and proceeded to lead the dance himself with diabolical
frenzy. He pranced through the streets at the head of the procession, until they reached the Square of the Palazzo Vecchio,
where they followed him into a tavern. He bore no resemblance now to the melancholy, languishing individual of the
previous encounters. With dishevelled locks, his shirt open at
the breast, he played his guitar, which seemed to be bewitched,
until he had roused his companions to a Bacchanalian orgy.
Then this strange being suddenly disappeared, and none of

his young companions could ever discover anything about him.

"Some days later I heard that Paganini was to give a concert," the writer continued. "Eager to hear this matchless virtuoso, whom I had never seen before, I hastened to the theatre. The curtain rose. Imagine my astonishment when I recognized the mysterious stranger with whom my thoughts had been so busy. I need not describe the frenzied applause of the enraptured audience. I will merely say that he seemed that evening to have embodied in his playing the graceful apparition of the girl on the mountainside, the storm among the ruins, the bird song on the river bank and the delirious revels of the evening in the Square of the Uffizzi."

"Stuff and nonsense," said the Princess. Still, she considered that the influence of Pauline, who had made a conquest of her sister's captor, had been deplorable. Since his visit to Turin he seemed to think that he could take any liberty he pleased; she would have to show him. . . . But there was that tiresome newspaper cutting lying on her lap.

Forli. September 8, 1810.
Our theatre had the honour of a performance given by the sublime virtuoso, Nicolò Paganini, who evoked equal admiration and amazement.

Yes. This must stop. She had graciously allowed him to set out once more for Parma, Bologna, Cesena, with its ancient arenas, Rimini, Ravenna, Forli, Imola, Faënza. But where was his gratitude? What marks of affection had he given her? He did not even trouble to send her news, except an occasional flattering extract from a newspaper. One of these days she would have to speak to him as a sovereign.

His sensitive artist's antennae warned him of her mood. He came back with his nerves even more on edge than her own. If what he heard and guessed was true, he was to be curbed, and confined—while he was engaged in making a conquest of the whole of Italy. Well, let her try. . . .

At an official soirée at the court it had been announced that the maestro would first conduct a distinguished body of musicians and then give solo performances, on four strings, three strings, two strings, and finally on one string only. The great day arrived. In the midst of the usual confused sounds, there was a sudden hush. The audience saw, descending from the gallery, where Michelangelo's Conqueror leans his curly head towards the festival hall of Lorenzo the Magnificent, a figure in the glittering uniform of a Captain of the Royal Body Guard.

He faced the orchestra and the violins struck up.

Elisa was furious. In the interval she sent him a message, ordering him to retire at once and change into a black coat. The Captain claimed the privilege of his commission, which entitled him to wear his uniform whenever he pleased. She repeated her order, which he again refused to obey. With his sword at his side, he strutted about the hall, played his *soli*, bowed to the audience again and again, and finally joined in the dancing. Long after the fête had reached its zenith, a strange figure in glittering uniform could be seen, gliding through the mazes of the quadrilles.

Late at night, he decided once more on flight. He would make his art "felt" in Milan, Pavia, Turin. He pondered. Thirteen years! He had stayed thirteen years at Lucca. He bequeathed to Marie Elisa his Sonata in C, which he dedicated to her as an act of homage. But in spite of all her overtures, the Princess was never to see him again at her court, nor to receive again the nocturnal visits of this strange being, whom she had so often awaited "quivering with love" on the terrace at Marlia.

"FAREWELL! KEEP PURE AND CHASTE"

W̶AS it true that that angular profile of his, quivering in the candlelight, had once cast its shadow on the walls of a convent? That cell in the convent school, to which he had brought the girl, on the pretext that it would facilitate the solemnization of their marriage? Bending over his table, he examined a police notice that was spread out before him. This was headed, in round hand, in huge block letters:

THE HUMBLE PETITION

OF FERDINANDO CAVANNA, TAILOR,

TO THE ADVOCATE OF THE POOR

In 1814 Paganini had returned to Genoa, sated with honours, blasé and disillusioned. He had had enough of courts and jealous princesses. At thirty-three it was time a man ceased to be a page. He returned home a conqueror, deeming himself the equal of Christopher Columbus, his fellow countryman, arrogating to himself every prize, every reward. His footsteps echoed on the flagged floors of the taverns which Antonio used to haunt—there, and in less reputable haunts. The police, when appealed to, shut their eyes. After some wild prank, he would burst into peals of laughter. Ah, there was nothing now to recall the little mystic of San Lorenzo. His well-cut features were ravaged and wore a cynical expression. There were already wrinkles on his delicate skin. He wore a frock coat and gaudy waistcoats. His hair was plastered down with oil. Posing as a

cynic, he no longer felt at home in the old surroundings.
When he had first run away from Genoa, life lay ahead of
him, a glittering fruit that was hard to pluck. It was well worth
a few tumbles and a scratch or two. But when he had bitten
into it, it left a bitter taste on his thin, sensual lips, which were
curled in a perpetual sneer. Only continual change, or some
suggestion of the grotesque or the sardonic, brought light into
his eyes.

His first Concerto, which reflects this mental condition, is
strident, noisy, and gloomy by turns. The opening is grandiose.
The timbre of the violin, which is tuned a semitone above the
normal pitch, impinges on the heavier, more sombre tones of
the orchestra. There are passages of thirds that sound like
laughter, the biting irony of the *pizzicato*, the shrillness of the
stopped harmonics. The *Adagio* conjures up a tragic scene,
such as that in which Demarini, the celebrated actor, invoked
heaven from the depths of his dungeon. . . .

But one day in Milan he was dumbfounded by a fantastic
scene from Süssmayer's ballet, *Il Noce di Benevents*. It revealed him to himself. Those birds of the Inferno, those female devils who danced on to the stage, were his own familiars,
seductive till they became intolerable. As soon as he returned
home he wrote with a fiery pen *Le Streghe*, the Witches'
Dance. When he played it in Milan for the first time, flames
seemed to burst from his violin. The fame of it reached even
Germany. In Milan he gave eleven concerts, alternately at
the Scala and at the Teàtro Caraccino. Then followed five
concerts at Genoa, where his audiences were thunderstruck.

"Be he angel or devil," exclaimed the *Gazetta di Genova*,
"he is certainly the genius of music."

At Turin he was prostrated by another attack of his old
malady. The doctors were baffled. In earlier days his growing
fame had proved a sovereign remedy. Today he had another
specific, one that the Witches prescribed: his power over

women, of which he was fully aware. He was eager to try its potency on the *regazze*, young girls.

He made discreet advances to a young musician, Catarina Calcagno, a girl of fifteen with whom he played at the Teàtro Ré. But one evening, soon after his return to Genoa, he met at a ball a merry girl of seventeen, Angelina by name, who was the daughter of a tailor.

He thought her charming. Angelina! A tailor's daughter and just seventeen! Might he have the pleasure of seeing her home? Angelina! Angelina Cavanna!

"He had relations with her, which were by no means Platonic, in the cell of a convent school, to which he had lured her," the petition continued. "After apparently taking all the necessary steps for the solemnization of the marriage, he made the excuse that it could not be performed in Genoa, on account of his parents, and carried her off to Parma, without even referring to the marriage again."

This was in accordance with the facts. And further:

"It became evident that the union had been consummated. The girl had repeated attacks of nausea, which she herself, in ignorance, ascribed to worms. Without enlightening her, he promised to cure her and brought her ten packets containing a pinkish powder. The next morning, he prepared some barley water, added sugar and the contents of one of the packets, and made her drink it. Then he left her. . .

"The concoction brought on a violent attack of sickness affecting all her organs. She vomited the whole day, bringing up blood, as the two servants at the inn could testify. But unfortunately she cannot identify these men, one of whom was a Swiss, and the other a Venetian. She told them about the powder and showed them the remaining packets. . . ."

When Paganini returned, the girl refused to take any more of the powders, and so there were the expenses of her confinement to be met. Angelina overwhelmed him with complaints and reproaches and even threats. He soon grew exasperated, and tired of her. He sent for the police and told them to take her home to her parents, alleging as his excuse that he had been suddenly recalled to Genoa.

But Angelina, with only the clothes she stood up in, had fled to Fumerei in the mountains, to a woman who had been her sister's nurse and foster-mother. Here she spent the severest months of the winter, with only a little coarse bread for food and without news from her "inhuman" lover. She nearly died in the home of these charitable but poverty-stricken people. Her bed was a handful of straw, and the hut leaked so badly that her night-gown was soaked and she had to dry it at the fire during the day.

"She would certainly have perished," the tailor concluded, "had not Divine Providence revealed to the distracted father her place of refuge. He found the unfortunate girl half dead. A surgical operation had to be performed to deliver her of a dead child, which was imperilling its mother's life.

"Shortly before, in May 1815, Paganini had been guilty of a refinement of cruelty. He had come to Genoa, and, boasting of his right to do as he pleased, had deliberately insulted the family of the petitioner by walking past their windows to visit the house next door, thus parading his triumph and his iniquitous conduct. In view of this behaviour, the petitioner ventures to appeal to the magistrates to prosecute this wicked man."

❧ This time things were looking black. The case was proceeding. Surely he would not have to go to prison for a ragamuffinly tailor and a loose girl. He engaged an advocate. The defence affirmed that Angelina had been in collusion with her father, who was a notorious blackmailer. According to the neighbours, he had often turned his daughter out of the house, bidding her earn her living on the streets. She was free to come and go as she pleased, at any hour of the day or night, and took advantage of this license to attend festivals and public balls with suspicious-looking strangers, whom she would actually take home with her. Gossip was busy with her. The neighbours declared that she often used to spend the night away from home, and this had been her habit long before she had become acquainted with the defendant.

He reflected. If, in spite of all this evidence, Figari, his advocate, proved unequal to the situation, he would enlist the services of the only man in Genoa who, in his own line, was as gifted as himself. This was Luigi-Guglielmo Germi, an advocate who, in spite of his youth, had been elected member of the Sub-Alpine Parliament. His eloquence was the talk of the town, and he was, besides, an excellent musician. He, if anyone, would be able to save the situation.

But the cunning tailor was too quick for him. As if he had guessed his intention, he hurried on the case and secured a verdict in his favour.

On May 6, 1815, Paganini was arrested and conducted to the Tower. How blue the sky looked through the dirty, barred windows, how white the foam that flecked the sea!

The same day, in court, he signed an agreement to pay the outraged father a certain sum in damages, on Angelina's account.

He was released that evening, but on his refusal to pay the stipulated sum, the case was reopened. It was dragged through the courts, and at last, a year later (1816), the final Court of Appeal pronounced judgment as follows:

His Majesty's Senate, sitting at Genoa.
Concerning the Action brought by Ferdinando Cavanna and Angelina Cavanna his daughter, represented by Maître Ciocca, acting as poor man's advocate, against Nicolò Paganini, represented by Maître Figari, advocate. In view of the fact that sufficient evidence has been brought to prove that seduction under

promise of marriage was practised on the person of Angelina Cavanna, whom the defendant enticed away from her father's house, abducted to Parma, and after a short period of cohabitation, abandoned, the plaintiff is entitled to claim damages.

The Senate having heard the case presented by the plaintiff's advocate, and the defendant's advocate not having appeared before them, award to Angelina Cavanna £120 damages, the defendant to pay all costs.

M. GRATAROLA,
Clerk of the Court

Genoa, November 14, 1816.

The incident appeared to be closed. But, in fact, it had scarcely begun. His reputation, which was already doubtful, now became atrocious, and he could no longer rely on the favour of the Grand Duchess Elisa to bridle slanderous tongues.

"He is possessed," people said, endorsing in their own way the judgment of the Courts on the seducer. His very talent proved it, since it defied all human laws. He was capable of anything.

When little or nothing of the truth is known, facts become distorted and people believe the worst. That mistress of his, whose soul was imprisoned in his violin, where it gave vent to those long-drawn wails, those sudden rages . . . perhaps he had tortured her, or murdered her. And what of the supposed rival? Had he stabbed him in the back, or had he made away with him by poison? At first it was a mere whisper, but as each spectacular appearance of the virtuoso stimulated popular imagination in all the towns through which he passed, the rumour gradually increased, until it became an undertone to the clapping hands and the cries of bravo.

"I find Paganini's art infinitely disturbing," a lady wrote from Trieste to a friend, who was looking forward to hearing him in Venice. "I cannot tell you how greatly he delights me."

Eight years later the legend of Paganini reached the ears of Stendhal on his arrival in Milan:

"Paganini, the most eminent violinist in Italy and perhaps all northern Europe, is a young man of thirty-five, with black piercing eyes and a shock of curly hair. This ardent soul did not attain his sublime mastery over his instrument by eight years of patient study at a Conservatoire. He owes it to an amorous peccadillo, for which, they say, he was thrown into jail for many years. Abandoned and alone, in a prison, which might prove only a preliminary to the scaffold, nothing was left to him in his chains except his violin. In the long nights of his captivity, he learned to express his soul in music, and had ample time to perfect himself in that language." *

* Stendhal's *Life of Rossini*, Paris, Michel Levy.

FRIENDSHIPS

To the illustrious Signor Luigi-Guglielmo Germi,
Genoa.

Milan, September 3, 1816.
The kiss I send you comes from my heart. . . . All the sirens
in the world may go to the devil. All I care for is the continuance
of your friendship.

He had done with women. He had a horror of them: their
persons, their rapacity, the very scent of them, which led to
the Tower. He was still entangled in the after-effects of his
affair with Angelina and deeply mortified at all that Genoa
was saying about him. He settled in Milan, where he was
soothed by sympathy and adulation. But what had possessed
him to reject the advice of the famous lawyer Germi, the
"Paganini of advocates," whom he had summoned to his
rescue? He had consulted him, begged him to help him, and
had then done as he pleased.

"You must surely be aware," he wrote, still harping on Angelina, "of the questionable behaviour of this woman. You must
realize what humiliation and annoyance I suffered from the
police, at her instigation. I cannot understand how you can
urge me to acts of generosity against which my conscience and
my injured soul are in revolt."

What was he, this rescuer, who had come too late to save
him? Was he his judge or his friend? At first Paganini rebelled.
Although he was four years his junior, Germi, who was, despite

his youth, the chief ornament of the Ligurian bar, lashed him with irony. Had his client not realized to what a pass his doubtful morals, his vanity, his chicanery had brought him? Others, more powerful than himself, had come to grief when they had snapped their fingers at the law of the land. The voice of the preacher, that golden voice, trained to persuade, proved more effective than his words. Paganini, sensitive to lovely sounds, was touched by it. He still retained something of the nervous child, and the slight feeling of awe inspired by Germi was not unpleasant. Nicolò lowered his crest at his new friend's attitude and admired his wisdom, learning, and orderly way of life. Swallowing his pride, he questioned Germi and confided in him. What was he himself in his heart of hearts? A magician? A sorcerer? A Don Juan? No, he was better than that. He was a man like other men, and to this new friend he would at last unveil his real countenance.

For the sake of Germi and of his mother, he sometimes returned to Genoa, that cruel city. On each of his visits, Germi tabulated the documents in the Cavanna case. But one evening they abandoned the law in favour of music. Instead of poring over papers, Nicolò played quartets with the "adorable friend," who was a lover of Haydn and Mozart, and a sound interpreter of their music. Nicolò led the quartet; Germi played the second violin; the other instrumentalists hardly counted. Night fell. In the pauses of the music they could hear the subdued murmur of the sea. Facing Genoa, the superb city which lay taking its ease in its amphitheatre, its brow crowned with convents and palaces, they watched the lights of ships in the harbour kindled one by one.

Nicolò, bending over his friend as if he were helping a child, was on edge with anxiety. Whenever Germi made a slip, he played loudly to cover it up. During the *Adagio* his eyes were wet with tears.

When could they meet again? Perhaps not for months. Tomorrow Paganini was to set out for Milan, Bologna, and Venice. . . . He saw the musicians to the door. They were overheated from playing; Germi must put on his cape and be careful of the steps. Nicolò bent down to him. The ships were lying at anchor in the harbour; their lights glittered in the distance as they dipped up and down.

He could set out on his journey with his mind at rest. Germi, the beloved friend, had taken everything on his shoulders; his troubles, his family, his business, his successes, his plans, his health, his mistresses, his accounts, his critiques. What a tremendous burden! Absence, that serpent, lost its sting in the case of two such friends. Germi's steady affection forged a link between them; it was an axis, a centre for the wide circumference of Paganini's concert tours.

"Although I miss your companionship," Nicolò wrote from Florence, "you sent me such a dear and charming letter, that not content with reading it myself, I enlivened a brilliant conversation with extracts from it."

If a letter was delayed, his nerves tortured him with forebodings. Had Germi ceased to care for him? Had he left Genoa? Was he ill? Had he forgotten him? Was there a rival? Writing from Bologna, he complained:

"Two months of silence! And not a day has passed without my thinking of you. I am *curiosissimo* to hear what happened about the courtesan, who was so much taken with the quartet, or perhaps with the dedication. Tell me honestly, did you make her fall in love with you?"

Whenever Germi made a successful contract or investment, Nicolò hastened to congratulate him. He wrote from Naples:

"I apologize for sending you such a large sum of money through the post. If you were to withdraw your kindness, I should indeed be miserable."

He added a postscript: "The other day I noticed a well-behaved young girl in church and followed her a little way to

see where she lived. She is the daughter of a notary. What do
you advise? Shall I marry or remain a bachelor? Thank you
for the charming things you said about my quartet. Take a
look at Op. 15."

At last, in 1818, after two years of separation, they were to
meet again. Paganini, who was in Florence, preparing for his
concerts at the Pergola Theatre, was radiant with joy. He
crossed off the days to Germi's arrival on his calendar. He advised Germi to put up at the White Inn, which was the inn
nearest to his own lodgings, and he begged him to make haste.

> Let me soon have the joy of clasping you to my heart [he wrote
> impatiently]. I have so many things to say to you that will give
> you pleasure.
> Love me as I love you.
>
> NICOLÒ PAGANINI

❡ But although his affection for his friend filled his
heart and soothed his nerves, there were other influences besides Germi's at work. He had repeated attacks of his old
malady which sometimes prostrated him. Between the attacks
he was always on his travels. It was a mysterious disease. A
severe attack would affect every part of his body. In Ancona
in 1815, whither he had gone to give a single concert, he was
laid up for months. His nervous system and all his organs
were disordered. "The result of his excesses," said his enemies.
But was this really the explanation? How could he indulge in
excesses when he was pursuing so exacting a career?

"Once is enough," he pointed out to Germi, when he, in his
turn, was giving good advice; "leave Bacchus alone." (Had
Germi been drowning the sorrows of absence?) "He is a dangerous ally of that 'delicate harlot' Venus. Thank you again
for your own counsels on the subject of human temptations.
You must know that for the sake of my own peace of mind,
I have ceased to frequent a certain Signora."

Paganini travelled not only to give concerts himself but for the sake of meeting other musicians. He was keenly interested in violinists such as the German Spohr and the Frenchman Lafont, both of whom were touring in Italy. He read some of the classics and went to the theatre.

"This Carnival, the opera is by Rossini," he wrote from Turin, "it is called *Aureliano in Palmira*."

Although on days of depression he had doubts of his success, his star was in the ascendant in the Italian firmament. There was another star that was continually crossing his path. It was that of Rossini, the Swan of Pesaro, as he was already called. Nicolò's curiosity was aroused. Rossini was ten years his junior, and had actually dared to write, in succession to Paisiello, a new *Barber of Seville*. In spite of an unprecedented fiasco at the Teàtro Argentina in Rome, the opera had since been praised up to the skies. All the other capitals of Europe were fighting for it, and everyone was discussing the author.

Although he came of a patrician family, the Rossinis of Romagna, whose arms were a rose surmounted by a nightingale, he, too, was "born in the profession."

Gioacchino Rossini was born at Pesaro, where his father, Giuseppi, was town trumpeter. With the coming of Bonaparte, the Romagna was torn between the Revolutionaries and the adherents of the Papal party. Giuseppi, who was described as a strolling musician, was of the Revolutionary party and left Pesaro, taking his horn with him. His wife, Anna Guidarini, who was a baker's daughter, a dark, handsome woman with a very charming voice, made her début as *prima donna buffa*. As soon as he could toddle and had learnt his notes, Gioacchino followed in his parents' footsteps, like a circus child.

The Rossinis went first to Lugo, where they remained for several years. Here little Gioacchino received his first lessons from the Malerbi family. In 1794 the Rossinis settled in Bologna where stood the rose-red walls of the famous Philhar-

monic, of which Mozart was proud to be a member. Young
Gioacchino, who was amazingly gifted, had the same honour
bestowed on him at the age of fourteen. Up till then he had
studied *solfège*, harp, and violin with Padre Angelo Tesei. He
sang *soli* in churches, where his sweet voice and pretty, lively
ways endeared him to the choirmasters. When he had studied
counterpoint and accompanying, he went on tour by himself
as pianist and conductor. On his return he left Padre Tesei
and joined the counterpoint class of Italy's greatest teacher,
Padre Mattei, at the Liceo Communale of Bologna. At nineteen, Rossini's reputation stood so high that he was chosen
to conduct Haydn's *Four Seasons*, while the male soprano,
Marchesi, who had discovered Paganini in the Cathedral at
Genoa, led the *Creation*. When he felt that his boundless
imagination was backed by a thorough knowledge of music,
he took leave of the Philharmonic and of Padre Mattei. He
was off on his travels. He would now present his own works,
his own inventions, to the public. There would be scenes of a
new pattern, adventures in harmony and orchestration. (*Il
Signore Vacarmini* he was presently nicknamed.) The exuberance of youth expressed itself in a rush of new melodies, in
audacious tricks, such as the insistent reiteration of a single
note. Sometimes his operas were triumphs, sometimes they
were fiascos. His mother was informed of his failures by a little sketch of a *fiasco*, or broken bottle. He was soon to introduce the famous Rossini crescendo, which in the coming years
he was to use to excess.

In 1810 Rossini produced his first *opera buffa*, *The Matri-
monial Market*, at the San Mosé Theatre in Venice.

In 1812 followed *I due Bruschini*, or *The Fortunate Mistake*, which had a stormy origin. In revenge for the insolence
of an impresario he ingeniously introduced into the work all
kinds of outrageous tricks. The violins had to mark each bar
in the overture by a stroke of the bow on the tin lamp-shades

Elisa Bacciochi, Princess of Lucca and Grand Duchess
of Tuscany (Pinacotèca of Lucca)

Above: Antonia Bianchi.
Below: Paganini's son, the Baron Achille de Paganini. Lithograph by Dévéria (Bibliothèque Nationale)

above their desks. The audience hissed him, and Rossini made his escape to Milan, where another engagement awaited him.

In 1813 he redeemed this failure with the tremendous success of *Tancredi*, which contained the wonderful air "Di tanti palpiti," which all Venice was delightedly singing and humming. *Tancredi* was followed by *l'Italiana in Algeri* and *Il Turco in Italia*. Between 1814 and 1816 he produced *Aureliano in Palmira*, *Elizabeth*, and finally *Il Barbiere di Siviglia*.

Yet people said that he was lazy! The accusation was not unfounded. His last three operas had all to share the same overture. On one occasion Rossini was writing a duet in bed. The manuscript slipped down under the couch. Rather than pick it up, the maestro preferred to write another air.

According to Paganini, he had a charming, impudent face with sparkling eyes, which were set a little aslant. He was the complement of Paganini's genius, as Germi was of his heart. They completed each other even as light and shade, fat and lean, major and minor, piano and violin are complementary. At Bologna the paths of these two stars crossed again.

They met, in 1816, at the house of the great banker Pegnalver. No preliminaries were necessary. Rossini sat down at the clavecin while Nicolò took his violin. They improvised together while the audience listened enraptured.

"It's lucky for Rossini," said one of the listeners, expressing the composer's own opinion, "that Paganini has not devoted himself to lyric composition. What a dangerous rival he would have been!"

Nicolò delighted in his friend's exuberance, which was so closely akin to his own. Rossini's operas hummed with life, like a beehive on a sunny day. Paganini had only to capture one of these ideas to develop it on his violin in dazzling variations. From *Tancredi* he borrowed the famous air "Di tanti palpiti," which everyone in Venice was singing—duchesses, fishermen, laundresses—and filled it, like a crystal figurine, with exquisite sounds. He refined it, drew it out, gilded it, until it was iridescent with new splendour. Elated with his success, he took airs from *Cinderella* * and *Moses*.†

He endorsed Germi's opinion of his new friend: "What intelligence you showed in your appreciation of *Othello!*" he wrote to him.

Then a tiny incident roused the virtuoso in the musician. It was the arrival of a French violinist. After the usual affectionate ending to his letter to Germi, he added a postscript: "Yesterday at the Scala we heard a concert given by Monsieur Lafont. The worthy professor has certainly not the gift of stirring his audience. He is a sound, but commonplace, violinist. His wife sang, but her diction is poor. The two musicians were not as well received as they might have hoped."

Germi could read between the lines.

* *Non più mesta accanto fuoco.* Op. 12.
† The Prayer of Moses.

RIVALS

IN spite of Paganini's remarks, Charles Philippe Lafont, who was solo violinist in the chapel of Louis XVIII, was enjoying a brilliant success in Italy, and this was followed by similar triumphs in England, Germany, Holland, and Russia. It was exasperating to hear this fact repeated continually, especially after the previous year, when Nicolò had been overwhelmed with troubles and had had to spend months in Ancona, too ill to play. After he had heard the French virtuoso, he remarked, complacently, that there had not been above three hundred people at the Scala.

"Lafont has promised to come to hear me," he continued, "but we have agreed that he is to wait for my concert."

The day after Paganini's recital at Milan, Lafont became possessed with the idea of giving a joint concert with Paganini. It was to be a sort of tournament, in which the two celebrated virtuosi would contend with each other in strength and skill. Each had his own school, with its own characteristics and traditions. What a triumph awaited them both! Thus Lafont set the fatal ball rolling, and he did not improve matters by choosing an absurd dress to wear at the concert. The astute Genoese yielded to the persuasions of Lafont and his pretty wife. The encounter was to take place at the Scala on March 11, 1816. They were to play Kreutzer's Double Concerto, which had been first performed in Paris by the composer and Pierre Rode. Besides this, each of the protagonists would play compositions of his own, preferably pieces that required brilliant technique.

On the appointed day, all Milan was in a fever of excitement at the challenge. The famous theatre was bright as day. When the two artists appeared on the platform together, they were received with frenzied applause. Lafont began by carefully tuning his instrument, then turned to Paganini to give him the A, as was customary. But Paganini shrugged his shoulders carelessly, and at once attacked the famous Concerto, for which the audience were waiting so impatiently.

"In this concerto," wrote Paganini, "I kept faithfully to what was written, as long as the two violins were playing together. But in my solo passages I gave rein to my Italian imagination, and improvised, to Kreutzer's accompaniment, new variations, which made a great sensation, but did not appear to please my amiable rival."

Lafont, who was outclassed from the first, was disconcerted. While he himself faithfully interpreted the musical score that was plainly set before his eyes, Paganini's response consisted of strange waves of sound that seemed to be falling from another planet. It was like the utterances of an oracle. And in the *Adagio*, the phrasing, the chromatic slides indulged in by that man with the blazing eyes, were in the worst possible taste. Doubtless, in France, the impeccable, elegant Lafont, who was called the Alcibiades of the violin, would have regained the upper hand. His eyes strayed for a moment from the music desk, while he turned his head, with its curled locks, towards the hall. The audience sat spellbound, gazing at Paganini. Were they merely histrionic, those agonized faces, those eyes glistening with tears? They wore an aspect such as Lafont had never beheld before, such as he himself had never conjured up. A fulminating rhythm, drumming in his ears, swept him back into the dance. It carried him away, dazzled him, played havoc with his strings, and finally overwhelmed him in the presence of the ecstatic audience.

"Lafont perhaps surpassed me in beauty of tone," Paganini

admitted, "but the ovation which greeted my performance convinced me that I had not had the worst of the encounter."

As for the *soli* which were played in turn by each artist, the Frenchman's Russian Variations were drowned in the hubbub. All that remained in the memory of the audience was the theme of *The Witches' Dance* and the sombre figure of their maestro, whom Lafont had so rashly challenged.

In the meantime the fame of the "Black Cavalier" was spreading far and wide. It was heightened by the report of the contest, which was discussed by the other musicians. More than one bow was trembling in its sheath. Could not a single violinist be found, in the whole of Europe, skilful enough to discover this man's secret and eclipse his fame?

Germany was the first to answer the challenge. In October of the same year, 1816, she sent her envoy to Venice to confront Paganini. Louis Spohr was fair-skinned, sturdily built, with a fresh complexion. He had spent the winter in Rome and was now finishing his first Italian tour. Spohr, who was in the service of the Duke of Brunswick in Cassel, was considered to be the first violinist in Germany. He was also a talented composer.

"His genius," said the *Musikalische Zeitung* of Leipzig, "inclines to the grandiose and the sentimental."

He was ready to take up the challenge. What method would he employ? He dashed into the fray like a heavy dragoon.

"Paganini," we read in his autobiography,* "called on me this morning, and I had the opportunity of making the acquaintance of this remarkable man, of whom people have never stopped talking since I first set foot in this country. No instrumentalist has made such a sensation in Italy as Paganini. When I enquire into the reason, people reply that he extracts from the violin sounds that have never been heard before. Musicians, however, while they admit that his tech-

* Letter dated October 17, 1816.

nique is extraordinary, consider that his tone is poor, his phrasing in doubtful taste, and his bowing not sufficiently sustained. In a word they look upon him as a charlatan. His great reputation rests on *tours de force* and mountebank tricks, such as harmonics, *pizzicati*, variations played on a single string, the other three having been removed, imitations of incongruous sounds, such as the tone of the bassoon, or the voice of an old woman. In Germany we had a violinist of the name of Scheller, who caused an unusual sensation by much the same artifices. As I never heard Scheller, I am anxious to hear Paganini, who has all the resources of an unusual personality. I am convinced that he has great qualities. The story goes that his wonderful talent is the result of several years of intensive practising, when he was imprisoned for murdering his wife. He had had no education and can neither read nor write."

Paganini had been visiting Parma and Ferrara. He arrived in Venice still suffering from "an obscure malady." This time he was unable to compete and he resorted to a subterfuge. He paid Spohr a second visit, and began by overwhelming him with compliments on the success of his concert. When Spohr, who was surrounded by his friends, all of them excellent musicians, pressed him to play to them, he excused himself, alleging that he had had a fall and had hurt his arm. He and the great German violinist would, no doubt, meet again either in Rome or Naples, and then he would not wait to be asked twice. What an honour it would be. . . .

Spohr was taken aback. When he tried to insist, Paganini was nowhere to be found. It was a great disappointment.

"I am afraid I shall have to leave Italy," he said, "without having heard this worker of miracles."

This time the dragon was not to be drawn.

❡ The last of the "Three Musketeers" came from Poland, where he was director of the theatre at Lemberg. At that time his fiery talent, his elegance, his nervous sensibility, which resembled Chopin's, made Charles Lipinsky the idol of the public, especially the women. One evening in May 1818, without a word to anyone, he suddenly abandoned everything, and traversing Poland, Germany, Austria, and the Alps, arrived in Venice only to find that Paganini had just left for Verona. He followed him to Verona, and learned that Paganini had gone to Milan.

"A certain Monsieur Lipinsky has come all the way from Poland to hear me," Paganini wrote to Germi. "He will find me at Placentia."

At Piacenza fortune favoured him, and at last he found what he had sought for so patiently. His eyes lighted on a poster announcing a recital by Paganini. At the concert he happened to sit next to a friend of Paganini's, who smilingly presented him to the maestro. The young man, in a frenzy of admiration, had applauded all by himself, in the midst of a general silence, in the pause between the *Andante* and the brilliant *Finale*.

Just as Liszt had been charmed by Chopin, Paganini was won by the grace of the young Polish musician and the pathos of his playing. It was hard to resist the admiration of a disciple, whose chief delight was to proclaim his devotion from the house-tops.

"He hardly ever leaves me," said Paganini. "He adores me. When he returns to Poland he is going to study my methods. He says he never wants to hear any other violinist."

This time it was a friendly clash of weapons that threw off sparks of brilliant light. The musician made him free of the whole panoply of his art; he was permitted to handle and examine the maestro's tools. Other artists invited them to their houses, where they improvised together. In Turin they played, experimentally, Double Concertos by Pleyel and Kreutzer in public. They planned to tour the whole of Italy together.

The maestro laid aside his sarcastic manner and displayed

infinite tact in eradicating defects in the younger man's playing. This delicacy was astonishing in one who was usually so harsh. Lipinsky was living in a dream. He composed three Caprices which he dedicated to the "Eminent Professor, Nicolò Paganini."

But at last Lipinsky had to tear himself away from Italy and return to the North. His flight had been discovered, and he received peremptory orders to return to his post. He bade farewell to Italy, Italian music, and to a friendship which was unique of its kind.

Eleven years later, when Paganini visited Warsaw, the two artists sought to revive those radiant memories by appearing together on the concert platform. After the concert, one of the Polish journals praised Lipinsky at the expense of Paganini, whom it described as a charlatan. Other journals joined in the fray, defending Paganini and attacking Lipinsky, who rushed into print, disclaiming any share in the slanderous campaign against his illustrious friend. But he was embarrassed and uneasy. Paganini affected indifference. Time went on. The two men never met again.

CARNIVALS

In Rome, the Vicar-General, later Pope Leo XII, issued a flattering rescript, placing all the Fridays in the Carnival at my disposal for my concerts.

IT WAS indeed a concession. The sacred Fridays of Rome! Paganini was delighted at this little act of sacrilege. Everything conspired to entice him to the Holy City. It was first under the sky of Rome, subsequently under that of Naples, that his rival planet, Rossini, had made his home. In 1817 Rossini's *Cinderella* had had a reception as sensational as that of his *Barbiere* in the preceding year. At first it was received with ridicule, but soon afterwards Rossini had become the idol of the Romans. Like the *Barbiere, Cinderella,* the charming *opera buffa,* was now a universal favourite. Why did Paganini hesitate to join his friend and share his triumphs? Paganini was now convinced of his own unrivalled supremacy as a violinist.

"I did not play it as it was written," he said, referring to a quartet of Haydn's, "but there was an indescribable charm in my interpretation."

To win favour in the Holy City, Nicolò gave a gracious reply to the proposals made to him. He had himself decided to give no more concerts in Northern Italy after 1818. By way of compensation, he composed a Quartet, in which the violin had the only important part. It contained "a fantastic Minuet and a touching Trio."

But there was bad news from Genoa, and he had to postpone his departure. First it was his father, then his beloved friend,

57

and finally Teresa, *la mia carississississima madre,* who was ill. Without much enthusiasm, he completed a tour, to which he was committed, in the spring and summer of 1818. He gave concerts in Piacenza, Parma, and Cremona, the home of Stradivarius, where he was made a member of the Philharmonic Society. He played in Bologna, where he received an honorary degree at the hands of the celebrated Padre Mattei; in Pistoia; in Florence, where by general request, he gave five concerts in August. Siena was left out, because it was the custom for most of the inhabitants to spend Sunday in the country. He planned to reach Rome in the company of the tenor, Granti, whom he described as "extremely handsome and a very good fellow."

The morning tide would sweep him away to a new town, whence he would depart at night on the foaming crest of success. But he was weary of this rhythm, and eager to adventure farther, to embark on the great ocean itself. But there were days of lassitude and loneliness, when his mind dwelt on the idea of the firm earth beneath his feet, a settled home, and the company of young girls. It was indescribable how much he felt his solitude. He was forever chasing the "tempestuous petticoat."

"What ravishing young ladies they are, these convent bred girls! I met one of these Hebes on the staircase. Such encounters alas! are rare. But oh what a pleasure it was!"

In Turin he was so much taken with a child of "thirteen or fourteen, a Protestant girl of good family," that he asked for her hand in marriage.

"Her father replied that when she had finished her education, he would allow her to correspond with me, but that there was ample time to think the matter over."

The "sirens" too, were restored to favour in the person of the adorable Signora Taddea Pratologo, who lived at Naples. He pursued this love affair to the limit of his finances (that is to say the allowance he had instructed Germi to pay him). This lady had had "the education of a princess and was a trained musician." Finally there was a pupil of Crescentini who was "head over heels in love with him" and corresponded with him although her father had forbidden her ink and paper.

My one and only Treasure, [ran one of the letters in a hurried handwriting,] my pen cannot express the joy I felt when I received your charming letter. When you went away, only someone as madly in love as I am could have suffered as I did. But patience, patience! I entreat you to do all you can to come back to Bologna as soon as possible. That is the greatest happiness my beloved could bestow on me.

Farewell, my life, my all. Farewell.

Your most devoted lover,

MARINA BANTI *

As he went his way, tributes of love were showered upon him as a woman is garlanded with flowers. But now he hardly spared them a glance. He was weary of their perfume. Although he professed to have kissed the precious note a hundred times, Germi was again appealed to. " 'My only treasure'—do you care for that expression?" he asked anxiously.

Not many months after he had parted from his dear Marina in Bologna, he was begging Germi to supply him with a formula that would persuade the girl to regard him with the same indifference that he felt for her.

At last, on November 4, 1818, he arrived in Rome, at the same time as the Kings of Naples and Spain.

"This city surpasses in splendour all one's imaginings. The air is heavy, but my appetite is good."

Women continued to pursue him. But he saw through them now.

"They wish to rule over my heart and my finances, but I am sure you will approve of my decision, which I took some time

* Copied into a letter to Germi, date Florence, October 10, 1818.

ago, to send them all to the devil. I do not propose to let them ruin me. . . .

"P.S.—I am averse to the idea of marriage. I shall treat the ladies with respect. But no more love letters. *La libertà è un tesoro.* [Liberty is a treasure.]"

About a year before Paganini was making this confession of faith, the Austrian Chancellor, Prince Metternich, was bending pensively over a map of Italy. In the recent conferences at Vienna, Italy, by his authority, which he described as "the only existing anti-revolutionary moral force," had been officially divided up into four kingdoms: the two Sicilies, which had been restored for the benefit of a Bourbon; the Papal territories, which had been returned to the Pope; Piedmont and Sardinia, and Lombardy and Venice, which were annexed to Austria. Besides these there were certain duchies and principalities, whose rulers were dependent on the Empire.

These divisions were marked in pale colours on the map. But in contrast to the docile Austrian courts, Italy was in a ferment. She had been the first country to welcome the French Revolutionary troops and had never forgotten it. In Naples brigandage had been allowed to flourish and the *carbonari* to gain ground through the indolence of Ferdinand IV. Popular enthusiasm was excited by an expedition to Pernambuco in Brazil. In short, according to the report of Tito Manzi, Metternich's secret agent and a former minister of Murat, "the whole country was seething with unrest, and the conditions were favourable for the establishment of an Austrian Government which would be popular with the people."

In a quarter of an hour, Metternich, "Jupiter Conservator," made up his mind. In June 1817 he arrived in Florence, and this produced a deep impression.

"My presence in Italy," he wrote to his wife, "is exercising an incalculable influence on the march of events. I have had such a welcome as the King of all Italy would never have received."

Next came the bathing resort of Lucca, "a perfectly divine spot," which was built and developed by Madame Elisa.

"I know no other 'English' garden this side of the Alps with such a wealth of exotic trees and flowers; there are whole groves of magnolias. The climate of Lucca is infinitely milder than that of Florence. . . ."

But now Madame Elisa, with her musical bodyguard, was far away. On the other hand, cordial relations were foreshadowed between the Holy See and Metternich, who had decided to prolong his stay in Tuscany. He was enchanted with Italian music. This aspect of his stay he described in a letter to his family:

"Yesterday we spent a delightful evening at Madame d'Apponys' [*sic*]. She had invited a small party to hear Catalani sing. The two Archduchesses were present, as well as our entire suite. The audience were enraptured with Catalani's singing, and you would have been in ecstasies. If the Holy Virgin joins in the heavenly choir, her voice must surely be like that of this woman, who, however, is no virgin.

"I shall not decide about my journey to Rome for some days. The Holy Father is still too ill to transact business." *

The journey to Rome was postponed. It was in fact two years before this brilliant beginning had its historical sequence.

"My non-appearance in Rome is regarded with consternation," the Chancellor concluded; "I shall know how to take advantage of this attitude."

❡ *La libertà è un tesoro*, Rossini had hummed as he signed a renewal of the Draconian contract which bound him to Barbajà, the greatest impresario in Italy. Ever since 1815 the musical dictator had been watching the career of the young composer, whom he declared to be the "man of the day." He had seen him write the score of an opera in three weeks, snub

* June 20, 1817.

his captious public, and ingratiate himself with the women. Fame and the approval of the great Italian maestros awaited this young man, on whom the mantle of Cimarosa had fallen. The celebrated air of Zingarelli, "Wait for me, beloved shade," might well have been his answer. Such was the opinion of Barbajà, who had secured Rossini's co-operation and had proved his own ability to launch him.

Barbajà was originally a waiter in a coffee-house in Milan. He made his fortune with the invention of an ice cream, consisting of equal parts of coffee and chocolate and called *barbajata*. His next step was to establish gaming tables in the *foyer* of the Scala, where the audiences strolled up and down between the acts. He invested the millions he made in this way in buying up all the taverns and all the theatres in Naples. He had a taste for the arts and the proceeds of *barbajata* were translated into terms of architecture and music.

In 1816, when the San Carlo Theatre was burnt down and Ferdinand IV, arriving from Sicily, was plunged into such depths of despair that he forgot even the Austrian intrigues, a man came to him and said: "Sire, in nine months I will rebuild this magnificent theatre, which the flames have destroyed, and it shall be finer than before."

This man was Domenico Barbajà, and he kept his word.

"When he entered the new San Carlo theatre," wrote Stendhal, "the King of Naples felt that for the first time for twelve years he was King indeed."

The enthusiasm of the suburban population was indescribable. What need had Naples, with its brilliant orchestra, its new, unpublished operas, its galaxy of stars, to envy Milan its Scala? And to crown it all, there was the new theatre with its hall decorated in gold and silver, its boxes draped in deep blue, its torches in the shape of lilies.

Rossini's contract with Barbajà assured his future triumphs but he was committed to a vast amount of work. He could not desert Rome, but he had also to supervise the two theatres in Naples, the San Carlo and the Delfondo. On each city in turn there descended a glittering shower of operas: *Othello, Cinderella, Moses, Mahomet II, Mathilde de Sabran*, not to mention *La Gazza Ladra*, which was produced at Milan. Without a moment's relaxation he had to content the most critical and the most experienced public in the world. Around the young maestro revolved a planetary system consisting of stars of two sexes, or rather three, since the last of the male sopranos still held their ground.

Foremost among the ladies was Mademoiselle Colbran the singer, who was a magnificent Spanish *Elizabeth*.

"Hers was the most impressive kind of beauty," wrote Stendhal. "She had pronounced features which had a splendid effect on the stage, a superb figure, fiery eyes like a Circassian, a wealth of most beautiful jet-black hair, and finally a flair for tragedy."

Then there was Giorgi (charming as Rosina or Cinderella) and the exquisite Liparini. It gave Rossini no trouble to write parts to suit his favourite interpreters. Some of the old Neapolitan connoisseurs regretted that this man of genius had never known Madame Pasta, who was so great in classic roles, or la Catalani, who was in Florence making a conquest of the all-conquering Metternich.

The range of masculine voices was even wider. It included the four *bassi profondi*: Lablache, Galli, Zuchelli, Remorini; the celebrated male soprano Crescentini, and tenors such as Garcia, Rubini, and the charming younger Davide, whom triumphs were awaiting in Vienna. There was no end to the intrigues, the gossiping, the reiterations, the cackling; it was like an exhibition of fireworks. And to satisfy them all, he had to be continually composing, adapting, transposing, scolding, soothing, flattering, insisting, rehearsing, playing, courting, supping. . . .

But where a musician of a more serious temperament would

have broken down, Rossini handled the situation like a juggler. He was Figaro, coping with everything, joking at everything, laughing at everyone. But one day Monsieur Barbajà did not join in the laughter, for Rossini had stolen his mistress, Mademoiselle Colbran, thus securing for himself the sovereignty of Naples and the Two Sicilies, since he would henceforth write all the parts for the *prima donna*, this protégée of Barbajà, who was protected by King Ferdinand, who was under the thumb of Metternich, who, himself, was at the command of Francis II, Emperor of Austria.

The Emperor himself was soon to set out on his travels. Metternich persuaded him that his presence was necessary in Italy. He was to spend Easter in Rome, before proceeding to Naples. Faithful to his charge, the Chancellor went on ahead, arriving before the Imperial suite, and warned Count Kaunitz, the Austrian Ambassador in Italy, of the Emperor's intention.

"The Emperor arrived at half-past four," wrote Metternich, "and immediately proceeded to visit the Pope in his private apartments. His Holiness advanced to meet him, as far as his legs permitted him. The Emperor was received with great pomp, amid great rejoicings on the part of the populace."

The Emperor's arrival synchronized with the beginning of the Holy Week Celebrations in St. Peter's. In the Castle of St. Angelo, guns were fired and there was an exhibition of fireworks, "which ended with three girandolas, one above the building, and one on a lower level on either side."

Paganini was now in Rome and was to give musical expression to these arpeggios of fire.

"Tomorrow," wrote the virtuoso, "the Governor is entertaining His Majesty at a concert in the Tordinone theatre. The hall will be bright as day and (I), Paganini will be playing. A second concert is arranged for next week. The Marchesa Raggi is here; I had the pleasure of her company at the illumination of the Cupola and the fireworks which, however, were not a great success."

In the meantime Barbajà had engaged Paganini for a concert in Naples.* The Roman palaces were lighted up. The season had begun with all its accessories: gilded panelling, porphyry, chamberlains, cardinals, ambassadors.

Paganini breathed this ceremonial atmosphere as freely as if it were his native air. Many faces were reflected in the mirrors surrounding the august sovereign. But for whom was he playing that evening? What memories, what once-loved faces, were conjured up in the depths of those mirrors? Dida . . . Elisa . . . Pauline. . . .

Metternich, however, was ill and missed the performance. The next day he sent for Paganini to come to the Palace.

"To please the Prince," said Paganini, "I took up the first violin I could lay hands on. After he had heard me play, His Excellency was so much pleased that I repeated my visit another evening."

This time the drawing-rooms were deserted. There were no gay crowds, the mirrors were blank. After he had played, he was putting away his Guarnerius when a lady of a certain age, but still beautiful, approached him.

"You were a feast in yourself," she said.

"It was on that occasion," he added, "that Princess Metternich graciously invited me to come to Vienna. I promised her that when I left Italy, my first visit should be to that city."

* "At the concert last Thursday, the Cavaliere Crescentini came to see me in the green-room and invited me to dine with him on his estate. I spent a very pleasant evening in the company of Mademoiselle Colbran, and another lady, an amateur musician, as beautiful as Hebe, who made me fall madly in love with her, by her singing of the duet: *Per mare per fonti, cercando di Nice.* Signore Barbajà, the impresario of the theatre in Naples, sent me an invitation by Mademoiselle Colbran, offering me the theatre free of charge if I would come to Naples at the end of September." Bologna, July 1, 1818.

❦ Meanwhile, time passed between one carnival and another like water flowing under the arches of a bridge, and reflecting masquerading crowds. There was Nicolò himself, who looked more like a clown than ever with his hollow eyes and his cadaverous frame, and Rossini, still gay and sparkling, but already a little plump, a little bald. They were not to be a part of Rome much longer. They were soon to be carried off to the south by Barbajà. The impresario had made admirable arrangements. The Saturday after the party at the Braschi Palace, Paganini was to leave for Naples and go on to Palermo. He was worn out, and was to spend the winter in Palermo under the care of the best Sicilian doctors before returning to Naples. Here he was to undergo a rigorous cure before setting out for a tour of Germany, Russia, France, and England. Perhaps he would take a wife and have a baby boy or girl. But not yet! First he must recover his health, so that he could go to Vienna.

❦ Rossini, in his theatre in Naples, was contending with troubles of every description. Already last year, in *Moses in Egypt*, the public had invariably laughed at the Passage of the Red Sea by the children of Israel, which was grotesquely staged. The waves were of cardboard, six feet high, above the level of the stalls and the boxes, and were worked by stage carpenters who were supposed to be invisible. *Mahomet II* had involved him in other difficulties. His librettist, the Duke of Ventignano, was supposed to have the evil eye, and the composer was obliged to write his music with one hand while making the appropriate gesture with the other. Finally, when he returned to Rome for the carnival of 1821, on the very morning of the dress rehearsal of his new opera, *Mathilde de Sabran*, Maestro Bollo, the conductor, was struck down before his eyes with apoplexy. The music was unfamiliar, the cast inexperienced and nervous. There was every prospect of a complete fiasco.

At that moment Nicolò, who had just returned from the south, appeared in the proscenium, dressed in black from head to foot, like a Mephistopheles. He knew *Mathilde* as thoroughly as he had once known *Tancredi*. During the winter, when his friend was composing the opera, he had watched its creation bar by bar. He had deciphered it, handled it with his magic fingers, embroidered it with many variations. *Mathilde* was his god-daughter. He would present her to the public.

On the first night he conducted while playing the violin part an octave higher. The demoralized orchestra was completely galvanized. For three successive nights, replacing the leader and the horn player, supporting by turns the soprano and the bassoon, he led the whole hypnotized company to a triumphant success.

Like sleep-walkers who had come safely down from the roof, they were now ready to laugh at the danger and to joke with one another. King Carnival was the guest of honour. Nicolò's quartets for bows and guitar had the priority at all the musical soirées. He himself doubled the parts of violin and guitar, hanging the latter round his neck by a ribbon. He was no longer among strangers, but surrounded by friends and fellow-countrymen. The Marchese d'Azeglio, the youthful leader of the Italian patriots, sang a duet with Mathilde de Sabran, the pretty Liparini. One evening after supper they all dressed up. They covered up their evening coats and low-necked gowns with rags and paraded the town like a troop of street musicians. Rossini improvised as he tripped along, his plump little corporation shaking ridiculously, while Paganini's gaunt silhouette had a feminine look about it. A ray of moonlight glided over lips that glowed with kisses and over the polished surface of the guitars. This was the song the beggars sang:

> We are the blind,
> Blind from our birth.

> Be kind, be kind
> On a day of mirth,
> Spare us a penny,
> We are the blind.

Windows were opened; coins were flung down. Mad pranks were played till dawn on their more sedate friends, who had remained in their palaces.

The Carnival of 1821 came to an end, and the gay parties broke up. Paganini was preparing two concerts for the Argentina theatre and considering new proposals made to him by Barbajà, who was in Naples. Rossini returned to his San Carlo Theatre, while the Marchese Massimo d'Azeglio went back to his schemes for Italian Independence.

ROMANCE IN NAPLES

GERMI'S visits to the *Passo di Gatta Mora* became more frequent. Antonio Paganini had died on April 1, 1817, after commending his soul to his guardian angel and all the company of heaven. He left a disconsolate widow. Nicolò's sisters had made reasonably good matches, though they could not help comparing their own modest way of life and their unduly large families with the career of their brilliant brother, who was away in foreign parts. The elder, Nicoletta, had lost her first husband Gondolfo and was now Signora Ghisolfi. Domenica, wife of Giuseppi Passadore, was expecting another child. Carlo, the elder son, was making a living by playing in an orchestra and giving violin lessons. But Teresa had aged. It was now Germi's visits alone that kindled the old light in her eyes. Since she could neither read nor write, the "adorable friend" was her one link with Nicolò.

In July 1821 he made his way once more to the old quarter of Genoa bringing letters from Naples. He thought of young Columbus, who, like Nicolò, had escaped from this unchanging environment. He imagined himself, three centuries ago, bringing to the family of his friend, that daring sailor, a message in a bottle that had been cast up by the sea only that morning.

This time the bottle was full, and Teresa smoothed her brow. She still thought of her son—now a grown man—as the baby on whose behalf she had prayed one dazzling night: "Lord make him the King of violinists." But whenever he came back to her, feverish with his triumphs, or stricken by some mysterious malady, she bitterly accused herself of having cast a spell on him.

"This country," Nicolò wrote from Naples, "is enchanting, with its lovely climate, magnificent views, perfect wines, splendid carriages, public parks as radiant as Gardens of the Hesperides, and charming women. . . ."

But Paganini was living austerely, like a prudent Genoese.

"This first time I played at the great San Carlo Theatre the public broke a social law for my benefit. All demonstrations of approval or disapproval are forbidden until the court has led the way. This time, however, the public did not wait for the signal. They clapped and cheered and applauded enthusiastically. I have made the acquaintance of a most charming girl of seventeen, beautiful as an angel, with the education of a princess, with such a sweet expression and such a divine voice that everyone is in love with her. She sings divinely and her name is —guess!—Catalani. She is the daughter of the foremost advocate in Naples, one of its richest citizens. The girl would like to marry me, but her father would never give his consent. Neapolitans do not like their daughters to leave the nest. God forbid that I should form any ties without due consideration. Liberty is a man's most precious possession. . . ."

Still the same Nicolò!

With a smile, Germi took another sheet of more recent date, which was scrawled all over with Nicolò's large writing. This letter referred to plans for tours of Germany, Russia, France, and England.

"Suppose I were to take a wife!" he added.

Teresa pricked up her ears. But there was other news, exciting news in the same letter. Nicolò was making provision for his mother. He was settling on her an annuity of £1,200 and had bought her a house, near the church of Nostra Dama delle Vigne.

"Now there will always be a room for me, when I come home to see her and to enjoy some of that excellent minestrone, which she makes so divinely."

Perceiving that the old lady was overcome with emotion, Germi, like a practised orator, led up to the climax: Nicolò was engaged to be married.

"At last," he wrote, "I have decided to follow the dictates of my heart, and, as befits my circumstances, to take a wife. She is a charming girl belonging to one of the best families and combines beauty with a strict upbringing. She has really touched my heart. Although she has no dowry as yet, I have chosen her of my own free will and intend to be happy with her. I can think of no greater bliss. If heaven permits, my years will pass joyfully and I shall see myself again in my son." *

Three or four documents were required to complete the arrangements for the marriage. Nicolò begged Germi to help him. There were two points that troubled him. In the first place, Teresa had to sign an act of consent and she could not write.

"When she goes to the lawyer," wrote Nicolò, "she must pretend that she has a whitlow and keep her thumb bandaged. That will save our bacon."

The other point was an even thornier one. According to the baptismal register, Nicolò was in his fortieth year. If Germi could persuade the *curé* of San Salvador, who was the parish priest, to state that he was "under forty" it would be a great relief to him.

"And whatever you do," he wrote, "be quick about it. You know my nature, my hypersensitive nerves, my feverish imagination, and you will realize what a state I am in. If you would not have me consumed with love and impatience, make haste. I am longing to show you my Venus. You will have to admit that in love, as in everything else, Paganini shuns mediocrity. When

* Naples, June 22, 1822.

you and my mother see the object of my affection, you will be unable to resist her. You will thank heaven, as I do, for having created a child with every grace of body and soul."

Germi was sceptical; Teresa pensive. "Is that all?" her expression seemed to say.

As he was folding up the letter, Germi concluded his reading: "The marriage seems to have been made in heaven, so we may well hope for happiness."

There he stopped. He thought it would be ridiculous to read her the ending: "How are you, *mio caro?* Do you still love me? I shall love you till my dying day."

A CURE OF ASSES' MILK

HARDLY had the required documents been despatched when the engagement was broken off. No one knew the reason. Germi alone had some inkling of the truth.

"Beloved friend," wrote Nicolò, "I am sorry I have not written to you before. For your own private information, I will confide to you that the girl was such a scatterbrain that she was never of the same mind for two minutes at a time. That is why I have broken off our engagement, after four days which seemed like four years."

The truth was that his fiancée, Carolina Banchieri, the child who was endowed "with every grace of body and soul," had been in too much of a hurry. She had left her father's house to follow Paganini to Parma. As in the case of Angelina, both the elopement and the betrothal had come to an untimely end. A peasant woman of the neighbourhood had been put in charge of the girl and, in case of inquiry, would maintain that Carolina had been in her care ever since she left home.

"Thus," said the seducer, "perhaps people will believe what is not strictly true."

Apart from his private life, there were different opinions concerning the impression made by Paganini in the south. He continued to play more and more as if he were inspired; improvising, it seemed, his great Fantasias with Recitative and Variations. Sometimes he accompanied singers in Rossini's Cavatinas. Poets compared the effects produced by his music to the seraphic ecstasies of St. Francis. Others referred to the cold-

73

ness shown him by the Sicilians and the poor reception he had had in Naples. In that city, it was said, a conspiracy had been hatched between certain jealous instrumentalists and the composer Danna, who had placed the almost indecipherable manuscript of one of his cantatas before the maestro. But it was child's play to Paganini, who read it at sight, even turning it upside down. On another occasion, his innkeeper, suspecting from his appearance that he was suffering from consumption, which was regarded in Naples as a contagious disease, had actually put his bed out into the street. One of his pupils, a 'cellist of the name of Ciandelli (who, except for a young violinist called Camillo Sivori, was Paganini's only pupil in Naples), took the Master into his house, gave him bed and board, and administered a beating to the innkeeper.

Whatever the truth may have been, he left for the north in the autumn of 1821, with the intention of visiting his home on his way to Vienna. But in the course of the winter he was prostrated with fresh attacks of his malady, first in Parma and then in Milan. He was laid low until the spring and envied Rossini who was more fortunate than himself. Rossini had entered into a new contract with Barbajà, and was now on his way, with all his best executants, to Austria, London, and Paris.

"You will be hearing the news of Rossini's marriage to Mademoiselle Colbran," Paganini wrote to Germi. "They have made a fool of Barbajà. And shortly before the marriage, which was performed post-haste in Rome, Mademoiselle Colbran took eighty-four ducats off him. All his company are assembled in Vienna, and they are all, including Rossini and Davide, delighted with the city."

Vienna! The name echoed in his ears like a summons. Paganini, in thought, was wafted to the Danube on the wings of a certain phrase, which was worth a thousand compliments:

"You were a feast in yourself," Princess Metternich had said to him in Rome.

He was eagerly awaited in Vienna. But alas for the irony of it! Here he was, coughing his soul out. When his intestines were recovering, the mysterious enemy stabbed him in the back. What was it, this microbe that was torturing him, attacking throat and lungs and every part of him? How could he fight it, when each of his organs in turn basely surrendered?

Nevertheless he would not give in. First he must have rest. One of his friends, a general, who had borne a great name during the Napoleonic epoch in Italy, was living in retirement at Villanuova, near Como. He invited Paganini to stay with him. What could be more soothing to his nerves than spring on the Italian Lakes? What would be lovelier than Lake Maggiore, the Barromian Isles, the villa Carlotte, with its paradise of giant azaleas which perfumed the breeze with a thousand blossoms? The General, who had been dismissed by the Austrians, was a passionate lover of music, especially Paganini's. Nicolò would show him his latest compositions for the guitar, which was a favourite instrument of his host.

"I am going to stay at Field-Marshal Pino's country place on Lake Como," he wrote, "where I hope to be completely restored to health."

⟨ But he suddenly grew worse. His anxiety about his health increased. He left Milan and went to the University of Pavia, which was famous throughout Italy, for a diagnosis. After a thorough examination, the doctors exclaimed in unison:

"What madness to treat such a condition with old wives' remedies! What is required is a severe régime. . . ."

The celebrated Dr. Borda was summoned from Milan, which was close by, for a consultation. He confirmed the opinion of his colleagues, ordered asses' milk, and forbade the patient to take wine. The racking, persistent cough was due to a microbe, which would disappear as the result of an intensive "negative cure." Did they think it was consumption? Borda refused to commit himself.

"What a horrible cure it is!" Nicolò complained. "I have already had massage fifty-five times—thirty treatments at a drachma each, ten at four deniers and fifteen at five, without having derived the slightest benefit. Borda himself is puzzled by a malady, which is so obscure yet so persistent. He says it will take months, but in the end he hopes for a complete cure, so I must pluck up courage!"

Everything conspired against him, the rainy weather, the fever, which delayed his departure for Lake Como where a *belissima* she-ass and a lovely cow had been bought for him by the General. How could he help putting on weight! These setbacks, which at first he thought would be a matter of a few days, had already lasted more than a year, from June 1822 to August 1823. Except for a concert of Catalani * in Milan to which Paganini had dragged himself, he had remained "already buried" at Pavia. During these dark days, which dragged on and on, there were two rays of light that comforted him. One was Germi's affection, the other his own faith in his star. He even poked fun at the "admirable Borda," who declared that his malady was "something quite new," with a virus of its own that had not yet been discovered.

"Then patience, dearest friend, and look to the future," the sick man wrote in a mood softened by suffering. "If only I could tell you how much I love you! If you really love me till death, send me news of yourself. I was worried about my pulse, which continues to be feverish and irregular, but a letter from you

---

* "She has a perfect instrument in her strong and flexible voice," said Paganini, "but she has no sense of rhythm and no musical understanding. She would have more soul, had she been trained by famous masters, such as Crescentini, Pachierotti, Babini. . . ." Milan, June 18, 1823.

makes me feel well again and even my cough stops troubling me."

In the meantime, even the milk of asses and goats proved ineffective. Borda decided to take risks. In his feverish condition Nicolò began to dread the ministrations of the attendants, who massaged him, syringed him, and bled him by the doctors' orders. In an attempt to discover the cause of the cough, he was given large doses of mercury.

"I felt as if they had bought my body for their experiments," the patient complained. "Their proceedings seemed to me to smack of immorality, ignorance, and dishonesty. As a last resource I was given large doses of opium, and although the drug soothed my cough, it paralysed all my bodily functions. I could hardly stand and could not digest even a small cup of chocolate in twenty-four hours. Asthma set in; my stomach began to swell. Imagine what I looked like! Happy the man, dearest friend, who is permitted to escape to the other world without the aid of doctors."

At last he gave his nurses the slip, escaped from the torture chamber, and made his way into the town. He was a walking skeleton and seemed to be alive only by a miracle. He scribbled off an account of his escapade to his friend. He was at the end of his tether, and collapsed in a café, where an American doctor, who by a happy chance was present, came to his rescue. He revived him, but startled him by warning him that, unless he followed his advice, he would be in his grave within a month. He had had experience of similar cases, including the cough, which he said was due to extreme nervous exhaustion, a malady with which Italian doctors were not familiar.

"Here I am. I put myself in your hands," exclaimed the sick man in a loud voice, while all the other customers gathered sympathetically round him.

"He gave me pills of his own concoction," continued Nicolò,

"and put me on to a wholesome diet of grilled veal chops and good wine. In a few days I was restored to health and now I am feeling splendid. . . . In Milan the American * doctor is the talk of the town because of this miracle that he has performed. My cough is gradually disappearing. At the end of a week I shall return to General Pino, where I shall be better looked after and able to take riding exercise which is recommended by my American. We all detest Borda for ruining me not only physically, but financially, and making me waste nearly two whole years in misery.

"Excuse my bad writing. My American doctor allows me only five minutes of concentration at a time. One kiss, Your affectionate *Nicolò Paganini*." †

Once more his star was shining brightly in the firmament.

* He was actually a German. Paganini met him fourteen years later in Marseilles, where he was known as Dr. Spitzer.

† Milan, November 26, 1823.

ANTONIA BIANCHI

IT WAS some time since Bianchi had first come into his life, but his illness had stood in his way. There was also that strange prejudice of his, the morbid distrust of women, which was continually crushing his dream of a one and only love. Except for the passionate days of his adolescence, when he lay at the feet of Dida, he had often been attracted only to be disillusioned. And with each fresh reincarnation of his dream, a new and fairer image presented itself, which, he grudgingly admitted, gave him at least some precious moments. In his letter to Germi, announcing the breaking off of his engagement to Carolina Banchieri, he had added a postscript: "As this woman vanishes out of my life, that other one, of whom I have told you, is recalled to my mind."

Antonia Bianchi had heard him for the first time in Venice, in the season of 1816–1817, and had fallen in love with him on the spot. But his head was full of the lovely, aristocratic ladies, who were his friends, and he did not spare a glance for the humble singer at the San Samuele Theatre. While she was rising, step by step, in her career, this man, whose heart seemed to be of stone, was continuing his meteoric career.

But it so happened that he himself had suffered a rebuff. "I was slightly enamoured of that Venetian lady, but letters reached me with such lurid reports of her behaviour that I never want to hear of her again. She has given up her music, declares that she does not love me and that she sets no value on my friendship."

Bianchi now permitted herself to hope. On one of his visits to Venice, Antonia was singing at an evening party at which he was present. This time her rendering of Rossini's *Cinderella* was so charming that he fell in love with both the singer and Rossini's variations.

"Learn to sing," he said to her, "and I may be able to engage you for my concerts."

What declaration of love could have equalled that one curt remark? To crown it all, at the end of seven years of perseverance and endeavour Antonia actually appeared with Paganini at a concert in Genoa, on May 14, 1824, with which he celebrated his return. To be allowed to share the glamour of that triumph was a truly royal gift. None of his subsequent successes in Italy banished the memory of the great ovation he received, or of the fever of anticipation with which his concert was awaited. He had not played in Genoa since the Cavanna scandal, some ten years ago. Reports of his concert tours had reached Genoa, accompanied by long commentaries on the part of friend and foe. Then came the rumour of an eclipse.

"We hear," said the *Genoa Gazette*, "that since his recovery from his long illness he has made great progress."

Progress? What was the meaning of this word, applied to so dazzling a career? Interest was further stimulated by the rumour that, after his magnificent performance in Milan the previous week, and after tomorrow's concert, to which all Genoa was eagerly looking forward, he was to leave Italy for a prolonged tour of Europe.

All expectations paled before the reality in the Sant' Agostino Theatre. In spite of a deluge of rain, the hall was packed. Paganini received a frenzied ovation.

"It is impossible," said the *Genoa Gazette*, "to describe in words the expression, the unearthly sounds, which he draws from his wonderful instrument. The most skilled musicians, the most learned professors, are baffled. It is Paganini's secret.

His fingers attain a rapidity, his notes a velocity, which neither the ear nor the eye can follow. Hearers and onlookers are spellbound. He has adopted the habit of playing from memory. He stands on the platform, alone with his violin. One might well say, an Apollo. . . ."

Others described him as a sorcerer, an angel, a devil, who could transform his violin at will into a flute, a guitar, a 'cello, or even a human voice. The least enthusiastic referred to him as a prodigy.

"Bianchi," the *Gazette* added patronizingly, "made a favourable impression and was recalled several times."

Antonia Bianchi, white as a sea-gull in her snowy veils! When she was animated, her eyes sparkled ingenuously beneath her dark locks. The pearly smoothness of her skin was set off by her velvet bodice. Her voice and talent were mediocre, but she possessed undoubted charm. Paganini was aware of it; he was disturbed by her magnetism, while he amused himself by troubling the peace of one who was already in an ecstasy of emotion. He sunned himself in the lingering glances she bestowed on him.

"I am not handsome," he said complacently, "but when the women hear me play they come crawling to my feet."

She made up her mind to captivate the great man.

And what of Paganini? Returning from those dark regions of suffering, he threw himself with the ardour of one raised from the dead into this new love affair, which he vowed was the real thing at last. He was proud of Antonia, who charmed his friends; proud even of her absurd but flattering jealousy, proud of his own genius, his own virility and of his kindness to her. She owed everything to him; he would speak to Barbajà about her and push her on, and even perhaps. . . .

Yes. He decided, after an additional concert on May 21, 1824, to make her a promise. In the autumn they would appear together in Venice, where their romance had begun. But until then she must work.hard. In the meantime he, the maestro, had to devote himself to those perennial mistresses of his, the cities of Milan, Brescia, Bergamo, Udine, Verona, Padua. . . .

In Milan he supped with Ugo Foscolo, who, recalling the concert Paganini had just given, evoked the Iliad.

"All Homer appeared before me," cried the poet. "The grandiose first piece conjured up the arrival of the Greek vessels before Troy. The charm of the *adagio* reminded me of a tender scene between Achilles and Briseis. When shall I hear you play the hero's lament for the death of Patroclus?"

"When Achilles Paganini finds his Patroclus among violinists," replied Paganini, in staccato tones.

At last in lovely Venice, Nicolò rejoined the fair Bianchi.

It was the Venetian autumn, heavy, voluptuous, golden, saturated with music. Venice herself, fair, languorous, and feminine, was reflected in her innumerable mirrors. Nicolò was like a lark, caught in full song. He had fallen in love again. He could breathe. He could create. He composed a second Concerto, sparkling with vivacity, with a finale which had the accompaniment of a tinkling bell. The celebrated *Rondo à la Clochette* was to see the light of day. The horizon was brightening.

To the familiar ripple of the canal, his public life went on, with the engagements, successes, and disappointments common to his profession. In Rome the Pope gave further proofs of his favour.

"Do you know that His Eminence, the Cardinal Secretary of State, who is eighty-four years of age, said after he had heard me play, that never in all his life had he spent such a delightful evening. He intends to obtain a decoration for me from His Holiness. To be sure a decoration of this kind does not amount to much, but outside Italy it is valued highly."

But the summer of 1824 in Venice was stiflingly hot. Besides, the Opera refused to extend its hospitality to him, out

of spite "because my concerts had done it harm." The famous
passage about an "amorous peccadillo" in Stendhal's *Life of
Rossini*, which was now in its seventh edition, caused a great
deal of talk. All society was excited about it and Germi's aid
was once more invoked.

"Your kind letter about the author's calumny in the *Life
of Rossini*, is causing a great sensation in Venice. All my
friends are delighted. I am infinitely obliged to you."

But in Rome tongues were wagging.

"I was surprised to hear that I had learnt to play the violin
while in chains. You must get me a certificate from the Governor refuting all these fabrications, so that I can obtain what
I want" (*i.e.* a Papal decoration).

In the meantime the centre of gravity of his whole existence
had shifted. He was overwhelmed by emotion at the news
which Antonia gave him: she was with child. "I shall see myself again in my son," he once wrote to Teresa.

He spent Christmas of 1825 in Rome, and joined in the
celebrations. There were to be no more lapses. Those days
were over. The devil had reformed and become a monk.

"Here I am, joining in processions and singing litanies, for
it is Holy Year. Although there are few foreigners here, they
have asked me to give a concert. I shall do so, provided I can
obtain permission to open one of the halls."

He was, however, chiefly concerned with finding a retreat,
an oasis, to which he and Antonia could repair to enjoy their
love in private. But everything, including his own family, conspired against this plan. His sisters pestered him to set up his
nephews in life. He was rich and powerful. Surely he ought
to help them and send them money. Luckily Germi was there
to act as a watchdog and transact the necessary business.

"I told my mother that I never wanted to hear the Passa-
dores and the Ghisolfis mentioned again. As a reward for her
forbearance, I will help them. If my precious family do not

love me, I certainly adore you. Give my love to my mother."

He had to take a more accommodating tone with Barbajà and carry out his contracts, which took him to Florence, Sala, the Argentina in Rome, the Del Fondo in Naples. It was to the advantage of Bianchi's career as well as his own. "I am making Bianchi sing, to get her name known," he said to the impresario.

At last in the spring, his professional ties were relaxed. The oasis had been found and the lovers set out to enjoy the balmy climate of the south.

"On April 22d, 1825," wrote Nicolò, "that is to say the 22d of this month, I am leaving for Palermo."

Palermo. How much it stood for: spring, palm trees, music, relaxation. It was a Nirvana of perfume, peace, liberty, and happiness. During the summer, he gave only four public performances (May 28, June 17, July 8, September 16, 1825), but with his first concert he made a conquest of the Sicilians. In this Eden there was no registry office, no giving in marriage. On July 23, 1825, a son was born to them who received a baptism of sunshine and joy. He was called Achileo, Achillino, Achillininetto. The lovers were inseparable. Time passed in a dream. Paganini realized one day, to his surprise, that for nearly a year invitations to himself had always included Bianchi.

"As soon as Professor Samengo, the well-known amateur, heard of our arrival he insisted on our going to stay with him."

Samengo was a rich Genoese merchant, who had settled in Trieste. When his famous compatriot agreed to give a concert in that town, he extended a magnificent welcome to Paganini and his companion. The audience at the Teàtro Nuovo were equally demonstrative. At his first concert, the general enthusiasm was expressed by a voice from the stalls exclaiming: "*Angelo del Paradiso.*"

It was Meyerbeer, who for the next few months accompanied the maestro wherever he went.

The violinists in the orchestra learnt their lesson from Paganini and accepted it philosophically.

"We may as well make our wills," said one of them, Benesh by name, to an Austrian of the name of Jähl.

"It's too late," said Jähl. "We are dead already."

In Venice the strange pair were lionized. Count Paruchini, a descendant of the Doges, sent his gondola to meet the steamer on which the great man was travelling. Nicolò had given a successful concert in Trieste, but he was out of sorts. He was nervous and on edge and was dressed all in black, as at the concert, except for a yellow nankeen waistcoat, which greatly shocked Pancaldi, whom the Count had sent to meet him.

"He was most improperly dressed himself," observed Pancaldi in his *Memoirs*, "although he had made la Bianchi put on evening dress. After keeping the company waiting, all of whom were dying to see them, they were announced at Paruchini's reception as Madame Bianchi and Professor Paganini. The rooms were packed with elegant *signore* and *signorine*, who all turned to look at them. To my horror, Paganini was still wearing the same atrocious yellow waistcoat which he had worn on the steamer. With much dignity he presented Signora Antonia to the ladies, and invited her to sing, but when he himself was earnestly entreated to play, he flatly refused.

" 'The Count played me false,' he said to me. 'I understood that there was to be only a handful of friends, but he has invited the whole of Venice. I do not feel inclined to play this evening.' "

When he returned to their lodgings, he was in no mood for amorous dalliance. One of those terrible revulsions of feeling, with which he was only too familiar, was beginning to work havoc with his romance. He had recognized the symptoms some time ago. Antonia had annoyed him at Paruchini's party. In public she was embarrassingly jealous; she was vulgar, absurdly pretentious, and without real talent. He had transferred all his affection to Achillino, whose hair was already beginning to curl. He remained with Antonia solely for the sake of the child. Antonia, who had a temper of her own, was becoming uneasy. She pried, she made every possible *faux pas* and only succeeded in widening the breach.

"You know," he was soon confiding to Germi, "Bianchi, who is still with me, has one great defect, she flies into a rage over the merest trifle."

One day he left her alone in the house for a quarter of an hour, and she attempted to break his violin. It was only saved by his valet, after she had hurled it to the ground four times. Two days later, instead of leaving her at home, he took her with him to the house of some Spanish grandees. It was here that the climax was reached.

"The son of the house wanted to talk to me about the peculiarities of a certain fervent devotee of the violin. Bianchi interrupted us, and, out of jealousy I suppose, asked me to take her home. I wanted to know the reason. Whereupon she boxed my ears violently (*gifle puissantissime*) and uttered such infernal screams that she alarmed the whole assembly. She shrieked till she nearly burst, and we thought we should never bring her to her senses."

Alas for Palermo, its spring, its palm trees!

The oasis had concealed a volcano.

❦ The Pope sent him a decoration—that same Leo XII who had once in Rome made him a present of all the Fridays in Lent. On April 25, Nicolò became Chevalier of the Golden Spur.

Chevalier! With a flaming bow in his hand! What was he—Archangel or Lucifer? It was all one to him. He served a tyrannical power, which he would never betray. He made a final tour of some of the Italian cities, but his eyes were once more fixed on Vienna, the focus of all his plans. He persuaded his cousin, Lazzaro Rebizzo, to meet him in Vienna. Forty-two spare bows had already arrived there in perfect condition. He had sent his twelve-year-old pupil, Camillo Sivori, to London to prepare the way for his visit, and the boy was doing wonders. Catalani offered Paganini a most tempting contract to give concerts with her in Vienna. Beethoven himself was calling him, in those quartets of his, which he played so enthusiastically in Bologna with doctor friends who were amateur musicians. When would he be able to obey the summons?

One obstacle after another presented itself. Achillino broke his leg and the fidgety maestro sat motionless for hours on end with the child on his knees. Then he himself caught a "severe cold." Again the doctors despaired of his life. But he discovered a wonderful new remedy, the *Elixir le Roy*, which purged him and reduced his blood pressure and enabled him to dispense with the doctors.

After this he received a wound in his hand, which, however, healed up miraculously. Then the city of Genoa begged him to become director of their new theatre, Carlo-Felice. Bianchi, too, was regaining lost ground. He was weakening. She looked so pretty recently at the Scala and sang his *rondo* in such a masterly way that she was greeted with a storm of applause. She was certainly making progress. Once more Paganini yielded to her entreaties and declined Catalani's proposals. He settled on his mistress an annuity of a hundred Milanese ducats.

"At last," he sighed, "Bianchi is satisfied."

Should he take her with him? She clung to him with might and main. And Milan, too, was clamouring for him to give a concert at the Teàtro Ré.

"I shall be proud," he said, "to come to the rescue of my dear Milan and the students of Pavia.

"I may give another concert on my own account. I want to

hear myself play my third Concerto with the Polacca, which has never yet been performed, and my Variations without orchestral accompaniment, in which I shall play all the parts."

Would he ever get away?

At last, on January 2, 1828, the Alps were drawing near. He breathed deeply as he studied the map.

"I am having a comfortable carriage prepared for the journey," he wrote, at last, to Germi, "and I am leaving with Bianchi for Vienna early next week."

PART II AUSTRIA
GERMANY
POLAND

THE PASHA OF EGYPT'S GIRAFFE

WHAT is the explanation of this thing called fashion? How and when does it originate? Its chief promoters and patrons are great cities, great fortunes, and great ladies. Vienna was rising again after her overthrow at the hands of Napoleon. She was revelling in the joy of life and in captivating melodies. The secret of her exuberance was her passionate desire for pleasure. While Beethoven, deaf and lonely, was composing his Mass in D, Prince Metternich had returned home and was rapturously greeting his friends from Rome again. As early as 1818, when Catalani was touring Austria, he introduced and fostered with his kindly patronage amateur concerts and theatricals.

"At the first rehearsal of the concert, which was held at my house," the Chancellor recorded, "Goethe arrived. I presented him to Madame Catalani, and told her that he was a man whom Germany delighted to honour. Valabrègue, her husband, said: 'Who is Goethe?' I told him he was the author of Werther. The unfortunate man remembered this. Some days later he went up to the poet and said: 'My dear Goethe, what a pity you didn't see Potier playing the part of Werther. You would have died of laughing.' "

In the spring of 1822 the whole company from Naples, presented by Barbajà, with Rossini himself at the head, had been transferred to the Kärntnerthor Theatre. After the first performance of Zelmira, it was evident that in Vienna, as in Naples, triumphs awaited the "spoilt child of fortune."

That was how Weber somewhat jealously described his

91

brother composer, in spite of the ovation which his own *Freischütz* had received a few days earlier at the same theatre.

"It was a wonderful inspiration of mine," said Metternich, "to persuade the Italian Opera to come to Vienna."

He gave a pensive sigh. It appeared that he was hoping for a still more remarkable visitor. But it was clearly a case for patience.

Two years later Italian music had conquered all Austria, including Hegel, the philosopher, who admitted frankly to his wife:

"My taste is now so perverted that I infinitely prefer Rossini's *Figaro* to Mozart's. It is the same with the Italian singers, who act and sing infinitely more *con amore.*"

If both the minister and the philosopher confessed to this preference, public enthusiasm was likely to go to all lengths. But it so happened that in January 1828, at the very moment when Paganini, under Bianchi's jealous eye, was stepping into his carriage, tenderly watching over his Achillino and his Guarnerius, Vienna, the object of his journey, the artistic capital of Europe, Vienna, but lately widowed of her Beethoven, had gone mad over a giraffe.

The giraffe was the latest gift of the Pasha of Egypt to the Emperor Francis, and the Viennese, who delighted in anything exotic, were never tired of trooping in family parties to the Zoological Gardens at Schoenbrunn to admire it. They doted on its silky coat, its tiny horns, which the goldsmiths reproduced in miniature in gold. It was the fashionable craze. Everyone was wearing spotted gloves *à la giraffe.* This ridiculous cult had an astonishing vogue, which originated in the Ring and the Boulevards and almost rivalled the nobler joys of the opera and the concert hall.

Music lovers, however, saw a most interesting item of news in the *Theatrical Journal* of March 1828: "The famous Genoese violinist, the Chevalier Nicolò Paganini, has at last decided to undertake a tour beyond the confines of Italy, and to dedicate his first performances to Vienna, the City of the Arts."

The notice in *The Review of Art, Literature and Fashion* was more detailed, and predicted that Paganini's playing "would give pleasure of a high and unusual quality." It indulged in phrases such as "universal admiration," "a technique that had become proverbial," "unparalleled audacity." It added that concert-goers, when they went to the Theatre of the Redoubt, where the recital was to take place on March 28, would find that the price of seats had been doubled and that most of them were already booked.

Paganini the composer, who was a fanatical admirer of Beethoven and Rossini, roused as much interest as Paganini the virtuoso with the lightning fingers. And what of the man himself? He had arrived some days ago, as early as the 16th, and so far no one had contrived to see him, except Prince and Princess Metternich, whose drawing-room was the only one in all Vienna where he had condescended to play. He was thought to be a strange man, possessed, it was said, by occult powers.

Amateurs and professionals, all the violinists in Vienna, were waiting impatiently to hear him—the Böhms, the Strebingers, Jansa, Slawich, Mayseder, Léon de Saint-Lubin, and many others. They would judge for themselves. The frivolous city was pouring out money like water. The receipts had reached an astronomical figure.

❡ The orchestra had played the Overture to *Fidelio*. Immediately afterwards, above the dazzling row of footlights, the maestro himself appeared, pale, with ravaged features and flaming eyes. With the first stroke of his bow, "almost, one might say, with his first step on to the platform," Schilling remarked, "his reputation in Germany was made." The sound of his violin was like an electric flash, flooding him with light, "like a wonderful apparition in the world of art." This radiance suffused everything he played: the Concerto in B minor, the *Military Sonata* on the G string, the Larghetto, the Fantasy on Rossini's *Cinderella*.

The *Theatrical Journal* * of Vienna was rhapsodical: "When a new star appears in a trajectory, of which one can divine neither the chord nor the radius, the keenest observer can offer mere conjectures. If one speaks of inconceivable difficulties, which are executed as easily as the simplest air; of miracles of double-stopping, harmonics, incredible *staccati* performed in the most rapid *tempo*, yet with the most perfect tranquillity; if one says that in his hands the violin transcends the most moving human voice, that his ardent soul kindles the vital flame in every heart, that every note is pure and perfect, that every singer could learn from him everything he needs to know, it all amounts to nothing. It is only a gleam from the glittering mirror of his playing."

The ball had been set rolling. The publicity campaign reached delirious heights. Vienna was in the grip of a new frenzy. And what a frenzy it was!

"It is magic," wrote the correspondent of the *Leipzig Journal*, describing Paganini's masterly playing. "We are all of us bewitched, chained to the strings of his violin."

"In his own sphere he stands alone. He is unique," another journal declared. "His most distinguished colleagues are racking their brains to discover his secret."

By May 11 the new Orpheus had given six concerts. He performed almost exclusively his own compositions, "exalting more than any other artist of his generation, the pure and romantic spirit of music, which sprang from the divine spark of Prometheus." A correspondent in Vienna wrote, in June 1828, to the *Revue Musicale* (of which Fétis was the editor): "Paganini has been received with the utmost enthusiasm. He has actually started a fashion which, according to the *Austrian Observer*,

* April 4, 1828.

bids fair to rival the vogue of the giraffe, recently presented by the Pasha of Egypt, and the object of much admiration. On May the 11th, Paganini gave his sixth concert, which was to have been his last. The programme was as follows: 1. Overture to *Lodoïska*, by Cherubini. 2. Concerto, by Rode, consisting of *Allegro Maestro* and *Adagio Cantabile* in double stopping, especially adapted for this concert by the maestro. 3. The last air from the *Last Days of Pompeii*, sung by Signora Bianchi. 4. Sonata on the *Prayer of Moses* (which was encored) on the 4th string. 5. Variations on a theme from *Armida*, by Rossini, sung by Signora Bianchi. 6. Caprice on the theme of *La ci darem la mano*, composed and executed by the maestro. This concert, which took place in the day time, attracted a great crowd. The house was packed; every seat was occupied two hours before the concert began, except a few that had been reserved for H.M. the Empress, the Archdukes and duchesses and other persons attached to the court."

These impassioned panegyrics were soon reflected in the literature and in the light music of the day. At the height of the season, the great Strauss himself, the King of the Waltz, wrote *alla Paganini*, and his example was followed by Fischoff. Quantities of sonnets were written on Paganini, and acrostics were made on his name. Italians and Germans vied with each other in inventing striking epithets: "The Prince of virtuosi," "the god of the violin," "the son of the gods." Painters competed for the honour of a sitting.

The price of the seats was now five florins each. In the grip of the universal mania, grave men left their politics and children their play. Throughout the social scale, from high to low, everyone was worshipping this strange divinity, for whose presence the infatuated population was clamouring everywhere. Every shop window displayed his portrait, in all sizes, from the huge lithograph to the tiny engraving on a signet ring. It was on the lid of every snuff-box and on the knob of every walking-stick.

"The maestro ravishes the ear," ran an advertisement for a bakery, "but the other senses, too, have a claim."

So there were edible busts of Paganini in marzipan and icing sugar. Rolls were baked in the shape of little violins. *Menus à la Paganini* figured in the restaurants, where people went to sup after hearing an operetta, in which Paganini was the hero, at the Theater an den Wien.* His fair admirers wore their hair parted in the middle and arranged in curls, like the locks that framed the illustrious brow, while a whole generation of Viennese tailors drew their inspiration from the same source. Paganini was godfather to a hat, a tie, shirt-studs, cigar-cases, handkerchiefs, shoes, and tie-pins. A brilliant stroke at billiards was called *à la Paganini*, while gloves *à la giraffe* were completely out of fashion. Instead, they were embroidered with a violin on the left hand and a bow on the right. How could hands so gloved fail to clasp the dream? Dresses were printed with musical symbols. Lamps in the shape of a lyre shed a discreet light. Tiny napkins embroidered with minute representations of the virtuoso appeared on the tables of the Redoubt dining-room.

Musicians, it was said, were pawning their clothes to buy a ticket. Cab drivers adjusted their charges with the price of the seats. "It was weird," said the gossips; "it was positively uncanny."

The Court, not to be outdone, took a hand in the game. On May 23 the Emperor conferred on Paganini the title of "Virtuoso to the Court." On July 10 the city fathers presented him with the Gold Medal of St. Salvator, which was engraved by Joseph Lang. The inscription on the reverse was *Perituris sonis non peritura gloria*, while on the obverse there was a reproduction of the maestro's violin and bow, crowned with oak leaves and resting on a page of music, on which the first bars of *La Clochette* were written.

* *The False Virtuoso*, or the Concerto on the G string. Farce in 2 acts by Meisel. Music by Glaser, leader of the orchestra. (May 22, 1828.)

At the palace of Schoenbrunn, embowered in bushes of flowering lilac, there were brilliant receptions which recalled the gay days in Rome. Francis II (for whom Paganini had written variations on the National Anthem, "God save the Emperor," which caused a furore) was still on the throne, while Metternich was still his Chancellor. To the Princess, Paganini remained "a feast in himself," but at her side, there was another princess, who inspired yet another fairy tale.

"If I had not been ill," he wrote to Germi on July 5, "I should have given my fourteenth concert, but I hope to give it either this week or the next, in obedience to the *obligeantissime* request of the Archduchess Marie-Louise. I am to let her know when I have recovered."

Paganini's head was completely turned. "People seem never to tire of hearing me," he continued. "Is there another Paganini in the world, do you think?"

He himself was like a violin, which was too tautly strung and played upon by a redoubtable hand. His own hand obeyed a mysterious control, which, ruthless and insistent, dealt in contrasts. In frivolous, worldly Vienna, Paganini felt the influence of Beethoven's mighty shade. Once when he was conducting one of the Symphonies, he was overcome with emotion and burst into tears.

"*E morto!*" he sobbed. "He is dead!" He was introduced to Beethoven's last quartets, all four of which he heard played by the best professors in Vienna, "who did me the honour of coming to my house. Afterwards I had the joy of playing them myself."

But his own implacable genius was not to be denied.

"I have composed two *Adagios*," wrote Paganini, with the same pen that had once paid homage to the *Witches*. "One of them brings tears to the eyes. The other, which is religious in tone,* overwhelms the hearer with a feeling of remorse."

* After a performance of this composition in Frankfurt on March

These were immediately succeeded by a dramatic sonata, entitled the *Tempest*. It consisted of eight episodes: 1. Approach of the Tempest; 2. Beginning of the Tempest; 3. Stormy seas; 4. Prayer; 5. The Whirlwind; 6. The Height of the Storm; 7. Calm; 8. Finale brilliante.

This romantic tornado may have been inspired by the *Pastoral Symphony*. Franz Liszt and François de Paule may well have walked on such waves as these.

When this new flow of inspiration had subsided, it was followed by a fit of deep depression, which damped his ardour and affected his whole system: stomach, throat, teeth, and especially his nerves. The *Elixir le Roy*, with which he was saturated, had ceased to be effective. He tried the homoeopathic treatment, which Hahnemann had recently introduced and which was the subject of much discussion. Then he tried a cure at Carlsbad, before putting himself into the hands of an Army doctor, Marenzeller by name. "A thousand and three!" exclaimed his valet, a true Genoese Leporello, who bore the suggestive name of Casanova. "Don Juan had a thousand and three lovely ladies, and you have a thousand and three doctors."

Another discordant element was Antonia, who was becoming more and more jealous and embittered. "I have washed my hands of her," he wrote. "She is a beast, an iniquitous beast."

What had he not done for Bianchi since his arrival in Vienna!

25, 1831, the anonymous correspondent of the *Frankfurt Journal*, Paris, wrote on April 3, 1831, as follows: "Hitherto we had contented ourselves with paying homage to Paganini's miraculous violin playing. The public had not realized the sparkling beauty and originality of his compositions. The concert on Good Friday must have carried conviction to the least experienced ears. He played an introduction which he modestly described as 'religious' but which his audience unanimously acclaimed as divine. To compose melodies so sweet he must have been carried away in an ecstasy to hear the singing of the cherubim. It vibrates with the awe, adoration and love that nature feels in the presence of the Creator."—(MS. preserved in the Theatrical Museum in Trieste.) *Paganini intimo*. V. Codignola.

He had given her a good place in his programmes and had presented her to the critics, who agreed that she had sung her great air by Paër in very good taste. He had taken her into society, although, even before his illness, his only reward had been scenes and bitter reproaches.

"I shall really have to send Bianchi away," he wrote at last to Germi; "she grates on me terribly. . . . I am going to separate from her. Tomorrow I am giving my tenth concert at the Italian Opera which will be entirely for her benefit."

The result of the concert was three thousand florins. And so ended the Venetian romance. The little Cinderella of the San Samuele Theatre had wrecked her career with her jealousy. She had to leave the ball while it was still at its height.

There remained the question of the child. On that point Nicolò was adamant. He referred the matter to the law courts in Vienna; they decided that Antonia's annuity should be commuted for an immediate award of two thousand Milanese scudi,* which was paid to the Viennese bankers, Arnstein & Eskeles, and that she was to be allowed access to her son. Assisted by a tutor, Herr Hammer by name, Paganini became responsible for the education of his beloved Achillino, who had grown into "a most charming child, sensitive and intelligent. I will tell you the whole story when I am calmer. But I never, never want to hear her name mentioned again."

This was his last reference to Antonia Bianchi. Achillino was now all that was left to him.

Finally a whisper from the past trailed like a serpent over the leaves, blighting the flowers. The public, who were at first amazed at his incredible supremacy in his art, now accepted all the old Italian tittle-tattle, which, Heaven knew how, had crossed the Alps, in the wake of the maestro.

So that was the explanation! Oh indeed!

* Grove's *Dictionary of Music and Musicians*.

"Prison," hissed this knot of vipers. "Murder! Mistress! Evil Eye! Witchcraft!" How else explain the fact that in the Scala in Milan he had made his violin pronounce distinctly the name of a lady with whom he was passionately in love?

With even more detail than formerly, Amati, the correspondent in Florence of the *Fashionable Gazette* of Leipzig, described the uneasy atmosphere of a concert at which he had been present. He was seated by a lady, whose melancholy beauty and magnificent hair had attracted his notice at the Polnischer Hof. She drew his attention again by the heart-rending sighs with which she accompanied Paganini's famous *Air on the G string*. This young lady was accompanied, and appeared to be protected, by a cavalier of sinister aspect, whose lips were curled in a sardonic smile, which, when the violinist, disturbed by the lady's sighs, turned round, appeared to match the smile that hovered upon the maestro's own lips. There was, it seemed, a link between them.

"Now," exclaimed the journalist, "I know the explanation of that smile."

In fact everyone was aware of it, and had long suspected that Paganini and Satan were in league with each other, if they were not actually one and the same person.

After reading such diatribes (for not a single critique escaped his eyes), Paganini was deeply chagrined. Was that Satanic shadow, that menacing double, the offspring of that early romance, to pursue him all over the world? What had this sombre image to do with the artist, who had earned official recognition as Virtuoso to the Imperial Court, and Chevalier of the Order of the Golden Spur, which had been conferred upon him by His Holiness Pope Leo XII?

Per Bacco, the possessor of all these dignities would know how to defend himself. For the first time in his life he replied, in Italian in the *Osservatore Triestino* and in German in the *Theaterzeitung*, to these slanders, "deeming it his duty to defend his honour and to enlighten the public on the subject of these vague rumours, which were being spread abroad and were wholly without foundation."

He had never, at any time, in any place, under any government, for whatever cause, been compelled to lead a life that differed in any way from the normal life of a free man, a respectable citizen, a staunch upholder of the law. This could be vouched for by the authorities under whose protection he had been able to live his life in freedom and honour, devoting himself to his family and his art. On the strength of this blameless record, he had ventured to appear before a public as indulgent and appreciative as that of Vienna, the first city outside Italy in which he had had the honour to give recitals.

It seemed as if Teresa, in far-away Genoa, had been troubled by the repercussions of these old woes. She hastened naïvely to comfort him.

Dearest son [she dictated]. It is now seven months since I wrote to you in Milan. I have just had the joy of receiving your letter of the ninth of this month, through the kind offices of Signore Agnino. I am overjoyed to hear that when you return from Paris and London, you intend to pay me a visit. I pray to the Almighty every day to keep both you and me in health, and to grant that I may see you again.

My dream has come true and God has kept His promise to me. You have won a great name, and by God's grace your Art has brought you fortune. You are loved and esteemed by your fellow citizens. In my arms, and in the society of your friends, you will enjoy the repose that your health demands. Dear son, pray keep me informed of all that concerns you. If I can count on hearing from you, I feel that my life will be prolonged and that I shall some day have the joy of clasping you again to my heart.

We are all well. In the name of the whole family I thank you for the money you sent. Do all you can to make your name immortal. Resist the temptations of the great cities, and remember that you have a mother who loves you tenderly and never ceases to

pray to the Almighty for your preservation. Give my love to your charming companion and a kiss to little Achillino.
Love me as I love you,

Your affectionate Mother,

TERESA PAGANINI *

But letters and articles were soon forgotten, while the scandals persisted. As he was considering how to deal with them the idea of an official biography occurred to him. Perhaps it might be published in the French *Revue Musicale*, in Paris, in which Fétis recorded his triumphs and the programmes of his concerts. Paris? Why not?

Paris attracted him. His friend Fontana Pino, who lived in Paris, urged him to join him, because there was a rumour to the effect that Paganini did not venture to measure himself against the French violinists.

"Make haste and come, and put the sceptics to shame," insisted Pino. "This one laurel leaf is lacking in your crown."

Pino was right. It was good policy to hit back and to split up the enemy forces. He would escape from the Viennese fusillade, and go to see his cousin Rebizzo in Dresden. In the winter of 1829 he intended to visit Munich, Prague, Berlin, Frankfurt, Stuttgart, Strasburg, Châlons, and Paris. And in April he would go to London. Nicolò fixed July 24 for his farewell concert in the hall of the Redoubt. His programme included his *Tempest* and the first performance of his third Grand Concerto, which was his adieu to Vienna.

Early in the following month, Bianchi left for Milan, where she remained permanently, while Paganini went to Bohemia. After a rest and a cure at Carlsbad, he hoped to reach Prague in November. He left Vienna on August 2. His tour of Europe had begun.

* July 21, 1828. Letter published by Fétis. *Biographical Notes on Paganini*, Schoenenberger, Paris.

THE SORCERER'S APPRENTICE

PRAGUE, DRESDEN, LEIPZIG, BERLIN

THE wooden floor of the Berlin echoed under his feet as the wooden frame of his fiddle resounded under his fingers. The carriage, which was as dry as the broomstick in the old fairy tales, clattered and jolted along, striking sparks from the paving stones. Europe was in a ferment of excitement. All its cities were clamouring for him at once. He was forever on the road.

His realm consisted of a box on wheels some two yards square. His violin case contained, besides the Guarnerius, all his valuables: his jewels, his gold, a little fine linen, and the famous red pocketbook, worn at the edges, in which everything was jumbled together—snatches of themes, receipts, accounts, contracts, concert tickets, critiques, and love-letters. His only other piece of luggage was a hat-box. Wrapped in a cloak, winter and summer, he leaned back in a corner of the carriage, which was hermetically closed, with his eyes shut or glittering with fever, taking no interest in the landscape.

When he was well, he would rise early, take a decoction of herbs or a cup of chocolate, and set out on his journey. Once in the carriage he would talk over his plans with his secretary, or any friend who happened to be travelling with him. The rumble of the wheels excited him. As he sat there, fasting, with a face of waxen pallor, he would work out anxiously the times when it would be necessary to change the horses. Often he was in great pain from his stomach or his throat, and would try to forget his sufferings in conversation. Then a fit of coughing would interrupt him.

"Never mind," he would say resignedly. "Later on, when we get to the conversational part of the road."

This was his name for the soft, sandy roads in the heather country.

When he put up at an inn, he insisted on absolute silence.

"I get my fill of noise in the great cities," he would say. "When I am travelling, I want peace."

On reaching his room, he would throw open the windows and "take a bath of fresh air." Almost at once he would fall into a heavy sleep. He often dreamt that he was still bowling along in the carriage. Roused by a fit of coughing, he at once reached for his red pocket-book.

"Where is it?" he exclaimed. "Where are my manuscripts . . . my rehearsals . . . my Achillino?"

It was thirty years since his travels with Antonio, when he himself had been the child.

The pocket-book was under his pillow. He was nodding again, and soon he was once more fast asleep.

This cyclonic fame that he had aroused sometimes raised his spirits to the skies, but now and then it beat him down as if he were a boat carrying too much sail. Against what hostile forces had he now to contend? He had left Vienna on the crest of his popularity, but he arrived at Prague to find himself plunged into a vortex of jealousy and bitterness. His room at the Black Knight rang with his imprecations, because, for the first time in his career, in spite of the financial success of his concerts, which he gave in quick succession on December 1, 9, 13, 16, and 20, 1828, aspersions were cast on his playing.

On December 10 the anonymous correspondent of the *Hamburg Exchange* wrote: " 'Tis a mad world, my masters! Oh these Viennese with their strange tastes, their crazy raptures! They talk of virtuosi! I cannot understand, how, after hearing Romberg, Rode, Spohr, Lafont, the public can listen for one moment to such foolery."

The critic himself had no intention of ever again listening to such a cacophony of noises as issued from the fingerboard of Paganini's violin. "It was more like the twittering of sparrows than any legitimate musical sound." He had attended one of the Italian's concerts, but once was enough. Paganini's bowing was incredibly weak. In Prague none of the violinists were tempted to break their violins, as was said to be the case in Vienna. *They were all laughing at him and his Viennese.* True, one sentimental lady had been reduced to tears, but as no one had followed her example, the incident was not considered significant. As for his compositions! "His compositions (and he plays only his own, which have probably been performed more than two thousand times in the last fifteen years) are beneath contempt. The Turkish drum, the cymbals and the trombones play the principal part. Just imagine: in the *Prayer of Moses* by Rossini, of which he has made a complete hash, the accompaniment consists of tambourines and cymbals. And the so-called 'Clochette' with which the Viennese are infatuated!"

But although it was shortly before Christmas, the public continued to buy the tickets, the price of which had risen fivefold. (He must avenge himself as best he could!) He himself admitted that he had greatly increased the prices.

"You would hardly believe how many enemies have been stirred up against me," he wrote to Germi. "I have never injured anyone, but people who do not know me, describe me as the most vicious, miserly, repulsive of men."

These hostile rumours reached the ears, the sensitive antennae, one might say, of Frédéric Chopin. He took fright.

"I have been urged by my friends to appear in Prague. But I do not wish to spoil the success I have enjoyed in Vienna.

They gave even Paganini a bad reception. I shall stay here in peace." *

Although he was "burning to reach London in the spring," he was unable to leave Prague. He was suffering from an affection of the throat, and an emergency operation had to be performed on his jaw. Thanks to the enforced delay, Nicolò had the satisfaction of witnessing the reaction to the article in the *Hamburg Exchange*. Two champions, who were strangers to him, Professors Schottky and Müller, both eminent men in Prague rushed to his defence. Müller referred to the critic, who had talked of the twittering of sparrows, as an ass. At Paganini's second concert, which did not begin till ten oclock at night Schottky was greatly impressed by "the unprecedented manifestation of artistic perfection" on the part of "this fallen angel," "who wore the tragic mask of antiquity." So much so that after the concert he sat down and sketched his portrait.

"No one was ever so incredibly lean as Paganini; with this he has a pale complexion, a sharp prominent nose like an eagle's beak, and long bony fingers. He seems too frail to bear the weight of his clothes. When he bows to the audience, his movements are so strange that one dreads lest his feet should detach themselves from his body and the whole man disintegrate and crumble to a heap of bones. When he plays, his right foot comes forward, and in the quick rhythms beats time with a vivacity that is almost comical. His face, however, never loses its death like impassiveness, except when the storms of applause break out. Then it lights up with a peculiar smile. He shoots out his lips, his eyes dart hither and thither, but there is no trace of benevolence in their gaze. In the difficult passages he twists his body into the most grotesque attitudes, poking his head and his right foot forward until he forms a kind of triangle.

"*Schade!* What a pity," he wound up, "that Hoffmann never

* *Chopin's Letters.* Introduction by I. J. Paderewski, Société d'éditions. S.A. May 1935.

knew him. He would have made him the hero of some fantastic story!"

When he read the article, Paganini jumped at it. Schottky should be his champion, his biographer. He wrote to him.

"I was told that you have published an article, in which you expressed the intention of writing my biography. But I have heard nothing more. My keenest interest is aroused, as well as that of my cousin, who was my informant. Pray let us see some portion of your work. How happy I am to find a champion, whose name alone will suffice to stamp out calumny.

"Your probity and your talents will be the despair of my enemies and you will have the satisfaction of having performed a generous act."

An official authorization was sent to the Professor, followed by reminiscences and documents relating to the childhood of the virtuoso.

"I came into the world," said Paganini, seizing this opportunity to knock a few years off his age, "in February 1784. My mother had a dream. . . ."

But how was he to continue? How could he convey in words the world of sound, with its boundaries, its laws, it ecstasies? How could he express all that a musician discovers or constructs as soon as his ears are opened? Nicolò fell back on facts, such as he saw them. But they were distorted by his memory, his imagination, his own passions, the passions of others, by the halo that surrounded his name, and by his prodigious artist's vanity. He did his best to follow the clue, spinning the strands like the insect which he so closely resembled. On this gossamer thread hung, quivering like dew drops, music and legend. . . . Here, caught in a spider's web, was harmony, and fame, and the sensibility of the sensitive, and the amazement of the insensitive, a rainbow of adoration and awe. Bewildered, ecstatic, he hovered over all the kingdoms of the earth, while at his feet lay the capitals of Europe, waiting to hear him.

"I cannot refuse the flattering invitations of the neighbouring countries," he wrote to Germi. "So I shall be in Paris at the end of September and in London at the end of March 1830." But in the preceding winter and early spring he was expected in Dresden, Leipzig, and Berlin.

"It was ecstasy!" said the Berliners, describing the ovation which Paganini received. "Such a demonstration of enthusiasm has rarely been witnessed in theatre or concert hall."

The attitude of the city in general, however, had been sceptical and unfriendly towards this compatriot of Rossini (who was detested in Berlin), whose strange reputation had preceded him to Germany. But the first notes of the *solo maestoso* provoked such a burst of applause that it "put even Sontag's successes to shame."

The Schauspielhaus presented a curious spectacle at his first concert on March 4, 1829. Fair-haired Gretchens leaned over the balconies at risk to life and limb. This magician of the south, as he was called in Berlin, with his livid skin, damp curls clinging to his forehead, and moist lips, found a short cut to the hearts of his square-shouldered, square-headed audience. He had to bow an incredible number of times before he was allowed to wrap himself up in his furs and go home.

When he returned from Saxony at the end of January, he was accompanied by his cousin, the poet Lazzaro Rebizzo, whom he had mentioned in his letter to Schottky. The previous year Rebizzo had promised to join him.

"Rebizzo is a perfect treasure," exclaimed Nicolò, who made him his inseparable companion.

Besides his cousin, he brought from Dresden more thalers and a snuff-box, which had been presented to him by the King. In Leipzig he had some trouble with the orchestra.* This inci-

---

* In the latter town Paganini had tripled the price of the seats, while declining to raise the orchestra's fees. They refused to assist at a concert arranged for February 16, and it had to be cancelled.

dent put his back up, and he became haughty and insolent. But it made him all the more anxious to see the Prussian capital subjugated to his "magic." This wish was gratified.

"It is my Viennese public over again!" he exclaimed.

While he was in this triumphant mood, he gave two additional concerts on April 6 and 29 in aid of the victims of the floods in Prussia.

After one of these concerts, old Zelter, one of the most captious of musical pedagogues, who had a grudge against Paganini because he was the idol of the day, dropped a line to Goethe. After mentioning other items of news, he wrote: "As I have no money, I could not go to hear Paganini. But I have seen a portrait of this *Hexensohn* [witch's brat]. He will be carrying 10,000 thalers away from Berlin—unless he loses them first at faro."

Zelter had the good fortune to be present at the second concert, and was so well placed that he could see every movement of the maestro's hand and arm. He was able to form his own opinion.

"Thanks to their suppleness, strength, and elasticity, they are untiring; they are as precise as the works of a clock—a clock with a soul."

Among professional critics in Berlin, Rellstab of the *Vossische Zeitung*, who was "all the law and the prophets," could hardly believe his ears. "He cannot be said to overcome difficulties," his article began, "because none exist for him. All great violinists have their own style, their own method. But Paganini transcends himself, he becomes the living embodiment of joy, cynicism, madness, pain and agony. He is the old *Hexenmeister*, the master magician."

To another critic (Marx by name) he was Dr. Faustus, issuing rejuvenated from the infernal cauldron. "He stood there, kindling the orchestra with scattered sparks of sound, with phrases, which he left unfinished, dissonances which he did not trouble to resolve, until suddenly he broke into the most mellow, the most unearthly melody that has ever been played on a violin. Then his eyes began to glow with a deeper, darker flame, while sounds, more rapid and more piercing, came pouring forth. He seemed to be striking his instrument, like the unhappy youth, who after conjuring up the image of his murdered mistress, destroys it again in a fit of amorous rage; then once more seeks to revive it with tears and caresses." *

The nerves of the musical public were quivering; chords were vibrating with the thrill of legend and poetry. The madness spread.

But where the Italians and the Viennese, even in their wildest moments of enthusiasm, kept their feet on solid ground, the Germans were carried away by Paganini's magic and conjured up visions worthy of Jean-Paul, Hoffmann, and Goethe. This, then, was the meaning of that shadow, that mysterious double, which had been seen in Vienna, which the virtuoso nourished with his music. Was it an image or a phantom? An evocation or a vampire, weaving around the bloodless medium a network of mysterious communications?

Paganini himself encouraged these legends which were more piquant than the truth. At each of his concerts, with its storms of passion and tenderness, he seemed more charged than any professional medium with some strange magnetic fluid. He completed the circuit between his audience and his own morbid sensibility. He would have chosen to renounce the world rather than abstain from his trances.

Bisogna forte sentire per fare risentire. "One has to feel, before one can make others feel," he wrote to Schottky, and this phrase became the keynote of his biography.

❡ It was human nature strained to excess; musical and technical expression pushed to grotesque extremes. Finally

* *Allgemeine musikalische Zeitung.* No. 16.

there was that suggestion of the supernatural which roused the population to a frenzy. Of such elements the miracle of Paganini was compounded. Was he conscious of it or not? From 1829 onwards this problem exercised critics, composers, and doctors. But he remained shrouded in mystery, leaving them only the cast-off garments of the magician. Yet it should have been easy enough to find the answer. They had only to listen to his daily practices.

But according to contemporary reports, many people dogged the footsteps of the maestro, following him from hotel to hotel all over Europe in the hope of hearing him in private and surprising the secret of his technique. An Englishman who was passionately fond of the violin had pursued him for six months and at last arrived at a certain town at the same time as the maestro. At enormous cost he secured a room next to Paganini's. A single, disused door separated the two rooms. After one glance through the keyhole, the Englishman gave a sigh of relief. Yes, Paganini was there in his sitting-room, seated on a sofa, and he was drawing the precious violin from its case. But what was happening? Five minutes elapsed and he had not heard a sound. Although Paganini was running the fingers of his left hand up and down the strings as if making sure of new positions, he did not touch the bow. Then, as if satisfied with having run through the Concerto on the silent strings, he put the Guarnerius back in its case without having played a note.

In despair the Englishman called for his bill and crossed the Channel again.

Even in his letters to Germi, Paganini seldom referred to any practising, except when debarred from it by ill health or by an injury to his hand. Indeed, rehearsals and concerts, which followed more and more closely, almost daily, on each other, took the place of regular practices. By work he meant composition, rather than practising scales and exercises, or concertos by other composers (whose works were gradually dropped from his programmes). It was not because he despised or disliked practising, but because, by virtue of the mystical intensity of his early studies, his violin technique had become merged in his creative faculty.

"I have my own personal method, to which I adapt my compositions. If I am to play the works of other composers I have to rearrange them to suit my style. It is less trouble to write compositions of my own, in which I can give free rein to my musical feelings."

George Harrys, his secretary, who, shortly after Schottky, began to write his *Life of Paganini*, received this profession of faith. More than once he referred to his master's exhaustion after playing to a few friends, and he maintained that, paradoxical though it appeared, apart from concerts or rehearsals, *Paganini never practised.*

The morning before a concert he would sit, motionless, absorbed in thought, gazing into space and consuming vast quantities of snuff. He tested his strings, and looked through the orchestral parts. But no one ever saw the manuscript of the violin parts, such was his dread lest they should be stolen. Did they indeed exist, except in his own brain?

His tall silhouette could be seen gliding along close to the wall, as he made his way, in frock-coat and black cravat, to the concert hall for a rehearsal. He was on his guard against inquisitive interlopers, whom he snubbed.

"We all have our little secrets, my dear fellow," he replied to Mayseder, the Viennese.

"I have worked hard enough in my time to acquire my skill," he sometimes remarked; "I deserve a little rest."

The rehearsal began. If the members of the orchestra were nervous and made mistakes, he would dart flaming glances at them and stride up and down the platform.

"Speak up," he would say if he wanted them to play more

loudly. Sometimes, as at Hanover, he exclaimed: "Courage, gentlemen!"

If, however, he was pleased with them, he would say: *"Bravissimo!* You are all virtuosi to a man."

He indicated the rhythm with a few *pizzicato* notes. When it came to the *cadenza,* the solo, for which the orchestra had been eagerly waiting, he sometimes said with a sarcastic smile: *"And so forth,* gentlemen. The fireworks will be for tonight."

When he returned home, he threw himself on his bed. If he felt the slightest doubt about his memory, he glanced at the orchestral score. Soon the carriage came round. He dressed, with a face that was whiter than his linen.

"If I were in Paris," he sometimes said, "I should not play tonight."

By the time he arrived at the hall his blood was up. He was anxious about certain important details.* Were there enough trumpets and trombones? Where was the big drum? Was the hall crowded? He looked to see. It was full of warmth and life.

"Good people," he said approvingly.

But he did not scruple to keep them waiting a long time before he appeared on the platform.

"I was not at my best at first. But I warmed up," he said sometimes to the fanatical admirers who lined the streets all the way from the concert hall to the hotel. He smiled at the artists, the instrument-makers, the students, the young people. His triumph soothed him like the comfortable supper he enjoyed after the concert. The next day there was always a crowd of visitors, whom he handed over to his secretary. He was inundated with invitations and could have dined out six times a day. As a rule he declined these invitations, but occasionally

---

* It was said that Paganini was in the habit of inspecting the cash receipts before playing. This lacks confirmation and is not in accordance with the preoccupation he showed.

he accepted one and he always regretted it. It meant eating meat, drinking all kinds of wine, and missing his siesta.

Tomorrow it would begin all over again.

The critics hurried home to write up their reports.

He followed his course, like a stone that had been flung, and the problem of this miraculous man continued to baffle generation after generation. On December 14, 1829, the *Morgenblatt* prophesied that Paganini's name would be world famous in musical history; it credited him with all the powers that legend had ascribed to Orpheus. Fifty years later, after the meteor had vanished, Wasielewski delved even farther back into Grecian history for illustrations: "Though this wonderful artist lives on in his compositions, the divine afflatus cannot be transmitted. His works are like the riddle of the Sphinx, which none but Œdipus could solve."

EASTERN EUROPE

FRANKFURT-ON-ODER—WARSAW—BRESLAU

ONCE more the road stretched before him like a ribbon. In May 1829 he left Berlin for Poland and had soon reached the Oder. Here the landscape wore a different aspect and the trees were planted in straight rows. The mansion of Princess Zyelinska, who was to be his hostess, was in the neighbourhood of Frankfurt.

She was a very great lady, almost a queen among the Silesian yokels. She cut a dash, like the horses that drew her sleigh in the winter. No one knew how old she was—she was ageless. In the daytime she always wore a man's leather jerkin. At night, she changed her brown wig for a white one and appeared in full evening dress. When she was asked why she did not decide always to wear a white wig, she replied:

"Do you suppose my heart is always white?"

She was passionately fond of music and had made elaborate preparations for fêting the incomparable virtuoso. This explains why the Frankfurt concert was "so much better organized than might have been expected," said the *Musical Gazette*.

The virtuoso had arrived at eleven o'clock on the previous evening and had received a great ovation. Late at night the party returned to the château for supper. The table glittered with silver-plate and candelabra. But what was it that sparkled in the eyes of the Princess? Two tears or merely the reflection of the shining crystal? Bells were heard tinkling merrily in the great avenue of the park. Was it the stage-coach already?

Paganini had slipped into the hall without realizing that his hostess had followed him. He intended to take French leave, but in the gloom two bare arms embraced him, two hands held him fast. The footman vanished discreetly. White hands wrapped his fur coat around him, imparting to it their warmth and fragrance. Two lips sought his own. How could he leave her without one word?

It was cold outside. He was feeling ill. Eastward ho! The door of the coach slammed to.

❦ It was spring in Warsaw. Paganini arrived there on May 22. His concert was to take place on the 23d. A slim young man with an aristocratic profile was in the audience. This was Frédéric Chopin. He was not yet twenty-one, but he was to be haunted all his life by the memory of that evening. There was another slender figure in the concert hall, that of Lipinsky, the fanatic, who had traversed the whole of Europe to hear him, and whom Nicolò had dearly loved. Now the two were rivals. A controversy arose. Lipinsky was said to represent the "classical," Paganini the "romantic," school. Nicolò shrugged his shoulders. It appeared that Germi was the only friend who remained to him. To console himself, he wrote him a detailed account of his triumphs.

After his twelfth concert in Berlin, the public insisted on his returning for the wedding of the King's son on June 20, 1829. His Majesty appointed him to be honorary first director of music. Spohr and Meyerbeer vied with each other in showing him attentions.

"My health is tolerable," he added. "I am careful not to over-tax my strength. On the occasion of the Coronation of His Majesty, the Emperor of Russia, here in Warsaw, he bestowed on me a ring set with brilliants."

Many plans were proposed to him, but he declined, as too exhausting, an invitation to visit Russia.

Elsner, the director of the Conservatoire, formally presented him with a gold snuff-box. He was credited with many successful love-affairs, but that was no new thing.

According to the *Warsaw Gazette*, it was reported in the newspapers in Italy, where a close watch was kept on his career: "Paganini is to marry Signora de L——. She is in love with his genius. She is a Florentine by birth, and has pursued the maestro for the last three years, but, owing to adverse circumstances, she never succeeded in hearing him play till she reached Warsaw. She is twenty and beautiful."

At forty-eight his own description of himself, in the early days of Antonia, still held good: "I am neither young nor handsome, but when the women hear me play, they come crawling to my feet."

It was not surprising that the German worship of his music frequently developed into a sentimental passion. In his rare moments of leisure, he was once more obsessed by a yearning for love.

But he had had enough of dashing young girls. Enough of authentic princesses and tragedy queens—one Bianchi sufficed. But now, in the heart of life, crowned with success, in failing health, he was alone. He longed for tenderness and support.

The Warsaw affair came to nothing.

"My heart leapt when I saw your writing," he replied to Germi, who had sent him the newspaper cutting. "There is no truth in the report. I am still a bachelor. It is more than two years since I looked at a woman. My only happiness is the knowledge that you are my faithful friend, and the guardian of my modest fortune."

But on his return to Germany, the effect of his playing was so magical that the most exalted personages, the most gracious ladies, were raving about him.

"I must not repeat to you all that the confidante of a queen told me concerning her royal mistress. You would be amazed if you could see my letters from a ravishing young lady of twenty, recently married to a Baron. She is ready to abandon her family and unite herself to me for life. But her father is one of H.M.'s councillors and a man of too much distinction in Germany. So, in the interests of morality and my own fair fame, I must relinquish the happiness of possessing her. Some day you shall read her letters. They will bring tears to your eyes."

(Breslau (July 24 and 28, 1829). Scene: the Aula, the festal hall of the University. Just before the end of term Paganini consented to play to the enthusiastic students. In return, they composed and produced in his honour a *Melodramatic Vaudeville*. They rehearsed every day, under the direction of Herr Just, the director, who was a great lover of music. Paint, masks, cotillions, were smuggled in and hidden away in desks, but this time there was no fear of punishment. The corridors were seething with excitement. At last the scenario had reached the proper pitch of perfection. The subject of the libretto was a fairy-tale:

"The Princess Harmonica de Technophile was about to crown her people's wishes by marrying again, but none of her suitors pleased her. She refused the learned Hoffmann and the Chevalier Agatho. At last, however, she threw herself into the arms of the brilliant virtuoso, Zaganini."

CAST

Herr Just	.	.	.	*Zaganini*
Masks	.	.	.	*à la Paganini*
Music	.	.	.	*à la Paganini*
Receipts	.	.	.	*à la Paganini!!!*

The Kingdom of Technophile was *en fête*.

HEADQUARTERS: FRANKFURT ON THE MAIN

Frankfurt, Leipzig, Darmstadt, Mainz, Mannheim, Halle, Magdeburg, Dessau, Halberstadt, Weimar, Erfurt, Bamberg, Rudolfstadt, Coburg, Gotha, Nüremberg, Munich, Tegernsee, Ratisbon, Augsburg, Stuttgart, Frankfurt, Cologne, Düsseldorf, Bonn, Cassel, Hanover, Hamburg, Bremen, Brunswick, Baden-Baden, Frankfurt, Carlsruhe, Frankfurt, Carlsruhe, Strasburg

IT took him a month to reach Berlin again and to complete his triumphal progress across Germany. At last he reached the banks of the Main. He made his entry into Frankfurt, the town of Goethe's birth, on August 27, 1829, on the eve of the celebrations for Goethe's eightieth birthday. Scenes from *Faust* were being performed at the theatre. Nicolò seemed so perfectly at his ease in these festive surroundings that he might have been a personage who had escaped from the wings. He was charmed with the old city, the capital of the ancient Germano-Roman Empire. At the first concert he gave, the conquering hero was received with almost military honours; with fanfares of trombones and trumpets accompanied "with transports of enthusiasm on the part of the orchestra."

For the audience the trumpets were the prelude to experiences fraught with mystery and terror. This man with the long black hair and the pale countenance opened to them with his violin a world which they had never imagined, "except perhaps in dreams." There was in his appearance something so supernatural that they looked for a glimpse "of a cloven hoof or an angel's wing."

In September, when the universities were reopening, all the

119

turbulent young students flocked to his concerts and were entranced. Among them were the poets, composers, and virtuosi of the future.

"In Paganini's *Adagio* I heard the singing of an angel," Schubert had said the previous year in Vienna.

Henri Vieuxtemps, on the threshold of his career, was passing through Frankfurt. He was only ten years old when he heard Paganini, but he always remembered the "magnetic chains" which the maestro had woven around his audience.

Among the students from the Heidelberg University who had come over to Frankfurt for one of Paganini's concerts, was a young law student of nineteen, Robert Schumann by name, who wore the orange cap of the University. He wrote in his diary: "In Frankfurt this evening I heard Paganini! What ecstasy! What transports of the soul!"

Three years later, Franz Liszt, returning to his room at his hotel after attending Paganini's first concert in Paris, unburdened himself in a letter to a friend: " 'I, too, am a painter,' cried Michelangelo, when he first beheld a masterpiece. Humble and poor though I am, since I heard Paganini play I keep repeating Michelangelo's words to myself. René, what a man! What a violin! What an artist! What suffering, what anguish, what torture those four strings can express! Look, here are some of his phrases. . . ." *

Indifferent to all these reactions, Paganini had retired to his tent and was planning a "proclamation." Before he left for Leipzig, the citizens of Frankfurt were to be publicly thanked. He preened himself. He could hardly refrain from using the royal "we."

He received a deputation from Dresden, Darmstadt, Mannheim, Mainz, Düsseldorf, and Magdeburg, begging him for concerts. He received their spokesman, Lieutenant Couriol,

* Liszt's *Letters to La Mara,* May 2, 1832.

who undertook in future to manage his affairs in Germany, and he accepted their proposals. Then he returned to his proclamation:

TO THE CITIZENS OF FRANKFURT
> *The undersigned, moved by sentiments of the*
> *deepest gratitude for the cordial and magnificent*
> *reception . . .*

The next day Darmstadt welcomed him with equal enthusiasm, which was expressed by a serenade performed outside the windows of his lodging. Soon his room was invaded by admirers, clamouring for souvenirs; one asked for a broken string, another begged for a kiss. In the meantime he was working out his plan of campaign. After a visit to Mainz, Düsseldorf, and Mannheim, he hoped to arrive in Magdeburg on October 17, 1829, Halberstadt on the 20th, Magdeburg again on the 23d, Dessau on the 25th, Weimar on the 30th, Erfurt on November 2d, Nüremberg on the 9th, Stuttgart on the 11th, Carlsruhe on the 13th, Brunswick on the 16th. By the beginning of October everything was ready. He broke camp and left the banks of the Rhine for those of the Elbe.

This systematic planning, which he now adopted, proved to be surprisingly efficacious. It canalized the eddies of his life. He was also enjoying a respite from his malady and had in fact almost forgotten it. He had no time to brood over the harsh paradox on which his life was based: "to live by music and to die of it." He was too busy now to be obsessed by love or the want of it, or to be desperately anxious about his health, while doing everything to undermine it. He was a mass of contradictions: humble and arrogant, sceptical and superstitious, a son of the people with a passion for the life of courts, a moody Italian who had won the heart of Austria, a seducer who had been brought to book, and the tenderest of fathers.

In those halcyon days, his faculties, no longer rebellious, no longer disordered, were like a disciplined crew who would steer his ship past those dangerous reefs: sickness, anxiety, jealousy.

❰ He had hardly reached the Elbe, when, like Napoleon, he took twenty towns in his stride. He was compared by the local press, like all the great conquerors in history, to a natural force.

A violent thunderstorm happened to be raging when he appeared in the great theatre of Magdeburg. He seemed to conduct the lightning with his uplifted bow.

Dessau battened for a whole week on visitors who had come for a concert that had to be postponed. They could be seen strolling disconsolately up and down the river banks.

❰ Weimar, October 30, 1829. The orchestra was conducted by Hummel. All the visitors had flocked back from Dessau to hear the great maestro. According to the recollections of one of the violinists * in the orchestra, although the price of seats had been doubled, the hall was so closely packed that an apple dropped on the crowd would not have touched the ground till the end of the Concerto.†

Goethe himself was present. This was recognized as a supreme mark of favour by all who were aware of the poet's increasing dislike of crowds. Goethe wished to form his own opinion, and to test the truth of Zelter's description in the letter from Berlin in April.

Never perhaps had the "magician" made an appearance so spectacular, or indulged in such an outrageous exhibition of charlatanism. Around his cadaverous form, described by Schottky, hung the black frock-coat of atrocious cut, with its sagging shoulders, which was soon to become famous. Long

* Zobe, *Musical Recollections from Weimar.*
† E minor.

black trousers flapped about his heels. Was it carelessness? Parsimony? Arrogance? No one knew. As for his behaviour, he began by manifesting an almost servile obsequiousness towards his audience. But he at once redressed the balance by a gesture of symbolical significance. He "swept his bow down to the ground, like a general on parade saluting his sovereign with his sword."

What would Goethe, who was wont to say that he would like to awake in a museum surrounded by godlike marble statues— what would Goethe make of this Titanic mountebank and the adventitious aids with which he created his atmosphere?

On November 1 he wrote briefly to Zelter, who was still in Berlin: "I heard Paganini yesterday evening."

But the following week he gave a more elaborate description of his impressions. "From the point of view of pleasure," the poet confessed, without commenting on the virtuoso's exterior, "which for me always hovers in a sphere midway between the senses and the intellect, I can find no base for this column of flame and cloud. I can only say that I heard some meteoric sounds, which I have not yet succeeded in interpreting."

"The first time I heard him," wrote Zelter, by return of post, "he reminded me of Moses, performing his tricks in the presence of the Egyptians. I found it irritating.

"The thing in him that captures and retains the attention to such a high degree," Zelter concluded, "is perhaps a certain mixture of the fantastic, a weird imagination and a longing for liberty. He is not so much a lunatic as a *poseur*. His playing was like musical *hors-d'œuvre*, a kind of prairie oyster, which one swallows down with the aid of pepper and vinegar."

❲ Halberstadt, Erfurt, Bamberg, Rudolfstadt, Coburg, Gotha were child's play. He left Thuringia and hurried south to give a recital in Nüremberg on November 6. In the genial atmosphere of that pleasant town the cordial, rather than the fantastic, side of his nature was uppermost. He congratulated the orchestra fraternally, and "the memory of the new Orpheus was engraved on the heart of the ancient, art-loving city."

In Munich he was elected *Meistersinger*, and Stutts, the conductor of the Royal Orchestra, crowned him with a laurel wreath amid scenes of indescribable enthusiasm. At his third and last concert, the doors of the theatre were thrown open for the benefit of the crowds who had been unable to obtain admission to the hall. The ground floor was packed with royalties: the reigning family of Bavaria, the Duchess of Lichtenberg, and Prince Karl. The only absentees were King Ludwig I, who was ill, and the Queen Mother Frederica-Wilhelmina-Carolina of Baden, widow of Maximilian-Joseph. Paganini was invited to pay homage to them at Tegernsee, which was the country residence of the Court. Here there was a charming incident.

The concert was about to begin, when a great uproar was heard outside. The Queen inquired into the cause and was told that some sixty peasants from the neighbourhood who were aware of the arrival of the famous Italian violinist, and had heard how the doors of the Munich theatre had been thrown open, had gathered outside the castle in the hope of hearing him. They begged that the windows might be left open so that they could enjoy his music.

"Her gracious Majesty," said the newspapers, "in her readiness to meet their wishes, gave them more than they asked for. She ordered them to be admitted to the *salon*, where the discreet manner, in which they showed their pleasure, was as much commended as the decorum of their behaviour."

At this epoch, musical education was made compulsory in all the schools in Bavaria.

He could see the rocks ahead more clearly now. At Augsburg his partisans were jeered at as "drunkards." In Cassel his old rival Spohr contrived maliciously to make him miss a concert.

On his return to Frankfurt in the winter of 1830–1831, he had to endure daily contact with Guhr, a violinist and conductor, who had vowed to make a technical analysis of the maestro's methods. "Wretched tyro, let him try!"

"In the meantime," wrote Spohr, "he is very gay, not to say exuberant."

It was the rapture of the creator. At least twelve of his works were composed in Germany. His damascened weapons were the brass instruments of the orchestra.

"I have finished the Concerto in D minor and have begun another in F major, which will be my favourite, but I shall not have time to finish it, as I still have to orchestrate the former, before transferring myself to Paris at the beginning of the month. I have written a Sonata with Variations in *Beffa* [in joke] which I still have to orchestrate." *

His thoughts were busy with his visit to France. "You had better address your letters to Paris to the Hôtel des Princes, rue de Richelieu No. 109. That is where all the great put up. Meyerbeer and his family are staying there. Do you know, all the Paris newspapers are saying most flattering things about me?"

All fashionable Paris was expecting him in a flutter of excitement. Paganini's works were being published. The following notice appeared in the *Revue Musicale:*

"At this moment, when all Germany is amazed at the genius of Paganini, and France is hoping shortly to welcome the famous violinist, Monsieur Pacini, music publisher, Boulevard des Italiens No. 11, wishes to draw the attention of his customers, professional and amateur violinists alike, to the fact that he has already published the following works by the celebrated maestro: 12 Sonatas, 3 Airs with Variations, 24 Caprices or Études which embody innumerable phrases, passages, and new varieties of bowing. Monsieur Pacini possesses the original

* To Germi, Frankfurt, February 11, 1830.

manuscript of a duet which Paganini executes solo with amazing skill. It has a left hand *pizzicato* accompaniment, while the intricate melody which contains a great many quick passages, is played with the bow. The effect produced is that of two distinct instruments. This work, which the publisher describes as one of Paganini's prodigies, is now in the press. The price will be two francs. Monsieur Pacini proposes to publish everything that Monsieur Paganini has composed."

The ground had been well prepared for his arrival, but it was postponed till a later date. According to the newspapers, things were looking black in Paris in the spring of 1830. In May, Parliament had been dissolved by Polignac's Ministry, but it had returned to supreme power in July. Decrees were promulgated, suppressing certain liberties, which roused the press and the Universities against Charles I and inflamed public opinion. There was rioting in the streets, and the population was in no mood for plays and concerts. Barricades were thrown up; shots were fired; blood began to flow.

Paganini postponed his journey till the following year, "in the hope that by that time the troubles would be over."

As the way to Paris was barred, he decided to remain in Frankfurt. In the first place, Achillino had measles. He had, besides, a liking for the town. The Napoleon of violinists, as Dida, the Florentine Princess, had laughingly called him, now turned his attention to business. After a formal reception in his honour at the Museum, Paganini laid down his bow. He did not intend to play again in public in Frankfurt. In thirteen months he had amassed an incredible amount of booty. The "black eagle" relaxed his claws and surveyed his hoard in amazement.

"In another two or three years," he wrote to Germi, "I ought to be in possession of about £80,000. Such are the fruits of fame. But what am I to do with all this money? Have you a taste for fireworks? Luckily I have a son. May God preserve him."

The pages of his pocket-book made illuminating reading. They contained a mass of figures, calculations, notes of contracts, stock-exchange transactions, purchases of land, investments. Germi had power of attorney. Paganini himself professed to know nothing about arithmetic. But, in spite of the preposterous methods he evolved, his figures, like the notes of his violin, never broke the invisible laws. Eskeles, his banker in Vienna, was amazed at this mathematical accuracy in a being from another world. A note sent from Carlsruhe to Eskeles, winding up the accounts for the year 1829, is an intriguing document. A copy was sent to Germi:

> *Vienna £1600; Vienna £400; Prague £480; Dresden £320; Berlin £1028; Berlin £287; Warsaw £928; Warsaw £120; Breslau £280; Frankfurt £520; Leipzig £400; Magdeburg £246; Nürnberg £447; Munich £337; Stuttgart £306. Making a total of approximately £7699.*

This was added to the receipts of 1828:

> *Milan £920; Bologna £960; Genoa £800; Vienna £2400; Prague £402. Making a total of approximately £3282. Grand total approximately £11,087.**

"He is said to be very fond of money," observed the *Revue Musicale.* "But for this he may be pardoned, when it is considered that he is amassing a fortune for his four-year-old son, to whom he appears to be passionately devoted."

After all his campaigning, after scaling such dizzy heights, how delightful it was to feel the kindly earth beneath his feet again and to kiss a child's cool brow. In a letter to Donizetti, referring to certain musical projects, Paganini opened his heart. "Achillino, my dear Achillino, is my only joy. He is steadily increasing in beauty and talent. He speaks German perfectly and acts as my interpreter. He loves me tenderly. As for me I adore him."

* The pound is reckoned at its gold-standard value.

At the time of their residence in Frankfurt, this son of his, who was "born in the purple," this *amatissimo* Achillino Cyrus Alexander Paganini, was a beautiful child, with black velvety eyes and long curls. He was graceful and had his mother's charming voice. From the age of two he had given astonishing signs of possessing a perfect ear. Nicolò was asked if he intended to have the boy taught music.

"Why not? If it will give him pleasure, I will teach him myself. I love him dearly and am positively jealous of him. If I were to lose him, it would be the death of me. I could not bear to part from him. He is in my thoughts day and night."

Achillino inherited his father's terrific imagination, which led him to make havoc of Paganini's household. The maestro's own room was a jumble of wooden horses, violins, toy swords, violin bows. If the intrepid visitor contrived to make his way through a barrier of furniture thick with dust, he was likely to start an avalanche, consisting of toys, half-finished manuscripts, boxes of biscuits, lumps of resin, boots, slippers, orchestral scores, all piled up precariously. Eventually he would run Nicolò to earth, in a yellow dressing-gown, with Achillino on his knees.

"The poor child is bored," said Paganini, "and I am worn out. I have played every game I can think of. I have carried him about. I have made him chocolate. I am at my wits' end."

One day, Achillino drew his wooden sword and attacked the author of his being.

"*Angelo mio*," groaned the Napoleon of violinists, sinking to the ground. "You have wounded me already."

Once, when it was time to start for a concert, a tragic situation arose: Achillino had hidden everything—frock-coat, music, socks. . . .

"*Angelo mio!*" entreated the maestro, the last shreds of dignity thrown to the winds, "what on earth have you done with my things?"

In return for a promise that he should never again be told to wash his hands, which was a practice he particularly disliked, the "angel child" restored the hidden articles one by one, while the audience in the packed theatre waited patiently.

Some day Achillino would be rich. He would be a Baron. Westphalia conferred upon Paganini the dignity of Commandatore, with arms and title transmissible to his heirs male. The son of Teresa Bocciardi was now a noble. He had cards engraved with the following inscription:

Baron Paganini

Commander and Chevalier of several orders

It was surrounded by a wreath of oak leaves.

Achillino was not the only one to introduce the joy of life into the heart of the conquering hero. His household was now comfortably organized. As a servant, he had an excellent young man who was well-educated and spoke four languages: Italian, French, German, and English. Finally, German beauties, to whom he referred in a letter to Germi, were ready to play the part of fair captives. Queen among them was the young lady of twenty, whom he had relinquished, on his return from Warsaw, in the interests of "morality and my own fair fame."

She had fair hair and a tender heart. Her father, Herr von Feurbach, was the most distinguished writer on jurisprudence in Germany and was chevalier of many orders, Privy Councillor to the King of Bavaria, President of the City of Anspach.

"Her name is Helena," Nicolò informed Germi. "Three years ago she was married to a German Baron, and is, consequently, a Baroness. But it was not a love match. She is passionately fond of music and sings tolerably well herself. She came from Nuremberg to hear me play and begged her husband to take her to my second concert as well. After she had heard me, met me, and spoken to me, she fell so violently in love with me, that, if I could not be hers, she would pine away and die. She has a charming face and is beautifully educated. Her letters are worthy to be published. In sentiment they are far superior to those of Abélard's Eloïse."

Spring came early to the banks of the Main, in the almost meridian climate of southern Germany. They met, and their friendship developed, in idyllic surroundings. Parties were arranged, with Paganini as the centre of attraction. Such was his fascination that he had only to appear in the audience—as he did at a concert in Ems—for the hall to be packed.

Paganini was not a little attracted by "this most gracious young lady." He went into society, and accepted an invitation from His Excellency the Austrian Minister. To please Helena and complete the conquest, he took to wearing patent-leather shoes and tight-fitting coats that showed off his wasp-waist.

"I intend to dance at a Ball at the Russian Minister's next Monday," he said complacently.

Helena's husband, however, suddenly became jealous and uneasy, and sent her back to Anspach. As soon as the warm weather began, Paganini was to visit Ems and other towns in the north, before going to Baden-Baden in August, where he was to take the waters. While the romantic young woman was languishing in the country, Nicolò arrived at this small cosmopolitan town, which was the rendezvous of fashionable Europe when the season was in full swing. Paganini paced the avenues of lime trees, which shed a sugary sweetness on the air, deciphering Helena's letters. She boldly chose to write in French, that being the language of love.

ANSPACH,

August 7, 1830

MY DEAREST NICOLÒ,

Hour follows hour; day follows day. Anxiously I count the minutes, hoping that the next will bring me at least a few lines of your handwriting. But I wait in vain. To hope, I see, is to despair; to love is to suffer.

Thoughts of your adorable self mingle with everything I do,

whether I embroider, sing or talk. Even in my dreams, we are together, but you do not always make me happy. Often I am haunted by terrible forebodings and I weep like an unhappy child. At other times I am a different person. I am in the wildest spirits, I joke and laugh and sometimes even dare to believe that Nicolò is thinking of me. . . . Nicolò and music, these are the two passions of my life. Music will never betray me. But what of Nicolò?

I hear that you are taking the waters at Baden-Baden. What do you think of them? Are they doing you good? I fear the pleasures of that charming spot will drive me from your thoughts. I am uneasy about that fair friend of yours. Forgive me, Nicolò. But how can I help it, when someone who shall be nameless, is so unkind that he will not write me the least little friendly word, although that one little word would have the power to destroy the pains of hell that torment this timid and sensitive soul of mine?

While you are enjoying yourself, I am pining away. You have forgotten me, while I faithfully cherish your beloved image. How different we are in temperament. Spirit of compassion, divine compassion, I implore you to seek out this man in the midst of his distracting pleasures. It may be that he has forgotten the very existence of poor Helena. Go to him. Convey to him but one of the thousand sighs that are imprisoned in this heart of mine, which, unhappy though it is, will remain faithful till death.

O Nicolò, why this long and terrible silence? I have written to you repeatedly, but have received neither a reply nor your picture. . . . But, hush! I have learnt to suffer in silence. Yet, do not dream that I shall ever forget you. I possess no painted portrait of you, but love has engraved your image on my heart. It will outlast all the sorrows in the world. In the letter I sent you to Frankfurt, I asked you to come to see me. But you continue to preserve a diplomatic silence, never caring how unhappy you make me. Yet I cannot believe that this is your intention. You were enjoying yourself at Ems, Wiesbaden and Frankfurt. Time must have flown. It was natural that you should have found the pen a troublesome intermediary between two parted ones, when there were companions at hand ready to talk to you and amuse you. I keep making excuses for you, but in vain! I cannot rest. You have learnt the secret of mastering me and I am your prisoner forever. Soon my days of liberty will be over. My husband will return, and the bird will go back to its cage.

Helena's plans were ripe. Her choice was made. She would exchange one Baron for another. She would follow Nicolò. Yet she still endeavoured to plead her cause:

Do not blame my weakness. I have told myself a thousand times that my sentiments for you are a grievous sin. But how can I resist it? To try to efface your image would only cause me useless pain. To give up Nicolò would mean giving up life itself. *Without Nicolò I should die.*

And now, beloved friend, a thousand farewells. I will not try your patience further. But though I end my letter, I cannot prevent my loving thoughts from seeking you out. I would not spoil your pleasure, but, amid the distractions of your life, let your imagination sometimes conjure up the image of your most faithful friend. Well, I must wait to see what that spirit of compassion will do for me. God comfort me, and preserve your friendship, your memory of me. May Nicolò, who still inspires my hopes, NEVER DRIVE ME TO DESPAIR.

Your ever loving

HELENA

 In his old age, Don Juan had embarked on a new adventure, he was again cherishing the hope of love. He replied to Helena's letter. Yes, he would give up everything for her. He would join her at the end of the month. An emaciated, impressive figure in his black cloak, with his glittering eyes, he left the coach at Anspach, not far from Augsburg, and hastened to the rendezvous.

It was midnight. In the gloomy inn, which sheltered the lovers, they agreed in the interests of secrecy to give out that he was "architect to the King of Prussia." From motives of prudence they received no visitors, for this was the city of which Herr von Feurbach was President and where everyone knew Helena. These three stolen days were irradiated with Helena's love—Helena, who was so white, so blonde. At night, to avoid scandal, they broke off their passionate communings. At the end of the three days, Nicolò went back to Baden-Baden.

Helena was bent on obtaining a divorce. She intended to marry Paganini and to renounce all claim to her own fortune. But once his passion was satisfied, Nicolò began to deliberate. If he "married this young lady," he would secure "a good wife, and a good mother for Achillino," he wrote to Germi, whom he consulted as usual. "It would be difficult to find a woman who would love me as much as Helena. It is true that when they hear my violin all the women are moved to tears. But I am no longer young. I am no longer handsome. In fact I am as ugly as sin (*bruttissimo*). Think it over and give me your advice. Her letters reflect her thoughts. Her conversation and her voice are enchanting and she knows as much about geography as I do about the violin." *

In some perplexity he thought about this domestic angel, who had come down to him from heaven. Perhaps this was his last chance. Germi might set him a good example. Nicolò was aware that Germi was becoming more and more enamoured of his fair friend, Signora Camiglietta. She was of the servant class, but so charming a mistress that she was the envy of many a great lady. All Germi's letters bore witness to his affection for her. Perhaps this was the road to happiness: tranquillity, affection, a normal, middle-class way of life.

But at each of these words, that had charmed him only yesterday, he seemed to hear an answer, an evocation: the mention of a date, the name of a country. Even as he lay in Helena's arms, he began, carelessly at first, then feverishly, to plan new

* Baden-Baden, August 30, 1830.

itineraries. What was this insidious malady that was sapping his strength in the guise of love? The sands were running out. Time was draining away the blood from the artist's veins, and there was nothing to show for it. He knew well enough what it was that was arousing him and goading him on. He must needs go. He must needs play his violin. Once more he must wear himself out on the roads, in the great cities, where everyone recognized him and gazed at him with awe, as if he were a phantom (*La Beffana*). If ever he wanted to travel incognito, he would have to wear a mask. Incorrigible wanderer that he was! Monster, nourished by the thousand-headed public, gorged with fame, with concert programmes, figures, patrons, fresh supplies of adulation! What place had a woman in his life?

"Times are not too auspicious," he wrote to Germi, "but life is too short. It bids us not to waste it. Heaven send that I may see you again before I die."

It was the end of Helena's romance. He decided to break with her. He tied up her love letters with a violin string. He would never reply to one again. In a corner of one of the packets these words may still be read: "Nineteen of Helena's letters."

In one of the letters, worn away at the folds, these broken phrases are still legible: "My friend . . . my beloved Nicolò . . . persist . . . silence if you wish to . . . longing for you is killing me. . . ."

He took his departure from Frankfurt, leaving in his landlady's charge his most precious possessions, his Achillino and the manuscripts of his Concertos. He had solved the problems of love and marriage. At the end of a letter to Germi he said: "I'll tell you some other time about my love affairs."

"THE DEVIL MUST HAVE GUIDED MY HAND"

"He was wearing a frock-coat of dark grey, which reached to his heels and gave him an appearance of great height. His long dark hair fell to his shoulders in twisted locks and formed a black frame for his pale, cadaverous face, on which sorrow, genius and hell had left their ineffaceable stigmata." *

— HEINRICH HEINE

I VISITED many towns: Cassel, Hanover, Hamburg, Bremen."

It was the month of June. In the Alster Pavilion in Hamburg, two men of note crossed his path: Heinrich Heine, the poet, and Lyser, the painter.

Lyser was old and deaf, but had a passion for music. He even wrote musical criticisms for the Hamburg and Viennese journals. To a poet, sounds conjure up a world of images; to a deaf man, images reveal the realm of sound. With a sketch-book in his hand, Lyser took notes at plays and concerts. He would lean over into the orchestra and read the counterpoint from the faces and finger movements of the musicians, like a conductor studying his score.

"What was surprising in that?" asked Heine. "In the players' gestures the deaf painter could see the sounds. To some men, sounds themselves are only invisible symbols, in which they can hear colours and forms."

The illustrious Beethoven, who was deaf himself, had already been the victim of Lyser's vein of painful irony. Many of Lyser's

* *Florentine Nights*, Heinrich Heine.

135

well-known caricatures of him are still to be found in Austria. And now Paganini, acrobat and sorcerer, had arrived in Hamburg—Paganini with his signs, his incantations, and his airs of a millionaire. Lyser dogged his steps, observing his triumphs, and his maladies. He drew his silhouette in that grotesque frock-coat; he painted him naked; he painted him flayed and disembowelled. He painted him as a skeleton playing the violin. He painted his grotesque and angular attitudes, his violin bow, his left arm, his fingers executing *arpeggios*, sixths, thirds, and octaves. He painted his hat, his female admirers, his bows, his phials, the sneer on his face, and the voluminous cloak in which he wrapped himself. He painted the dark, bitter features of that fabulous countenance, "which seemed to belong to the sulphurous nether regions." Then Lyser stopped. There was a buzzing in his ears. "I really think that the devil was guiding my hand," he declared to Heine.

While they were chatting in the Public Gardens, waiting till it was time to go in to the concert, Lyser told the poet, who was on a visit to Hamburg, the legend that was believed throughout Germany. Paganini had sold himself, body and soul, to the devil, who, in return, had made him the best violinist in the world, able to earn millions with his bow. But first and foremost he had to be liberated from the accursed galleys where he had languished for so many years. It was thanks to this bargain that he was able to blackmail the two of them that evening, to the tune of two thalers each.

Heinrich Heine burst out laughing.

"Look, there he comes," persisted Lyser, "with that doubtful familiar of his. Doesn't he walk as if he still had the iron bar between his legs?"

The "familiar" was a rosy-cheeked, dapper little man, who skipped along beside him in a grey coat with steel buttons. He was George Harrys, who was attaché to the Embassy at the Court of Hanover. In his enthusiasm for Paganini's playing, he became first his secretary, then his biographer. At the sight of this strangely assorted couple, the poet was reminded of Retsch's engraving of Faust, walking with Wagner outside the gates of Leipzig. But if Paganini, etched in broad daylight, under the green trees of the Jungfernsteg, bore so sinister an aspect, what effect would he produce that evening in the glare of the footlights?

"You are aware that I have musical second sight?" asked Heine, raising his voice for the benefit of his deaf companion as they strolled and talked. "I possess the gift of seeing the correlative shape of every sound."

❰ They had some difficulty in finding their two-thaler seats in the packed hall of the Comedy Theatre in Hamburg, which presented an unusual appearance. There was an "Olympian gathering of bankers, millionaires, sugar and coffee magnates, with their fat and lawful spouses, the Junos of Wandrahm Street and Dreckwall Alley." While the painter and the poet were still exchanging their ribald remarks, Paganini appeared on the platform. He was in gala dress: "black frock-coat and black waistcoat of atrocious cut," said Heine maliciously, "such as was perhaps the correct wear at the court of Proserpine."

But behind the footlights, which seemed to burn low of their own accord, in the midst of the profusion of flowers with which the stage was decorated, the virtuoso brought forth the strangest bloom of all. It was a monstrous flower of sound, unfolding its phrases like a whorl of leaves; its trills were like thorns, and the notes of his violin were like the deadly, velvety petals of carnivorous plants. The maestro was shadowed by that mysterious double—chimera or vampire—which had already become a legend, whose wings had brushed those distant shores, wafting to the poet their perfume, and fecundating with images the land of dreams. Thanks to his "musical second sight," Heinrich Heine himself was carried away to those nameless realms. He managed, however, to give a lucid analysis of the experience.

"With every stroke of his bow, Paganini conjured up before my eyes visible shapes and scenes. He told me, in pictures, many strange tales, in which he and his violin played the principal part."

Enthralled by the sights which the music evoked, the poet was presently overwhelmed by a nightmare vision: "It seemed to me that it was the hour of twilight," he wrote, long afterwards, with a pen that still trembled; "the illimitable ocean was suffused with the purple light of evening, which gained in intensity, while the voice of the waves grew ever more august as it blended mysteriously with the tones of the violin. But as the sea turned a deeper crimson, the sky grew paler and paler, till at last the angry waves were the violent vermilion of blood, while the sky had a corpselike pallor, a spectral whiteness, which was pierced by great stars of menacing aspect . . . and these stars were black, black as glittering coals."

Who was lord over this realm of anguish? The poet continued, doubtfully: "I hardly recognized him in the brown dress of a monk, which concealed rather than clothed him. His wild countenance was half-hidden by the hood. He had a rope round his waist and his feet were bare. Paganini stood there, on a rocky promontory, a lonely, defiant figure, playing his violin. At times, when he shook the loose sleeve of his gown from his long, lean, naked arm, and swept his bow through the air, he seemed more than ever like a master sorcerer controlling the elements with his magic wand. Frantic howls rose up from the depths of the sea, and, in their panic, the blood-red waves splashed high into the air, as if to spray the livid sky and the black stars with crimson foam. There was a pandemonium of roars and a noise as if the world were cracking, splitting and breaking up, while the monk continued to bow with relentless fury. By the force of his insensate will, he sought to break the seven seals with which Solomon sealed the iron jars, in which he imprisoned the conquered demons. The wise king had thrown those jars into the sea. It was the voices of those very genii which I thought I heard, mingling with the angry bass notes of the violin. . . . Then I saw, emerging from the blood-red waves, the heads of the liberated demons. They were monsters of fabulous ugliness: crocodiles with bats' wings, serpents with horns like stags, monkeys with sea-shells on their heads, seals with long, patriarchal beards, women with breasts in the place of cheeks, green camel heads, marine hermaphrodites of incomprehensible anatomy, all glaring with cold and baleful eyes at the fiddling monk and stretching long tentacles towards him. . . ."

The monk had vanished.

"All around him the horizon expanded to a space so vast that the physical senses were baffled and only the eyes of the spirit could grasp it. In the midst of it floated a great globe of light, on which stood a superb and gigantic figure, playing a violin. Was this globe the sun? I cannot say. In the features of this man, however, I recognized Paganini, but a Paganini invested with ideal beauty, divinely transfigured, with a smile of reconciliation upon his lips. He was the embodiment of virile strength. His noble form was robed in azure blue; his black hair fell in shining locks about his shoulders. As he stood there, strong and confident, like a noble statue of a god, and played his violin, it was as if all creation were obeying his music. He was the human planet, around which the whole Universe revolved, with due solemnity, to the rhythm of celestial harmonies."

Vain talk of demons, when he could command the music of the spheres. The thunder of the breakers, the roar of the sea, were merged in a mighty hymn which brought back the warmth of life. In the distance the poet beheld a band of pilgrims in white, flowing garments like fleecy clouds. In their hands they carried white staves. And it was the golden knobs of these staves, which he had mistaken for stars, glittering in ecstasy around the Titan of music. The music quivered with rapture and love, till at last it burst into a pæan of unbridled ecstasy. It was as if thousands of bards were sweeping the strings of their harps in a final song of triumph.

"It was music such as the ear can never hear," sighed the poet, "music such as the heart alone can dream of, when it rests at night on the bosom of the beloved."

⁋ The houses looked black in the early dawn. Ships in the harbour were getting up steam. In the principal street, in spite of the early hour, the gates of an hotel were quietly opened to allow a carriage, with windows hermetically sealed, to pass out. It was drawn by coal-black horses with flaming eyes, who snorted and pawed the ground, striking sparks from the paving-stones. They turned the corner and soon the carriage was lost to sight, on its way to an unknown destination.

PART III FRANCE
ENGLAND
ITALY

"THE LOGE INFERNALE, OR THE DEVIL'S BOX"

DR. VÉRON, whom on March 1, 1831, the Minister of the Interior to King Louis-Philippe, Monsieur de Montalivet, appointed to be Director of the Opera, was a strange kind of medical man. While still a child, growing up in the back premises of a stationer's shop, his only interest was anatomy. When he became a medical student, however, he developed a passion for literature and music. One day he sold a skeleton in perfect condition for twenty-five francs so that he could give a dinner to the artists and poets who were his friends.

Young Véron was not alone in exhibiting these symptoms, which heralded a new intellectual era. All Paris was quivering in the breeze which chased away the last vestiges of the July Revolution. The memories of the bloody riots, the sack of the Archbishop's Palace, that of Saint Germain-l'Auxerrois, though still so recent, were blotted out; the streets were full of flowers; the minds of men were full of new ideas. The battle was to be fought on the field of aestheticism, and the soldiers, the young romantics, were ready. They had patiently endured the Restoration and had been moved to tears by Lamartine and Châteaubriand. Now they were to speak the language of those poets. Eighteenth-century irony was out of date, and they shook off the shackles of the classics. They discussed everything, themselves in the first place, "the beautiful, the unbeautiful, the futile, the heroic, the grandiose." The enthusiasts harped on their catchwords: "irresistible, monstrous, tempestuous, Babylonian, Shakespearean, volcanic, satanic."

Ranged behind their leader, Victor Hugo, they fought the battle of *Hernani*. Under the auspices of Charles Nodier, high priest of the first literary coterie, the fabulous and the fantastic spread their great wings.

Véron threw himself heart and soul into the new movement. He had made a fortune out of a patent ointment for chest diseases, called the *Pâte Regnault*, of which he was joint proprietor. Thanks to this, he was able to found, in 1829, a literary journal called the *Revue de Paris*.

Its pages were thrown open to young writers: Sainte-Beuve (*Portraits littéraires*); Mérimée (short stories); Hoffmann (*Contes fantastiques*); Scribe and Rossini (hitherto unpublished compositions). A young novelist contributed serials: *La belle Impéria, L'auberge rouge* (The Red Inn), *Les Proscrits*. He signed himself Honoré de Balzac. But before long he was writing indignantly: "Véron has sent the *Revue* to the devil, as a man kicks away the ladder after he has climbed the wall." *

After editing the *Revue* brilliantly for two years, Véron was asked to take over the direction of the Opera. Once more he was the physician and the patient was *in extremis*. The Royal Academy of Music, which had formerly been heavily subsidized by way of propaganda by Napoleon I, and subsequently by the Restoration, was moribund. The public had lost their taste for entertainments that had been in vogue before the Revolution. *Armida, Orpheus, The Dumb Woman of Portici,* the ballet of *Flora and Zephyrus,* and especially Rossini's operas: *Le Barbier de Séville, Count Ory, Moses,* and *William Tell,* which was written in 1829, were out of favour. The tenors were in everyone's black books.

"Monsieur Guizot received sixty thousand francs for saving France," a future minister remarked, "the tenor Duprez received the same amount for saving the Opera."

Draconian conditions were laid down by Louis-Philippe.

* A. M. Berthoud, Cambrai. Paris, June 1831.

Article I of the contract presented to Véron was couched in the following terms: "The administration of the Royal Academy of Music, known as the Opera, shall be entrusted to a Managing Director who will run it at his own risk, on a basis of profit and loss, for six years."

Véron signed the document without hesitation. His diagnosis of the situation was as follows: "The July Revolution was the triumph of the *bourgeoisie*. They are now cock of the walk and determined to enjoy themselves. The Opera will be their Versailles, and they will flock to it. Foreigners must be attracted to Paris by first-rate performances of musical masterpieces, and the glamorous spectacle of a brilliant and well-filled house."

⁌ But this desirable audience had first to be created. Earth was shaking underfoot. The *salons* had collapsed in the Faubourg St. Germain, which now existed only as the refuge of a ruined aristocracy, and they had not been instituted by the New Rich of the Faubourg St. Honoré and the Chaussée d'Antin. Yet they were burning to show off their luxury and their ladies, and to have their own great men, their financiers, and their ballet dancers.

And now to work! Véron's first object was to make a success of it. His great, pale face and bright eyes were everywhere during the four years of his rule at the Opera, which he had vowed to make a second Versailles.

The façade of the Royal Academy was at that time on the rue de Peletier, but to reach his office, the director had to make his way by the rue Grange-Batelière, skirting the monument and turning at right angles into the courtyard, with its shady chestnut trees. Once across the threshold and past the cubbyhole of Madame Crosnier, the door-keeper, and the box-office, he arrived at his headquarters, whence the final orders for the evening's performance were issued. There, on the alert, he found his two henchmen, Contant, the stage carpenter, and

Auguste, the leader of the low gang that led the applause. After-wards these hirelings met to concoct their plan of campaign in a low tavern in the rue Favart. Auguste, a herculean figure in a red frock-coat, held defeat or victory in his fifty-one pairs of hands; that is to say his own, those of his two lieutenants, his four sub-lieutenants, and forty-four of the rank and file, whom he scattered judiciously about the hall to lead the clapping. There were no lengths to which actors would not go to secure the favour of Monsieur Auguste, who could at will make or wreck a career.

There was the singers' green-room, which was formerly the white and gold drawing-room of the great mansion, the Hôtel de Choiseul, which had been bought by the State to accommodate the Royal Academy of Music and Ballet. There were dressing-rooms for the principals: Mesdames Damoreau-Cinti, Dorus-Gras, Falcon, and later Pauline Viardot, Grisi, Stoltz, etc.; besides the green-room for the ballet. There were "last-minute favours" to be distributed to the protectors of the ladies of the ballet: a box for a financier, a stall for a critic, or a complimentary ticket for the husband of somebody's sister. The Opera was ready to attract the hosts of foreigners, vanguard and rear-guard, who, it was hoped, would flock to see these glittering stars in the guise of princesses, sylphs, and gipsies.

When at last the Director could escape from his office, he made his way down the private staircase which led to the first stage-box on the right. Through the padded and curtained door he could hear the murmur of voices, which was the prelude to the raising of the curtain. He opened the door cautiously and found himself in the very heart of the citadel.

"In those days," said Roger de Beauvoir, who was one of Véron's collaborators, "the so-called *loge infernale*, or devil's box, was a great power. It was almost like the King's own sanctuary."

This nest of intrigue, this hot-bed of gossip, was the rendezvous of all the Paris dandies, all the young bloods of France, with their notorious liaisons, their fantastic locks, their preposterous notions, their Byronic profiles. They argued; they laid down the law. They came to see, and what was even more important, they came to be seen. Their frock-coats, in romantic shades of puce, ash grey, "dust of ruins," with velvet collars and billowing cravats, made bright patches of colour. Outside the door, the little "tigers," three feet high, leaned against the wall, guarding their masters' voluminous cloaks.

Every evening, Madame Gentil, the head of the women attendants, took careful notes of the celebrities who were present, for entry in her diary. She described the *loge:* "It is hung with pleated silk the colour of lapis-lazuli, and is adorned with mirrors, which reflect the soft radiance of the candles within the box and the light of chandeliers, each with sixteen gas jets, which are on the outer side. For some years the box has invariably been taken by Messieurs d'Etchegoyen, de Boignes, Royer-Collard, and Latour-Mézeray; Monsieur de Balzac has joined them temporarily. Monsieur d'Etchegoyen, the least flighty of these gentlemen, who are the leaders of gay society, is the protector of an actress who, though lacking in glamour, has pleasing manners and a pretty wit. Monsieur de Boignes, who is dreamy but spirited, spends his time at the fencing school and in the company of actresses who have a reputation at the second-rate theatres. Monsieur Latour-Mézeray prefers to make his conquests among the *bourgeoisie*, while Monsieur Royer-Collard, who excels them all in wit, learning, and the irregularity of his bachelor life, confines his attentions to the ladies of the streets and boulevards.

"Monsieur de Balzac, who, however, has not been here for some months, seems to come to the theatre simply to show himself off. The light plays on his great round head, with its long, thick, straight hair and clean-shaven double chin. When he props his head on the dimpled hands that rest on the knob of his walking-stick, it looks ridiculously like a capital on the top of a grotesque pillar.

"Monsieur Véron is obliged to keep on good terms with these patrons and often has to give way to them. It is only by the most tactful handling that the astute director has managed to attach them to his interests. Since then, Nourrit has been pronounced an impeccable artist, Fanny Essler adorable, and her sister the most accomplished dancer of the day. . . ."

Véron was presenting *Robert the Devil* (libretto by Scribe, music by Meyerbeer). This was a new departure and, it may be stated, the crowning success of his directorship. With his hand on the pulse of the public, the wise physician had hit on the right régime for his patient. Steeped in the literature of a bygone generation, Véron remembered the literary tastes of his youth, the coteries, the gloomy ballads, the legends of Nodier and Victor Hugo. He pondered. The poets of yesterday had been fascinated by the fantastic and the occult. He would now try their effect on the public. They were ready. Secretly they were tired of *coloratura;* they were blasé about their wealth and conscious of inexplicable yearnings. It remained to be seen if they would react to the vampires and satans of a new musical fashion.

"Samiel," the Satan of Weber's *Freischütz,* had made his bow at the Odéon. Berlioz, the French romantic composer, had fortified his *Symphonie Fantastique* with a Witches' Sabbath. Véron, with all the stage effects of the Opera at his disposal, could do even better. In voluptuous contrast, he would follow up Meyerbeer's choruses of demons with an enchanting ballet. How piquant to turn from an accursed convent with sacrilegious nuns to an Eden of iridescent angels. There was one who, all by herself, could people Paradise: Taglioni, most exquisite of sylphs in the fashionable ballet of the day.

"Our pens still tremble at the mere name of Marie Taglioni," wrote Roger de Beauvoir. "That ethereal poem still echoes in our hearts. Every evening in her little *salon* in the rue Grange-Batelière, she dispensed most gracious hospitality. There we met Méry, Delacroix, Auber, Alexander Dumas and a score of others. At every step you trod on Russians, bank-notes, coronets and poems. We used to say to Marie: 'How enchanting you were this evening!' and she would reply: 'That was nothing. Wait till you see me the day after tomorrow.'

"Her rival, Fanny Elssler, appealed to us with her suggestive, provocative dances. Fanny was the gipsy of our dreams. We could think of nothing to send her, except castanets, but they were castanets fit for a queen, adorned with strings of emeralds and rubies."

The Director of the Beaux Arts, Viscount Sosthène de la Rochefoucauld, issued a decree ordering ballet skirts to be lengthened by several inches, and at the same time curtailing the duration of the ballets. Would the prudishness of the court spread to the Opera? Were the poets to be banished from the wings?

"What would the *loge infernale* say to that, those leaders of fashion, with their butter-coloured gloves? How would they like it, those advance patrols of public opinion?" wrote Madame Gentil in her journal.

"It was a treat to watch these gentlemen, backed by their friends in the audience, guiding public opinion by signs of approval or disapproval. Sometimes they were refractory and turned their backs on the stage, insolently scanning the boxes at the back of the hall through their ornate opera glasses."

The boxes were another source of anxiety to Véron. Unless they were let for the season, it would never pay to prepare and light the huge building even for a single evening. The Rothschilds, who were said to be more powerful than the King, and superior to the law, had a box next to the Royal box. Baron Aguado, Marquis de Las Marismas, a patron of the arts and a sleeping partner in the Opera, who was said to be so rich that he never accepted change from a tradesman, had his box, and so had the Duchess of Otranto, Fouché's daughter-in-law, whom her husband escorted on foot to the Opera before going off on some romantic adventure of his own. Another box was let to Madame Bodin, who, twenty years before, had eloped with the multi-millionaire Demidof, the owner of mines in the Urals. A stage-box in the Upper Circle was occupied by a mysterious trio of ladies, who were always dressed in white and escorted to the theatre by an equerry in a rapidly driven carriage. Véron could never discover anything about them, except that the box was taken in Lord Hawley's name, and that, in the opinion of the women attendants from the suburbs, these young princesses, who called each other "my dear," frequented the King's Theatre in London.

In the old days, at a ball given by the Duchess de Berry, there was a fair-haired young woman, who danced so lightly that her feet seemed scarcely to touch the ground. The beholder was struck by her grace, before he thought of her beauty. The Marquise de Castries was a fine flower of the Restoration, of which Lamartine's Elvira was typical. Now she was a Parisian of the July Monarchy, and had exchanged the hunts and race meetings of the old régime for a social career at the Opera. Her somewhat unconventional elegance, her steady nerves, her quick perceptions, had a solid foundation. An eccentric but resplendent figure in her foaming feathers, laces, turbans, muslin jackets, she rose out of her swirling petticoats like a butterfly emerging from a chrysalis. In reality she was a highly successful business woman. Money attracted her far more than music. But the brilliant Opera was not only a centre of social life, it also served as a mart for all kinds of financial transactions. She knew how to turn a financier's brief visit to her box to better account than all the profit made by her husband in a year's work on the stock exchange.

Success seemed assured. Between the acts, the Opera-house

hummed like a beehive. Authors, poets, painters, journalists emerged from the wings, and buzzed about, making honey. There was Théophile Gautier, shaking his flowing locks; Alphonse Karr; Victor Hugo, accompanied by his wife, and arguing with a young man in a white frock-coat, who said in biting tones:

"Hugo! Hugo! You are a poet. Poets are lucky. I am not a poet. I am a critic, do you hear? A critic! Oh it is a miserable trade. Do you suppose for a moment that a critic is still human? You are mistaken. He is no longer a man. He is a slave, a pariah. . . ."

This particular pariah was Jules Janin. He passed on to talk to other celebrities: Eugène Delacroix; Berlioz; Alfred de Musset; Castil-Blaze, of the *Journal des Débats*; Alfred de Vigny, a poet who was jealous of the success of his own prose writings; Heinrich Heine, who had come back to Paris, his spiritual home; Emile de Girardin and his wife "the Vicomte de Launay"; Rossini, who had been promised a fee of ten thousand francs for every two-act opera he composed, but who now never wrote a bar of music; the young Donizetti, with his florid complexion and shining eyes, who wrote the fourth act of *La Favorita* in a single night; Auber, the French Rossini, who sought his themes in the Bois de Boulogne; and two composers in spectacles, Adolphe Adam and Fromental Halévy.

The orchestra was another source of anxiety. It was notoriously insubordinate and frivolous under its hoarse-voiced conductor Habeneck. As a rule they reserved their worst pranks for the rehearsals of *William Tell*. Véron was on tenterhooks at every performance of this opera. When the tenor Ferdinand Prévost appeared, leaning only lightly on his oar, and exclaimed: "Behold the blood!" the orchestra, with one accord, uttered cries of horror. When William raised his eyes to heaven, which in the theatre was represented by the chandelier, and sang: "The dangers are great, but the pilot is here," all the members of the orchestra turned their heads and cast glances of Voltairian irony at the chandelier.

Once these danger-points were rounded, the Director could slip out through the famous stage-door and go off to meet his friends at the Café de Paris.

The hall was already empty, and the chandelier had been put back in its case. A hum of voices proceeded from the crowds as they descended the stairs with slow, majestic tread.

"The great staircase," wrote a contemporary, dazzled by the brilliance of the scene, "was crowded with women in exquisite gowns. It was like a wonderful Jacob's ladder, with an angel on every step."

On that celestial staircase, in blissful anonymity, people from the suburbs could rub shoulders with the great. First, there was Monsieur Thiers, and pretty, fair-haired Madame Thiers on the arm of Baron de Manssion, diplomatist and father-in-law of Marochetti, the "Benvenuto of the century." With them was Mademoiselle Dosne. Then there was the Princess de Beauffremont; the Vicomtesse de Noailles and her daughter, the Princess de Poix; Madame Sabine de Noailles, the "Grisi" of the drawing-rooms; Madame de Crillon; the charming Madame Pozzo di Borgo; the Duchess of Valençay; the Marquise d'Osmond and Madame de Lauriston, escorted by Monsieur de Belmont; the Duke of Coigny, President of the Commission on Lyric Theatres; the Prince de Kaunitz; two peers of France, of whom the Marquis de Dreuz-Brézé represented the legitimate party; and Monsieur Viennet, the writer of fables; Raoul Rochette, who had so many decorations that he was nicknamed Brochette ("spit"); Monsieur Guillaume, the gourmet who invited all Paris to his house, and thanked them when they accepted his invitations.

"At Monsieur Guillaume's balls, everyone knows everyone, except the host, who knows nobody."

And finally there was the much hoped-for foreign element:

the Princess de la Ligne, the beautiful Belgian Ambassadress; the Countess Merlin, who was a musical expert; Princess Radziwill with a green shade over her eyes; the Marquis of San-Yago, a Castilian who was thirty-two times as noble as the King; Baron Vidil, with red heels to his shoes; Monsieur Kniff, who always carried a box of jewels to give away; Captain Gronow; Prince Tufiakin with Mademoiselle Georges; a young, tragic actress of seventeen, Rachel by name, with her mother; the Marquis du Hallais; Messieurs de Montguyon, Jules de la Grange, de Lavalette, de Vaublanc, and many more besides: in short, all the gilded youth of Paris between the ages of twenty-four and sixty-nine.

❧ Such was French society after the Revolution, which Balzac eyed so keenly from the *loge infernale* under the brilliant gas jets of the chandeliers. Those glittering crowds, ascending and descending the great staircase, that new Jacob's ladder—Véron doubtless saw them in his dreams. But on March 1, 1831, when he first came into power, all this was only a vision of the future. The rehearsals of *Robert the Devil*, which he intended to produce in a sumptuous setting, would be protracted till at least November, and then there would still be the rehearsals of the ballets, which, needless to say, would likewise conform to the satanic motive: *The Lame Devil*, *The Temptation*, etc.

Véron racked his brains to think of some attraction to stop the rout, bring back the stampeding public, and fill the stalls, which were as empty as the Opera cash-box itself. Where on earth was he to find this great attraction, this wonderful magnet? Every day increased the deficit. The sands were running out. . . .

"IO VOGLIO SVERGINARE A PARIGI"
["I INTEND TO CONQUER PARIS"]

P AGANINI journeyed towards the French capital by long stages; Carlsruhe, Frankfurt, Strasburg were included in his itinerary. He knew nothing about the Parisians, but he had dedicated a Concerto to them, his Concerto in D minor, which was a jealously guarded secret. He intended to give its maiden performance in Paris with all due pomp and circumstance.

After his tour of Northern Europe, he arrived in Carlsruhe on January 31, almost completely restored to health, thanks to his cures at Ems and Baden-Baden. This was also the case when he went to Frankfurt for what he thought would be his farewell visit. But in this friendly city, which had fêted him, soothed him, worshipped him, he found two distressing letters awaiting him. One contained the news of Teresa's persistent illness, the other that of the death of his brother Carlo. These sad tidings received simultaneously plunged him in gloom. Carlo dead! Carlo, with whom he had fled, as a child, to Lucca, "towards fame and love," as the two boys told each other. Now he would be alone, always alone, until at last death came to him.

At Strasburg he gave two evening concerts and received two wreaths on the platform at the hands of the harpist.

"I shall keep the more elaborate of the two to place on the head of my friend Germi, when I have the joy of embracing him again," he said, affecting to smile at this ceremony which

154

had now become traditional and which had in reality raised his spirits. When he arrived in Paris this mood of lassitude gradually disappeared. There was a new light over everything. The past seemed to have faded and receded. Yesterday's depression and yesterday's laurel wreaths shrank into insignificance confronted with this formidable array of new experiences, the fascinations, the dangers of the unknown. And yet he had seen so many capitals in the last year! For months the French papers had never stopped writing about him and commenting on his approaching visit. But what kind of welcome would they give him? Paris was the peak to which he aspired, but how was he to scale it?

He put up at the Hôtel des Princes, rue de Richelieu, where he met Paër, the former director of the Parma Conservatoire and now director of the King's Chamber Music. The Court insisted that Paganini should play at the Palais Royal on March 2. What reply was he to make? Rossini was in Paris, the gay companion, whom he had left behind in Rome ten years ago. His star had guided him from triumph to triumph, from Bologna to Vienna, from Vienna to London, from London to Paris. He was still the spoilt child of fortune and had for his patron the Viscount Sosthène de la Rochefoucauld, director of the Beaux-Arts. He proposed to approach the governing body of the Opera * on behalf of Nicolò. Where would Nicolò find a more splendid setting, one more worthy of his first appearance in Paris? The "Swan of Pesaro" with his fair round belly was as amusing as ever and smiled affectionately at his sombre friend. Nicolò's silhouette, which was reflected on the wall of his room at the Hôtel des Princes, was more gaunt, more phantomlike than ever. It flashed upon Rossini that here was the Mephistopheles of Véron's dreams, the very person for his scenes of hell. Here was the attraction so anx-

* Consisting of the Duc de Choiseul and Messieurs d'Henneville, Armand Bertin, Edmond Blanc, Keratry, Cavé.

iously sought for, the splendid star for the great romantic ballet. He pressed Paganini, who had fixed on March 9 for his concert, but was still undecided on March 5. He was so nervous that he even begged Paër to make his excuses to the Court. His cough, he said, was so troublesome that he could not venture to play before His Majesty at present.

The newspapers, however, tactlessly continued to comment on his movements: his appearance at the Italian's on the very first day of his arrival, where he went to see Madame Malibran in *Othello*; his presence at one of the Conservatoire Concerts on February 27, when Habeneck was conducting Beethoven's C minor Symphony.

After each of these performances, tongues wagged busily in the green-room. Some of the artists had seen Paganini's remarkable profile. The maestro, it was said, wanted to engage an orchestra to accompany him at the Opera. There had been more surprising things than that. Habeneck, himself a violinist, with a taste for novelties, had succeeded in introducing Beethoven at the Conservatoire Concerts. Only fifteen years ago, at the Conservatoire, the orchestra had held their sides with laughter at the rehearsal of the *Eroica*, and had created such an uproar that Habeneck had to wait till 1828 before risking the C minor (No. 5), which was now a great attraction.

Nowadays many virtuosi were purchasing at Pacini's the famous Twenty-four Caprices of Paganini. But when they tried to read them, they proved to be insoluble enigmas, impossible to execute.

Paganini, it was thought, was not yet to inherit the sceptre of Viotti, who had died in London seven years ago—Viotti, with his pure and mellow tone, "his bow of cotton wool, wielded by the arm of a Hercules"; Viotti, who was beloved of Cherubini; Viotti, the director of the Conservatoire, whose Concertos were always set as test pieces for the violin in the annual examinations. His colleagues and pupils carried on the tradition of his serene style, his correct musical phrasing, his broad, sustained bowing, which was straightforward, but perhaps a little lacking in variety. One of his disciples was Pierre Rode, who had died the previous year, shortly before Kreutzer, to whom Beethoven dedicated his penultimate sonata for piano and violin, the ninth, which, however, Kreutzer never consented to play—at least in public.

Baillot had the distinction of having been the first to organize chamber-music concerts, at which the Beethoven quartets were performed in Paris.

Nicolò wrote, on March 1, regretting his inability to be present at one of these concerts: "My health will not permit it, especially as I am to play before the King tomorrow and must save myself for the occasion."

At sixty, Baillot, "the noble Baillot," was still head of the great French School of violin playing, which was deservedly famous. It was so carefully graded that it could include among its students dilettante pupils, professors at the Conservatoire, and even the first violin of the Orchestra, who was growing old at his post. The School produced a type of violinist who combined talent with poise: an aloof manner, a lofty expression, a dignified stance, with the elbows held at the correct distance from the body. What impression was the hysterical Italian likely to make on a public accustomed to this classical tradition?

There was one man in Paris who could give a full description of the strange virtuoso. This was Lafont, who was actually in Paris on a concert tour. Other musicians remembered that the two had met long ago in Milan, where they had played Kreutzer's Double Concerto together. And Lafont, it was said, had not had the better of the encounter.

"Pooh! How do you know? Paganini is just an acrobat, a mountebank, a woman-hunter, with a face like a vulture . . . and disgustingly rich. He has no need to play professionally.

He could afford to hire the Opera-house without having to worry. . . ."

For the honour of the city, however, a suitable welcome had to be prepared for the stranger. One fine morning, Balzac, tracking Véron down to the wings of the Opera itself, found him in the middle of a "Paganini rehearsal." Thanks to Rossini and Véron himself, two cronies who understood each other at a nod, an agreement had been reached. Véron had only to secure Paganini's famous silver G string and he would be sure of his receipts, sure of once more attracting crowds to the Opera-house. A satisfactory contract was concluded. Although the price of the stalls was raised to 20 francs * each and that of other seats in proportion, the house was sold out in a miraculously short time. The cashiers could hardly believe their eyes. Actors who were appearing at other theatres and could not attend the evening performance, signed a petition, begging for a matinée.

On March 8 there was an announcement in the *Courrier des Théâtres*: "Tomorrow we are to hear the famous Paganini. There will be a gala performance in honour of the occasion. The concert will be followed by a ballet. It will be a treat for music-lovers."

On the evening of March 9 the grand staircase at the Opera was a veritable Jacob's ladder. It presented a spectacle far surpassing in brilliance Teresa's humble dreams or even the visions of Véron himself. All fashionable Paris was there. Its officials, its men of letters, its artists, its leaders of society—all were reassembled for the first time since the troubles. And what is more, they were all instantly galvanized.

"*It was the most surprising, the most wonderful, the most miraculous, the most triumphant, the most bewildering, the most incredible, the most amazing, the most impossible, the most unexpected thing that ever happened . . .*" wrote Castil-

* About 2,000 francs today.

Blaze, in the *Journal des Débats*, quoting Madame de Sévigny and reproaching her for having, "a hundred and fifty years too soon," wasted on a young Gascon the very phrases he needed to describe Paganini.

"Tartini saw in a dream a demon, who played a diabolical Sonata. That demon could have been none other than Paganini. And yet Tartini's sprite, with his double trills, his weird modulations, his rapid *arpeggios*, was the merest tyro compared to the virtuoso we now possess. He was nothing but a timid little imp, one of those underground goblins, who see the sun only through chinks. You will notice that I have to have recourse to the devil himself to give you some idea of what Paganini is like, to explain to you what I felt when I heard him and what I felt afterwards, and to convey to you the excitement which robbed me of my sleep that night and gave me St. Vitus's dance. And yet I can never succeed . . ."

Words broke down; words recoiled from an element which was beyond their comprehension. After the first shock, they endeavoured to analyse the experience and to give the analysis literary expression. But at the Opera, the music performed its function and carried the hearers away to a dazzling country, where the first to enrol themselves were the members of the orchestra. They were as eager now as they had previously been reserved, and attacked the enigmas, which they had solved at last. They let off the fireworks that illumined the sky. The Italian maestro was well advised to choose a mythical setting. He himself was "better theatre" than all the Samiels and Robert-the-Devils in the world.

"Five-feet-six," wrote Castil-Blaze rattling off his description as if he were decoding a spiritualistic message, "the figure of a dragon; a long pale face with strongly marked features; a prominent nose; long, black hair, falling in curls over his collar; extreme cadaverousness; two furrows on either side of the mouth, engraved, one might suppose, by his playing, so exactly do they resemble the *f*-shaped sound holes of a violin; glittering eagle eyes, alight with genius and rolling in their sockets.

"The joints that connect arm and wrist are so supple that I can only compare his hands to a cloth fluttering in the wind at the end of a stick."

The public, who had failed to appreciate the "noble Baillot's" chamber music at the Hôtel de Ville, were carried away by this explosion of romanticism, which excited them even more than the sound of the trombones and the crisp *arpeggios*. The Italian virtuoso was a creator. After his technical fireworks had burnt out, it was for the critics to make their approach, but for the audience, the last note of the Satanic *Allegro* had hardly died away when it was succeeded by the solemn pleading of the *Adagio*. The tears that filled their eyes were promptly dried by the sparkling *Rondo* which made them laugh.

The second item on the programme, *Non più andrai*, was on a theme of Mozart's, but it was as if a "ruffianly hand" had seized it by the throat and were forcing it into startling variations and making it execute prodigious leaps and bounds.*
When the hearers had recovered their senses, they realized that the whole range of emotions, which had shaken them for nearly an hour, had been produced by a single string, the G, which had done the work of a whole violin.

In *Nel cor più non mi sento*, the last item on the programme, Paganini dispensed with the orchestra. He stood alone on the platform, a superhuman figure, playing the melody with his bow, while he executed a *pizzicato* accompaniment with his left hand. The musical critic in the *Journal des Débats* backed up his colleague in the *Revue de Paris*, and summed up the delirious enthusiasm of the audience by ex-

* *Revue de Paris.*

horting all who had been absent "to sell, or pawn, all their possessions, in order to hear Paganini."

"Woe to him who lets him depart unheard!" exclaimed the critic of the *Revue de Paris*, while his brother critic in the *Débats* replied in the vein of the Psalmist: "Let mothers, newly delivered, bring their babes . . . that sixty years hence they may boast that they heard Paganini."

The most surprising thing was that this display of fireworks did not burn itself out.

"I can give you no idea of the prodigious triumphs I have enjoyed in Paris," Paganini wrote to Germi.

At his second concert, on Sunday, March 13, he was so sure of his ground that he played not only his well-known *rondo, La Clochette*, but ventured to give a first performance of his famous Concerto in D minor, which was dedicated to the French people. It was a work of fantastic imagination, containing phrases of breath-taking audacity and orchestral passages, in which the shrill voice of the violin vied with the roar of the trombones.

The public were completely conquered; they were insatiable. All the eleven concerts at the Opera were crowded to capacity. Such a thing was unprecedented. "If I had only come a year ago, I could have pocketed a million," he boasted to Germi. "I have been advised to buy an annuity. It is astonishing to see the success of all these concerts following so closely upon each other."

At the end of April the cashier handed him, on behalf of the Opera, a note of his net earnings, which bore eloquent witness to his success. In six weeks the magician had made 125,000 francs in gold, more than ten millions at the present rate of exchange. According to the *Revue de Paris*, one of his fanatical admirers declared that he could if he chose, play the whole of Molière's *Misanthropist* on his violin—a new version of the old

Milanese legend which affirmed that his magic violin had been heard to pronounce distinctly the name of the woman whom Paganini loved. Paganini believed that he had conquered Paris without having to strike a blow, and he now began to open negotiations with the English.

"Laporte, who is the impresario of the London Theatre, has come to Paris on purpose to see me," he wrote to Germi. "The day before yesterday I signed a contract with him agreeing to begin a series of concerts early next month and to continue them for six or eight weeks. After the season I shall go to Scotland and Ireland. . . . Rossini is a true friend. I owe my favourable contract for my concerts at the Opera to his kind offices." *

Paganini's taste for courts had revived. He was anxious that His Majesty and the Duchess of Orléans should honour him by being present at one of his last concerts.

"I am giving this concert more for pleasure than profit," he said to Véron and begged him to add an attractive ballet. It is not known whether Louis-Philippe granted his request; as a rule he neglected the Opera. It so happened that his initials, L. P., which were emblazoned on the royal box, served some years later for Véron's successor, Monsieur Léon Pillet. The decorators had no need to change the letters.

After giving a charity concert on April 17, 1831, Paganini took leave of Habeneck and of Paër, whom he always flattered by referring to himself as his "very grateful pupil." It was now thirty-five years since a pale-faced boy, with a nose like an eagle, astonished old Ghiretti, who had taught Paër and was a master of the fugue, with his *Duos Brillants*.

Shortly afterwards, on April 28, he left Paris for England. On his way, he gave concerts, by request, at Lille, Douai, Boulogne, and Calais. As a tribute of gratitude to Rossini, he composed and dedicated to him a Sonata on the theme of the Romance

* Paris, April 6, 1831.

of Othello. It was called *Souvenir de Rossini à Paganini*. All Paganini's friends including his old master Paër, Pacini his publisher, and Bennati his doctor, thought Paganini exhausted by his triumphs. He was paler and thinner than ever. He was to return to France in the spring of 1832. But it was thought that the English fogs would be the death of him, even if he survived the crossing.

BREAKERS

As HE was feverishly speeding away from Paris he left rough water in his wake. He fondly imagined that Dr. Burney's description of the "divine Farinelli," which was written nearly a century before, could be equally well applied to his own reputation.

"He conquered all who heard him," Dr. Burney wrote of the famous male soprano, "connoisseurs, ignoramuses, friends and foes."

These words were certainly an accurate definition of Paganini's powers of fascination. But Paganini could not support his reputation with his compositions, because a complete edition had not yet appeared, and once the maestro himself, the magnetic pole, had disappeared, those same "connoisseurs, ignoramuses, friends and foes" were no longer under the spell of his playing. Disillusioned, distrustful, and no longer unanimous in his praise, they began quarrelling among themselves. Their reactions were like the eddies and breakers which persist long after the cause of the disturbance has vanished. The musician and his music were soon submerged by an outburst of scepticism, depreciation, philosophising, aestheticism.

Twenty-five years later the controversy still persisted. Eugène Delacroix and his friend Telefsen were discussing Paganini at the house of the Princess X.

"When I alluded to my memories of Paganini," remarked Telefsen, "Delacroix replied that he was undoubtedly an incom-

164

parable musician. The difficulties and *tours de force* which his works are said to contain are as yet almost unknown, because even the cleverest violinists have failed to decipher them. There you have the inventor, the right man for the special task. I can think of many an artist, many an architect, and many another man, of whom the contrary may be said."

In 1831, however, there was one man who sought to analyse this river of sound and to discover its sources by reviving in his mind each of Paganini's concerts.

In spirit, Balzac was still at the Opera, listening fascinated to the maestro and observing him more intently than ever. It appears from his letters that he endorsed the opinion of the biographers, who called him the Napoleon of music. But he was more than this; he was the creator of a strange fantastic world to which Balzac had the *entrée*. Each new phenomenon set a new problem, which, even when Balzac was on the eve of his greatest works, continued to obsess him.

"What is the secret of artistic creation? Along what trajectory travels the force that inspires this ailing man? This electric current which expends itself in a single direction: harmony? And whence is this force derived?

"Is it energy long pent up? Are there reserves from which the dreams of ordinary mortals are derived? It may be that in the case of the awakened creator, or rather the creator in a state of ecstasy, the explosion of these forces projects a vision so intense, that it survives the ecstasy and tries to perpetuate itself. Then comes the slow elaboration of a form, a mould, into which these original dream sights and sounds are poured, so that they may become visible and audible. What patience, what efforts, are required to express, interpret, and transmit them!"

There is the struggle against the terrible resistance of matter, which the author of *Louis Lambert* compares to a "kind of metal shell in which this force is confined." "Unless it can be broken down, the divine afflatus, which could animate worlds, the energy, which is so fecund in victory, may turn against the spirit, driving it to madness and destroying it. . . ."

In the case of Paganini, that magician, the resistance of matter was shattered and his path was strewn with the burning fragments, proof of the victory of the spirit. But by what means was the victory won? One half of the problem was solved, but it left the other half more obscure than ever. How define this creative force, which instinct apprehends, how locate those zones where it originates?

Could the spirit that triumphed over matter, in other words the brain of the inventor, prove to be a talisman that defied time and space? Balzac himself could feel stirring within him imaginary generations, which would some day serve as patterns to living men. Might it be that the Italian maestro felt himself the forerunner of a winged host of romantic virtuosi, who were about to descend upon Europe; envoys with curling locks, with the eyes of angels or demons, and endowed with almost super-human talents?

Finally, did genius depend on the perfection or the imperfection of the human brain? Was it born of a spark struck from another world? Among the breakers that surged around the personality of the maestro, waves of the materialism and spiritualism of the day could be discerned. But instead of following the subject further, the author of *Séraphita* added these ambiguous comments:

"I am at present marvelling at the astonishing miracles performed by Paganini in Paris," he wrote on March 18 to Monsieur Berthoud. And on the same day he wrote to a "Mr. V." of Bayeux: "Do not imagine that it is merely a question of his bowing, his fingering, or the fantastic sounds he draws from his violin. . . . There is, beyond all doubt, something mysterious about this man. But though I bless him and admire him, it is not only to indulge my egoistical passion, my artist's enthusiasm, nor for the sake of climbing up on to my bell, like the bell-ringer of Notre-Dame de Paris, that I go to every one of his concerts. No. . . . It is partly out of patriotism, for the pleasure of seeing the Opera-house packed to overflowing and the cashier raking in 20,000 francs a night, which leads me to believe that the word 'want' is only a joke and that there is money in plenty. I do not indeed suppose that these eager ears belong to people with empty stomachs. But I infer that the animal we call a capitalist is suffering from a peculiar malady with symptoms which have not been studied by our statesmen. How else is it possible that a fee of 100,000 francs should have been guaranteed to Madame Taglioni, if she would promise to dance on her hands, while at the same time we refuse to invest similar sums in commerce, industry, the State, or even a canal, although they offer enormous interest and absolute security? Why these eccentricities? Perhaps it is because the ministers know no parlour tricks. Not one of them has succeeded in captivating the public. Paganini seems to me to be the Napoleon of his profession. But we have no Paganini among our politicians . . . though it is not for the lack of violins, music, bows and orchestras."

It was proved by experience that even to a prodigy of imagination, a seer like Balzac, the profound originality of the maestro, that "mysterious something," remained obscure. But though the cause was never discovered, the effects were plain enough.

In every country through which Paganini passed, the impression made by his playing, which had always a powerful effect on the nerves, took a characteristically national form. In Italy, the reactions were superstitious and grotesque; in Vienna, social and fashionable; in Germany, where the hero was made a baron, aristocratic and mythical.

Paris—not the city of the literary coteries, or of the great romantic revival, but rather the Paris belonging to Dr. Burney's category of "learned cities"—the Paris of the intelligent, professional classes had no liking for myths or barons. As soon as it had recovered from its first surprise, it pulled itself together. Society women and poets might talk of the devil. That was a normal literary convention. But at least serious-minded people could disregard idle talk and stories of the evil eye, which might go down in Genoa or Frankfurt on the Main. This was France, the home of reason and lucid intellect. The origin of virtuosity, even of genius, could be rationally, scientifically explained, without the aid of ridiculous inventions.

As if in support of this view, science took a hand. The May number of the *Revue de Paris* published a long article, entitled "Notes on the Physiological Condition of Paganini," which was followed by a "Physiological and Pathological History." Both were by his physician, Dr. Bennati. In these articles, Bennati, who had already attracted attention by other contributions of this kind, threw light upon certain idiosyncrasies, which seemed to bear out the first of Balzac's two hypotheses, namely, that genius was the result of a physical organization peculiarly adapted for its manifestations. In support of his theories, Dr. Bennati boasted of his intimacy, nay, his friendship with Paganini. He had met the maestro for the first time in Vienna in 1828, when he had attended him professionally for a persistent cough, which had seemed to suggest consumption. As soon as Paganini arrived in Paris, he examined him stethoscopically and called in his colleague, Dr. Miquel, for a consultation, before expressing a definite opinion. He made a thorough examination of the nervous system, the epidermis, the mucous membranes, the teeth, the stomach, the intestines, the glands, the muscles, and the brain. Then he went into the medical history of all Paganini's previous illnesses and the treatment he had received for them. Several of the prescribed remedies, especially those containing mercury, had nearly proved fatal to the patient. Fortified by all these investigations, Dr. Bennati proceeded to reason like a precursor of Lombroso. Reconstructing Paganini's frame, piece by piece, he came to the conclusion that his genius, which some attributed to the devil, was due to the functioning and the secretions of certain organs, which were anatomically unique.

"I have no intention of analysing the magical effects of Paganini's playing or of describing the enthusiasm of his admirers. As the maestro's physician, I have a more difficult task, that of appraising his physical organism and studying the relationship between that organism and the development of his genius. These notes of mine will serve as a complement to all the biographies of this remarkable man, with this difference: I shall not seek the explanation of his marvellous performances in ridiculous legends. I shall look for it in the development of his sensibility and his musical organs. . . . The remarkable results reached by Lavater in physiognomy and by Gall in craniology have established beyond a doubt that a trained observer can at once detect in an individual, by almost infallible signs, a special aptitude for any particular branch of human knowledge. It is not, however, my intention to apply these systems to Paganini. I shall not analyse his features or lay stress on the bump of music, which in his case is highly developed on the outer angle of the forehead, but I hope to succeed in showing that the supremacy of the famous violinist is not so much the result of intensive practising, as has been said, as of a special physical structure. . . ."

Here follows a list of characteristics and deviations from the normal which were required for producing such an amazing freak of nature: "the unusual size of the cerebellum; the broad deep conch of the ear; the unimaginable delicacy of hearing; the hand, which although of normal size, has its reach doubled by the elasticity of the capsular ligaments of the shoulders; the pliancy of the ligaments joining the hand to the forearm,

the wrist to the metacarpus, and the phalanges to each other,*
and, finally, the unprecedented degree of nervous excitability,
which is the cause of all his ill health.

"Such then, is Paganini," he concluded. "According to my
diagnosis, which is confirmed by Dr. Miquel, his lungs are functioning perfectly. His leanness is constitutional and not a
symptom of tuberculosis. Were Paganini stout he could never
twist himself into those acrobatic poses while he is playing, as
when he almost crosses both elbows on his chest and turns
himself into a kind of triangle. And then he would not be
Paganini."

To Bennati the case was now perfectly clear, but his readers
and the general public stuck to their guns. Nobody would sur-
render his own opinion. The "materialists" were on the side of
the scientist, but the others were reluctant to abandon the infernal prestige enjoyed by Paganini. Even among the critics
opinions were sharply divided. There was Jules Janin, positive
and cynical; there was Fétis, a meticulous critic; and Castil-
Blaze who congratulated the Enchanter on being his contemporary: "He may well be thankful," he exclaimed. "Had he played
like that a century ago he would have been burnt as a sorcerer."

❡ Echoes of the controversy crossed the border and
soon reached Germany, where Goethe, though now in the evening of life and absorbed in the publication of the second part
of *Faust*, was one of the first to hear the new theory about the
Magician. The patriarch of Weimar was becoming increasingly
a legendary figure and an object of worship. He disapproved of
this cult, which helped to dissipate his energies—a temptation

---

* "Thus he imparts to the first joints of the fingers of his left hand,
which touch the strings, an extraordinary flexibility which, without the
hand changing its position, enables them to move sideways without ab-
normal tension, and this they do with facility, precision and speed."

of his early days. He considered that the enchanted world of the writer, the only one that existed for him, should be like "a citadel enclosed within its walls, with the drawbridge raised." Then let the tide of flatterers and detractors beat against the walls; let pamphlets, letters, books rain down upon the stronghold. But he had his own mysterious way of keeping in touch with any new matter of interest. In spite of his resolves, Goethe was like the Watcher on the Tower in the second part of *Faust*, who was "born to observe, and to watch," who took pleasure in the spectacle of the world. A tall, shadowy form now appeared on the stage.

To spare his tired eyes and damaged heart, he had Bennati's article read aloud to him. It was one of those evenings which his friends remembered till their dying day. Gradually the peace and charm of twilight seeped into the poet's house, while stimulated by some chance remark, a flow of wonderful talk issued from his lips—"like a river of gold," in the words of one of his enraptured disciples.

All the great problems of existence rose to that luminous surface. Perhaps Bennati's theory on the origin of genius, which conjured up Paganini's image, reminded the poet of his own comment on the maestro, when he heard him in Weimar.

"I can find no base for this pillar of cloud and flame," he had said in his letter to Zelter. Perhaps Bennati's theory would supply this base for which he was seeking. Paganini's strange personality seemed to provoke controversy wherever he went. Radiant and sombre, infernal and celestial, he symbolized in his own person the struggle between darkness and light. Goethe, less than anyone, could remain indifferent to such a struggle. In the theories of this man of science he found again the love of reality, the positivism, which he admired in the French, and which was such a contrast to German haziness. Yet the author of *Faust* might well shudder at the idea of one, who, for so many of his hearers, was an incarnation of Mephistopheles; at the artist, whose life, like his work, had so strong a dash of the diabolical.

Bennati concurred with him in recognizing that a peculiar physical organism is the penalty of genius, and that a difficulty in conforming to everyday life is the price that has to be paid. Goethe, too, had had to struggle against this hypersensitiveness, which handicapped him in his resistance to the shocks of life but made him receptive to "the celestial voices." Still, it was perhaps carrying it too far to suggest that the "celestial voices" were merely a by-product of this hypersensitive condition.

"In the *Revue de Paris*, No. 2, May 1st," he wrote to Zelter, "there is an extraordinary article on Paganini. It was written by a doctor who knew him and attended him for several years. He puts his finger very astutely on the incontrovertible fact that the talent of this extraordinary man was fostered by the conformation of his body and the proportions of his limbs, which enabled him to express the Incredible and the Impossible. One is led to ponder on the theory that the physical organism can produce and determine strange manifestations in the living creature. I am reminded of one of the most profound sayings that have been bequeathed to us by our ancestors: 'Animals learn through their organs.' When we consider how much of the animal still remains in man, and that man has the faculty of training his organs, we return again and again to those reflections."

Following the lead of Balzac and Bennati, Goethe considered the question of the physiological origin of genius. While an animal is instructed by means of its organs, man trains his organs while learning through their medium. This fact is illustrated by the training to which a natural bent is subjected. But what is the origin of this natural bent, and in what way does training affect it? The answer was still to be sought.

❡ The musicians, however, did not bother their heads about the origin of genius. Talent they could account for. As soon as their first raptures had subsided, they were irritated at this insistence on the diabolical in elements with which they were perfectly familiar, and which they handled every day. They could explain it by analysing the delicate structure of the violin—fibre, strings, bridge, bow, all of which helped to produce these so-called manifestations of witchcraft.

Two years before, at Frankfurt-on-Main, Karl Guhr, an excellent violinist, who was conductor of the orchestra, had dogged Paganini's footsteps, thereby causing the maestro some annoyance. It was said that in despair at never being allowed to see the coveted manuscripts, he had attempted to write down from memory the whole of the *Non più mesta* of Paganini, following the example of Mozart, who had once similarly transcribed the famous *Miserere* of Allegri. The result of his patient labours was a work entitled: "THE ART OF PAGANINI'S VIOLIN PLAYING: *An appendix to all the methods of violin playing that have been published up to the present, with a section on single and double harmonics. Dedicated to the great masters, Rode, Kreutzer, Baillot, Spohr.*" *

An extract from this treatise had been published in a translation, with a commentary, by Fétis, in his *Revue Musicale* in December 1829. But at that time Paris had not heard Paganini. Although he was Belgian by birth, Fétis was wholly Parisian in outlook. He was editor of the *Revue Musicale* and *l'Artiste*, and director of the Brussels Conservatoire, and he was engaged also on a *Universal Biography of Musicians*. Now Fétis, with ten times his former interest in the matter, was to let Guhr have his say in his *Revue*, and then to reply to him.

"It is obvious," Guhr began, "that Paganini is poles apart

* By Karl Guhr, leader and conductor of the theatre orchestras in Frankfurt-on-Main and Paris. Published by B. Schott & Sons, rue de la Chaussée-d'Antin, No. 10.

from all other violinists. With their technique and their musical sensibility they have invested the violin with power to move the human soul. But, however they might differ from each other through temperament or nationality, they have always had certain things in common, such as their method of bowing, their tone production, their execution.

"Then came Paganini, and with one stroke of his bow demolished all the barriers of tradition. He opened boundless horizons to fantasy, imagination and technique. This terrible originality, however, has its peculiar weakness. It is impossible for him ever to escape from his own creative self. That is why Paganini falls so far below his best when he plays the compositions of other masters. The more fervent and active his imagination, when he gives poetic expression to his own passions and sensations, the more he is hampered when he attempts to emerge from his own personality. . . .

"Although, when he plays the quartets of Beethoven and Mozart he is entranced by their mighty genius, he cannot escape from himself. Ideas of his own break athwart the conceptions of the great masters, and, carried away by his amazing facility, he has to be on his guard against introducing *tours de force* of his own."

There we have the gist of the matter: the charge of introducing brilliant passages in doubtful taste, the *tours de force* of which Eugène Delacroix accused him. The methodical German backed up his assertions by quoting various witnesses, but his own analysis remains the best guide:

The chief differences between Paganini and other violinists are as follows:

1. His method of tuning his instrument.
2. His method of bowing.
3. His practice of combining the sounds produced by the bow with a left-hand *pizzicato* accompaniment.
4. His use of harmonics natural and artificial.

5. His performances on the G string only.
6. His incredible *tours de force.*

1. *His method of tuning his instrument.* In certain works, such as the Concerto in E flat on the Variations *Di tanti palpiti,* the tone of the soloist flashes into sudden brilliance, contrasting with the subdued sounds of the orchestra, like a dragon-fly glittering in the rain. This effect is produced by a simple dodge. The maestro raises the pitch of his instrument by a semi-tone. Thus he plays in the key of D, while the open strings are tuned a semi-tone higher than the orchestral instruments. This contrast greatly heightens the effect of his brilliant arabesques.

2. *His method of bowing.* The peculiarities * of his attitude. Despite certain German critics, he is completely master of the bow. By means of subtle nuances he gives his melodies a tenderness, which words cannot express. But the chief innovation is his development of *staccato.* He is the first to use the flying *staccato* and the *staccato ricochet.* His *sautillé,* which he uses in certain passages, and his *staccato* in general, bear no resemblance to the ordinary form. He throws his bow upon the strings and executes scale passages of incredible rapidity, while the tones of his violin remain as round and smooth as pearls.

3. *His practice of combining the sounds produced by the bow with a left-hand pizzicato accompaniment.* This has the startling effect of two violins, played simultaneously, as in the *Duo Merveille.* It was a device practised by the old Italian School, especially in the time of Mestrino, but it had been neglected by the French and German Schools. It can only be achieved by the use of specially fine strings, such as Paganini habitually employs, which enables the G and D strings to be sounded firmly together,

* "He leans on one hip, with his right arm and hand on a level with the bow. From his attitude one might expect his bowing to be awkward and his arm stiff, but it is soon obvious that arm and bow move with equal suppleness, and what appears to be due to some malformation is in fact the result of intensive study, which enables the artist to produce the effect he desires. The bow is of normal dimensions, but so tightly strung that the stick is less curved than usual."—Fétis, *Biographical Notes on Nicolò Paganini.*

an effect which it is difficult to produce with thicker strings. The bridge of Paganini's violin is less convex than that used by other violinists especially near the E string. This enables him to finger three strings at once in the top register.

4. *His use of harmonics, natural and artificial.* As regards Paganini's "fireworks," his natural and artificial harmonics, which are sometimes overshrill and penetrating, sometimes positively celestial, are like the sting of some insect, deliberately piercing the startled ear of the listener. This, to be sure, is another very old weapon in the violinist's armoury, but it is brought to diabolical perfection in all his Concertos and Fantasias. Chromatic slides, descending and ascending, simple and double trills, whole passages of double stopping, are all executed in harmonics with the utmost ease.

5. *His performance on the G string only.* Here, too, harmonics play a part. The G string is tuned very high and has a range of three octaves—three storeys, as it were, in Paganini's magic structure. (The amazement of the public will be remembered on the occasion of the first performance of *Non più andrai*, the Military Sonata, on one string, at the Opera.) For Fantasias * of this kind, all the strings are tuned a major or minor third higher than usual.

6. *His incredible tours de force.* Besides these sensational acrobatics, there is his double stopping, the reef on which so many violinists come to grief. "To him it is child's play," says a German critic. His double stopping is like an elaborate double flower, with its impeccably accurate thirds, sixths, tenths and octaves, which are like petals flawlessly unfolding.

"The quality of his tone," wrote Fétis, "is beautiful without being excessively full. His fingering is peculiar to himself. Often he places one finger on top of the other. More frequently still he uses the same finger to play several notes. He has a quivering

---

* In the celebrated *Prayer of Moses*, Paganini moved the G string next to the E in the place of the A. This was copied by his pupil, Camillo Sivori

Facsimile of the manuscript of *Le Streghe* (*"The Witches Dance"*)

Paganini's Guarnerius

Paganini at the age of thirty

vibrato of unusual quality, like that of the human voice, while his chromatic slides remind one of the practice of certain singers who are justly blamed for bad taste. . . . He seldom finishes his trills and unlike other violinists often executes them with the little finger. Sometimes, to free his hand for certain feats of agility, he bends the left thumb back into the palm. His suppleness is such that I seem to have seen him pass his thumb across the fingerboard to reach a note on the E string."

When they appraised Paganini as a composer, both the Frenchman and the German paid homage to the high quality of his works, from which monotony, the virtuoso's bane, had been completely eliminated.

Paganini wrote with the consummate authority of a master. His compositions teemed with ideas, which ranged from the simple to the dramatic. In elegance, in wealth of harmony, in intensity of interest, they challenged comparison with the grandiose masterpieces of Rossini. They were indeed a change from those charming Concertos of Viotti! They contained new effects of orchestration, especially in the use of wind instruments.

And yet some vague instinct made both critics withhold unqualified admiration. Guhr regretted Paganini's way of abruptly changing from the incomparable artist to the musical conjurer. Although Fétis believed that Paganini's Concertos would exercise great influence on the concertos of the future, he remarked: "There is prestige, there is the thrill of the supernatural in these works of fantastic genius. Yet not once have I been touched, not once have I been moved by the emotion, which seems to me inseparable from genuine music. Perhaps Paganini sacrifices too much to his desire to strike the imagination. And these compositions, which he himself renders so incomparably, might well sound atrocious, played by lesser virtuosi. Has serious music really anything to gain from his influence?"

As if in answer to his own question, he said in conclusion:

"The art of Paganini was born with him, and it will die with him."

The ball, which had been served so adroitly, was returned, and the *Revue* became the court on which this volleying match took place. Although Fétis was now Paganini's friend and was an impartial judge, he acted as umpire. Shrewd hits were exchanged. A whole literature arose on the subject of Paganini. The tone, which at first was calmly analytical, became embittered. The first to take up the challenge were the professional writers on music, who upheld the purely classical tradition. They deemed it their duty to warn young musicians against the dangers and inconsistencies of "this monstrous eccentric, who led the way to a crazy romanticism." Their leader, Joseph-Marie Fayolles, who had collaborated in the *Quatre Saisons du Parnasse* and the London *Harmonicon*, thus revived an ancient feud in the musical arena.

"Music, too, has its reactionary innovations," was the heading of this writer's article. "To abandon the principles of the Masters of the Old School," it went on, "is surely to blind the eyes of young musicians and turn them away from the study of the classics. Are all rules to be abolished? Is there to be no check to the ardent imagination of the young, which they mistake for genius? Is there to be no *beau idéal* in the Arts?"

"In my opinion," retorted Fétis, "those who consider an ardent imagination to be synonymous with 'genius' are in the right. Imagination and genius are one. . . ."

"These so-called innovations," replied Fayolles, "are nothing new. They have been dug out from the old rubbish heap of discarded violin music. No. Beware of romanticism, which seems to have captivated the taste of the day as never before. This passion for innovation is the height of absurdity. Leonardo da Vinci, Alex de la Viola, Simon Arietto, Veracini, Corelli, Tartini and their successors Geminiani, Leclair, Locatelli, Nar-

dini, Gaviniès, Viotti, Rode and Baillot, have left nothing more
to be said concerning the science of the violin."

"Let Monsieur Fayolles beware! That is a statement that
concerns not only music, not only art in general, but the whole
of human existence. To say that 'the last word has been said'
on any subject is to make a direct attack on human perfecti-
bility. . . . If some unexpected ray of light reveals a new
order, everything that can apply to it must be said, and no one
is justified in saying: 'Ne *plus ultra.*' "

But in spite of these sharp interchanges, Paganini's detractors
were gaining the support of the experts almost everywhere. On
his return to Paris, Lafont boasted to his lukewarm friends that
he himself had been the victor in that old duel, long ago in
Milan. Anders, a writer on musical subjects, who was collecting
material for a biography of Paganini, raked up again the sore
subject of Paganini's imprisonment.

(Paganini was preoccupied with plans for his immediate departure for London, and the controversy did not at
first attract his attention. He was an artist, not a philosopher.
Once that terrible impulse had subsided, which drove him on
to the concert platform, as it drove the Pythoness of Delphi to
her Tripod, he took no interest in general ideas. The box-office
was his chief concern and, after that, good, sound articles about
himself, containing praises that could never be pitched too high.
These he studied intently. As for Romanticism. . . .

It was only by chance that his eyes were opened. Imperceptibly, as formerly in Vienna, all the gossip about his person was
handed down from the upper classes to the general public.
There was now not a shop on the quays that did not display a
caricature of him, as its "touch of Paganiniism." A lithograph
of Mantoux represented him balancing on a tight rope, which
consisted of a G string. Grandville's caricature, which was

adapted from a terracotta figure by Dantan, exaggerated his Dantesque profile and his awkward attitude, with the left hip thrust forward and the hands convulsively clenched. These were merely the penalty of greatness, and in any case he never went along the quays. One day, however, in the centre of Paris, a crowd gathered round him to compare a lithograph, which was exhibited in the window of a stamp dealer, with the original. It was signed by Louis Boulanger, who was a first-rate artist.

He approached the shop window and found that the old scandal, which he hoped he had left behind him for good, had again reared its venomous head. He saw a portrait of himself, in the prison setting, to which legend persisted in banishing him. This time he was distressed at the revival of the old familiar nightmare. Was it all to begin again? It seemed as if the devil, after all, had a hand in it. A youthful peccadillo, his escapade with Angelina, six hours in the lock-up (that was all it amounted to)—did he deserve on that account to be thrown to the wolves: critics, brother artists, doctors, painters, biographers, polemical writers, philosophers, and finally the caricaturists of the boulevards?

He hurried off to Fétis. While he was away, Fétis must come to the rescue. He must publish in the *Revue Musicale* an open letter, in defence of Paganini, written by the maestro himself. The two of them concocted a long screed, which was naïve but, at the same time, not without subtlety.

To Monsieur F. G. Fétis.

Paris,
April 21, 1831

Sir,

I received so many marks of favour from the French public, so many tokens of appreciation, that I could not but believe the assertion that my fame had preceded me to Paris, and that, in my concerts I had not fallen too far below that reputation. If any thing more were needed to convince me, it would be the care with which I see your artists have reproduced my countenance and by the numerous portraits of Paganini, lifelike and otherwise, with which the walls of the capital are plastered. But, sir, these manifestations are not confined to simple portraits. Yesterday as I was walking along the boulevard des Italiens, I saw in the window of a stamp dealer, a lithograph representing *Paganini in Prison.* "Dear me," I said to myself, "are these good people exploiting for their own profit a certain ancient calumny, which has dogged my steps for fifteen years?" While I was laughing and examining this caricature of myself, and all the details with which the artist's imagination had embellished it, I became aware that a crowd had gathered around me and that they were comparing my physiognomy with that of the young man in the lithograph and remarking how much I had changed since my imprisonment. I then realized that these loafers, these *badauds,* as I think you call them, were taking the matter seriously and that the originators were making a good thing out of it. It occurred to me that since everyone must live, I could provide the artists, who were kind enough to interest themselves in me, with further anecdotes, which would furnish them with material for more caricatures of myself. It is with this object in view that I beg you, sir, to be kind enough to insert my letter in your *Revue Musicale.* . . .

Then followed, in Paganini's vein of sarcastic humour, an official list of all the crimes of *opera buffa* which he had committed. He had stabbed his rival and poisoned his mistress; he had spent long years in a dank dungeon, with only his violin to solace his captivity; and finally, he had been accused of sorcery. In Vienna, after he had played his Variations, *Le Streghe,* a gentleman, who was described to him as "of pale complexion, with a melancholy air and fanatical eyes," declared that he had seen distinctly, while Paganini was playing, the devil standing beside him, guiding his arm and directing his bow.

"His resemblance to myself was a sufficient indication of my origin," said the virtuoso sardonically; "he was dressed in red, with horns on his head and a tail between his legs. You will realize, sir, that after such a detailed description, there could be no possible doubt of the truth of his story. Many people were persuaded that they had now surprised the secret of what they called my *tours de force*."

Finally there was an unhappy coincidence, which put the finishing touch to everything. There was a confusion of identity between Paganini and a Polish violinist, Duranowski by name, who had been found guilty of an attempt to assassinate the parish priest of a village near Milan, in order to rob him of his savings.

"Would you believe it? That is the foundation of all these scandalous rumours. The violinist in question had a name ending in 'i.' It must have been Paganini. You see, sir, how completely an artist's reputation lies at the mercy of individuals who are themselves too idle to believe that any man can work as diligently, while at liberty, as under lock and key."

He ended on a note of pathos. "Since, in spite of every proof to the contrary, these slanders persist, I must put up with them. But one hope remains to me. Perhaps, after my death, calumny will release its prey, and those, who took so cruel a revenge on me for my success, will let my ashes rest in peace. I am, sir, yours etc., PAGANINI."

The reply of the painter Louis Boulanger (May 1831, p. 160) appeared almost immediately in *l'Artiste*, a journal of which Fétis was likewise editor:

Sir,
You were kind enough to show me a letter in which Monsieur Paganini complains bitterly of the slanders that pursue him. Calumny, he says, will not relinquish its prey until he is in the tomb. As a lithographer I am accused of having pandered to that livid goddess. But I must clear myself; I am neither a calumniator, nor a practical joker, nor a hoaxer, who exploits the curiosity of the Paris idlers.

My only crime is this. Paganini came to Paris and was received with universal enthusiasm. I saw and heard him, and it was one of the great moments of my life. But I had not the pleasure of seeing the devil perched on his shoulder, like an organ grinder's monkey, dressed like a British admiral and complete with horns and tail, galvanizing the expectant audience. No, sir, I did not see this. But I saw instead a remarkable man whose appearance made a profound impression on my soul. I was fascinated by that noble countenance, which was animated by the divine fire of art. He was one of those men of destiny of whom Heaven is so sparing, men set apart from the vulgar throng, such as I have seen admirably depicted by Hoffmann, men whom the world seldom understands.

As I gazed on that pale brow with its marks of sorrow, I wondered if his fatal destiny had laid its iron hand upon his radiant soul, to penalize it for having received so much, for its pre-eminence among the rest of humanity. At that, the melancholy figure of Tasso, reclining on the stones of a dungeon, came into my mind. With this was mingled, confusedly, the vague rumour I had heard of Paganini's incarceration, of which I did not know the cause, and which I had imagined to be a far more serious affair. Yes, I said to myself, such is the fate of genius. Long neglected, often persecuted, in the end genius is sometimes rewarded for all its sufferings by the acclamation of the whole world. A fate to be envied!

I returned home, deep in thought, with my head full of Paganini, and I did the sketch you were kind enough to insert in your journal. The error was purely my own. I trust that these lines will convince Monsieur Paganini that I had no share in any plot that was hatched to injure his reputation. My ignorance was to blame, and I had no intention of confirming a story, which was a malicious invention. It would be absurd to attack a man, whom all the world esteems and admires. I trust he will realize that it was due to a misconception on the part of the artist, and that the piquant anecdotes he was kind enough to communicate to the cartoonists would not prove happy subjects for lithography.

Louis Boulanger

JOHN BULL

IN SPITE of his friends' forebodings, he survived the crossing. He arrived in London on May 18, 1831, and at once signed a contract with Laporte for six concerts at the Opera-house. Once he was comfortably installed in the Sablonière Hotel with his publisher Pacini, and Pacini's daughter, he accepted invitations to dinner and actually began, almost imperceptibly, to put on a little weight.

Somewhat surprisingly, the English, who had been prepared for it, treated the supernatural element in his art as a joke.

"This popular performer," they said, "is in the habit of stringing his fiddle with gut made from the intestines of the late Pope. No wonder his art is infallible."

This sally, which poked fun at the Pope, the Papists, and this mountebank with his shock of hair, was received with hearty laughter. But faces fell when a notice was posted up outside the Opera-house * doubling the prices of the seats. Such pretentions were an insult to British dignity. The fever of the elections, which were about to be held, was forgotten in the popular resentment against Laporte, the Italian maestro's impresario, for a preposterous proposal that could only have originated in the brain of a foreigner.

Paganini himself, "that audacious, insolent Italian," whom people began to compare to Samiel, the son of Satan, came in for his share of abuse.

"John Bull is a patient animal up to a point," scolded *The*

* Grove's *Dictionary of Music and Musicians*.

184

Times, "but when that point is reached, he is not to be trifled with. He is not easily provoked, but neither is he readily pacified. We understand that up to the present only two boxes have been taken."

"Poor Mr. Lindley, pride of British fiddlers," said the *Athenæum*, "you have only to reduce your cello to the size of a fiddle and put it under your chin, instead of between your legs, and you will make more money. . . ."

A certain "popular nobleman of most exalted rank" set an example of passive resistance by ostentatiously refusing to take his usual box.

"Evidently the honour of paying the highest prices was reserved for England," it was said sarcastically.

Paganini's friends had to intervene to conciliate the public. News of the squabble amused society on the other side of the Channel. They had already been fleeced, though not to the same extent, and could speak with authority.

"The violent language of the newspapers," said the *Revue Musicale* in Paris, "is worthy of a better cause. When all is said and done, John Bull is not obliged to go to hear Paganini. Unfortunately he is torn between his two great passions: curiosity and avarice. It is not only the populace who object to the increased price of seats in their gallery. The aristocracy, too, wish to decide what they are to pay for their pleasures.

"It appears that Paganini is alarmed at this outcry. One thing at least is certain, the concert, which was to have taken place on the twelfth of this month, has been postponed."

As if in confirmation, Laporte received a note from Paganini. It was dated May 29, 1831. The concert, which had already been once postponed, was to have taken place on the following day.

The note ran as follows:

Sir,

As I am seriously indisposed, I shall be obliged if you will kindly

convey my regrets to the public and inform them that the concert, which was fixed for to-morrow, cannot take place.

Your obedient servant

Nicolò Paganini

At the same time a note was sent to the editor of the *Star*
informing him that Paganini was anxious to conform to the
customs of the country and that the price of seats would be
reduced accordingly. The dispute, it seemed, was over. Had
Samiel at last met his match in John Bull?

❡ Once their pride and their purses were safe, the
British public flocked to the concert which took place, at last,
on June 3. Their sporting instincts were aroused.

"Other violinists," Paganini was reported to have said, "do
not get beyond the letter G. That is the limit of their achievement. As for me I have no difficulty in rounding Cape T."

What did he mean by that?

Another saying was attributed to him. "If a violinist is not
capable of producing, on occasion, with perfect clearness, a
hundred notes a second, he may renounce all hope of ever becoming a musician. He will never be able to profit by the revolution in violin technique, which will be my parting gift to the
world."

A hundred notes a second!

The Germans looked for the origin of this "revolution" in
the realm of the supernatural, while the French sought it in
anatomy. John Bull, however, ascribed it quite simply to the
virtuoso's superb "form." Paganini himself referred with increasing frequency to a famous secret of his, which enabled him
to train in three years a violinist, who would otherwise have
wasted ten years in daily practising. A document had been deposited in the hands of the composer Tomaschek in Prague,
which was couched in these terms: "Thanks to a magical proc-
ess, communicated to him by Paganini, Gaetano Ciandelli of

Naples has become the first violoncellist of the Theatre Royal, and could become the best in the world."

There was also the case of Camillo Sivori, the son of a Genoese merchant: "This boy was barely seven when I began to teach him the rudiments of music. In three days he could play several pieces perfectly and everyone exclaimed: 'Paganini has worked a miracle.' In a fortnight's time he appeared in public. . . . When my secret is known, artists will study more profoundly the nature of the violin, an instrument which is a hundred times richer than is commonly believed. My discovery was not due to chance; it was the result of intense research. Some day my system of study will be adopted. The present method which tends to hinder the pupil rather than hasten his progress, will be discarded in favour of mine, which requires only five or six hours a day of steady practising. It is, however, a great mistake to look for the secret in my method of bowing, or in the way in which I tune my violin. Brains are needed to profit by my secret."

That summer of 1831 John Bull was struck dumb with wonder at the performances of the Italian maestro. He was completely bowled over and could only say: "Encore, encore. Do it again!"

"At my last recitals," Paganini wrote to Germi, "I received such a frantic ovation that I decided to give six more concerts in the following week."

Besides his own concertos, he performed the *Carnaval de Venise*, the *Prayer of Moses*, *Cantabile* on two strings, and *Cinderella*.

The walls of London were covered with posters, which, like the musical critics, bore eloquent witness to his triumphs.

"Paganini's last concert," said the posters, advertising his fifth recital. But there was such a run on it that it was followed by ten more concerts (June 27 and 30, July 4, 15, 25, 27, etc.). After these came the "very last" and then one that was "positively the last," and finally his farewell concert on August 3 when he was "rapturously encored." He played likewise at the London Tavern and at Holland House.

Ladies who were "anxious to see this man, who looked like Samiel and played like a demon," at closer quarters than behind the footlights, prevailed on him to give them lessons. His brother musicians accorded him a generous welcome. But when they heard him, they were petrified with astonishment. One evening the first violin's stand caught fire, but it did not occur to the violinist to put out the flames. He had eyes only for "Samiel," who, pale and exhausted, supported by two attendants, tottered on to the stage to bow to the audience. Another violinist, Mori, declared that he would burn his fiddle, while the celebrated Lindley swore that Paganini was the devil himself.

Did he consciously prepare these stage effects and exploit them? Was he prepared to accept the consequences, the old penalties, the old implacable vengeance? It is not impossible that henceforth he fostered this myth of a Satanic double, with whom he had a silent, mysterious pact.

"Nowadays," he wrote to Germi, "people do not ask each other whether they have heard Paganini, but whether they have seen him. To tell you the truth I think the notion that I am in league with the devil has spread to all classes of society. The newspapers lay too much stress on my appearance and this gives rise to incredible curiosity."

(At the end of August he was engaged to play at the Dublin Festival, but Ireland did not give him a good reception. Bitter things were said with reference to the condition of the Irish peasantry. The contrast was too great between the violinist's success and his way of life and the wretchedness of the people. In certain districts the wages of a labourer were four and sixpence a week, while Paganini, in twenty-eight minutes, reaped a harvest of two hundred pounds. (This result was also achieved the following spring at Winchester.) That sum would suffice to keep an Irish family for many winters.

The newspaper *Harmonicon* preached a crusade: "Are the Irish gentry so little concerned at the miseries of their fellow countrymen that they can only come to the rescue by means of a fiddle and a fiddlestick? If that is the case, the legend of Orpheus has come true."

"Samiel," however, viewed the situation from a different angle: "After leaving London for Ireland I gave sixty-five concerts, including those at the Dublin Festival and in other towns of England, Scotland and Ireland, between August 3, 1831 and January 14, 1832. Taking into account the fact that I was ill for five weeks, the sixty-five concerts were all given within the space of about three months. I visited thirty towns travelling in a coach and four, in the company of a singer, Signora Pietrelia. My suite included Signor Chianchettini, who was Catalani's accompanist and is a master of the clavecin; my secretary, a perfectly charming young Englishman, who went on ahead to arrange my concerts, an idiot who acted as porter, and an excellent manservant. I hired a delightful carriage in London. You cannot imagine the fantastic expense of these journeys; with reference to this, I have the most amazing things to tell you about the customs of this country. . . . Had I come to London twelve years ago, I could easily have made my fortune. But now it is not the same place; there is so much distress everywhere. No one but a Genoese could have made anything out of it. Laugh!" *

But he did not always laugh. One day at Cheltenham, seeing that the hall was nearly empty, Paganini, in his own words, tried to "get out of playing." But when the manager announced that he refused to appear, the crowd surrounded the hotel at which the maestro was staying and made such hostile demonstrations that poor Paganini hastily returned to the theatre and played

* Manchester, January 15, 1832.

the programme that had been advertised. He left the town that evening. This incident was not recounted to Germi.

There was another incident on the occasion of his first concert in Dublin, on August 30, 1831. The theatre was packed and it was suffocatingly hot. When Sir George Smart, the impresario, escorted Paganini on to the platform, they both received a tremendous ovation. Before he began, Paganini, wholly at his ease, calmly tuned his violin and ran his fingers up and down the strings, until the public in the gallery called out impatiently:

"What are you waiting for? We're ready."

Paganini was furious and stamped his foot with rage.

"What do they mean by it?" he exclaimed, turning to Smart.

In the midst of an indescribable uproar he hastily left the platform. Many entreaties were necessary before the Irish public were at last privileged to hear him. But when he condescended to play, the audience as usual went into raptures. In his Concerto in B, with the *Rondo de la Clochette*, he scored such a success that an ecstatic gentleman in the stalls called out:

"Arrah now, Signor Paganini, have a drop of whisky, darling, and ring the bell again."

He was now such a familiar figure to all the rabble in the three kingdoms that, as he confessed to Pacini, he shrank from going out, because the people mobbed him. As "King of semiquavers," he felt obliged to make princely gestures. When a ragged beggar asked him for alms, he picked up his fiddle and accompanied his gift of coins with heavenly sounds. At his departure from Dublin in the autumn, he was the central figure in what almost amounted to a minor revolution.

In a deluge of rain, hundreds of paupers waited outside the hotel for the "star" of the Festival to appear.

At first they waited patiently; then they began to stamp their feet.

At last the "splendid equipage of the modern Orpheus" drew

up at the door, to carry him away to Southern Ireland, whence he was to cross over to England. When the crowd barred his passage, he graciously awarded to all those outstretched hands two sovereigns.

In the winter of 1831–1832 his visit to Bristol was heralded by a proclamation couched in the following terms:

FELLOW CITIZENS

It is with profound disgust that I have to announce forthcoming concerts by Signor Paganini in the near future. Why all these performances in a time of misery and want? Funds are being raised everywhere for the relief of distress. Why should this foreign violinist divert to himself resources and money that should be applied to the assistance of those in need? Do not allow yourselves to be led astray by the musical eccentricities of this stranger, who is exploiting the ingenuousness of John Bull.

PHILADELPHIUS

Dec. 10, 1831

John Bull, however, threw himself upon this flamboyant publicity, hostile or otherwise, like a bull in the arena charging a matador's cape. How could he avoid that magic bow, which was as keen as the sword of a matador? After the aristocracy, the officials were the next to receive its thrust.

In the succeeding months he was invited to play in the Assembly Room in Edinburgh, although it was the stronghold of his worst detractors in the Modern Athens. At Oxford he was given the degree of Doctor of Music. There are allusions in his letters to invitations to Holland House and the Mansion House, where the Lord Mayor expressed his anxiety lest "flea-parties" should give place to tricks on the G string. It was denied that he had refused a huge fee to play at the Duchess of St. Alban's and that when George IV desired him to reduce his fee of one hundred pounds by half, he had replied: "It would be much cheaper for His Majesty to come to one of my concerts."

But after he had played at Court the King presented him

with a diamond ring. When the court jeweller came hurrying to take his measurement, he extended with dignity the index finger of his right hand. The matador redoubled his thrusts.

In Leeds, tickets for his concert were a guinea each and were all sold by noon. In Birmingham, there was such an inrush of strangers that the town could not accommodate them all. In Brighton, a poster protesting against the price of seats was torn to shreds. Finally, in conventional London, which had been the scene of the first hostile demonstrations, he defied tradition by giving "eleven recitals at Covent Garden at a time when it should have been closed. My violin has only to be seen for the house to be almost completely filled. My playing, they say, is more miraculous than ever. To prove it, handkerchiefs and hats are thrown into the air amid cries of wild enthusiasm. . . ."

In the interval, at the end of April, Paris had received another visit from this "King of Fiddlers," as the English called him. He had brought back from England more than £20,000, and had given one hundred and thirty-four concerts, of which two were for charity.

Before he left England, Watson, a new London impresario, suggested that he should finance a concert tour in Belgium and France and pay Paganini a large fixed salary. This hiring of one-self to an impresario was an innovation. Paganini inaugurated the new fashion by signing the contract. There was some talk of a tour in America, but England insisted on engaging Paganini for 1833, whatever the cost.

"I did not intend to return to London till 1834," he wrote to Germi in January 1833, "but the impresario insists on my returning this year, because the whole country is clamouring for me."

Was it, perhaps, John Bull, who had met his match in "Samiel"?

THE LADIES OF THE NORTH

SINCE Paganini's love-affair with Helena, the German Baronness, Germi had received no more amorous confidences.

"I will tell you about my love-affairs some other time," he had written to his friend. But this promise was never fulfilled. From 1831 to 1834 he alternated triumphantly between London and Paris, but on the subject of his amours Paris was silent. Perhaps the explanation was partly sartorial. A new and fashionable type of romantic virtuoso was to be inaugurated: dandies such as Frédéric Chopin, and Franz Liszt, who had eloped with the Countess d'Agoult, one of the reigning beauties in Paris.

Intuitively the painters subtly stressed the differences between the lions of the day. Ingres's fine portrait of Paganini gives an academic pose to the virtuoso who cared nothing for fashion, while the portraits by Delacroix and Gustave Doré and the caricatures of Dantan, Mantoux, and Grandville, and all the English cartoonists emphasize the uncompromising character of the man.

"By the way," wrote Liszt to La Mara, "could you find out for me what has become of that picture, called *La Musique*, or words to that effect, which was exhibited two years ago by Monsieur Läwlein. You will remember that I was represented in it with La Malibran, Bériot, Rossini, Paganini, etc. . . ."

Shortly before this period, however, another reigning beauty of the Legitimist Society of 1830, the Countess de Lamothe-Langon, was anxious to meet the hero of so many sombre legends in everyday surroundings, and to form her own opinion of him. He accepted an invitation to her house, and she looked forward to his visit with scepticism mingled with trepidation.

"Certain melomaniacs, whose opinion I distrusted, had spoken to me of him with such enthusiasm that I was sure they were exaggerating, and I wanted to judge for myself.* A great friend of mine, Dr. Miquel, an excellent man, whose only defect was that he had been hit in the eye by the last bullet fired in the July Revolution, brought Monsieur Paganini to see me.

"I had my own preconceived idea of him. I imagined that his features would bear the stamp of his genius, and that if he did not possess regular beauty, at least he could not be positively ugly. I was completely disillusioned. I saw, entering the room, a man with a figure that looked almost lop-sided, huge ears, a long square face, framed in black hair falling over his collar in the old Directoire style. His nose and mouth matched the rest of his physiognomy, while his deep-set eyes, burning with sombre fire, gave such a touch of the satanic to his whole person that I glanced involuntarily at his foot to see if it was cloven.

"Such was my impression of Paganini: a grotesque individual, with intense emotions, fantastic humours, a vivid and disordered imagination, creating poetry with his bow, exploiting by turns the true and the false, nature and art, and combining in himself the charlatan and the man of genius. Not content with being distinguished from other men by his talent, he must needs, it seems, surround himself with all the glamour of a miraculous past.

"He talked intelligently on subjects that had no connection with his art, but when he spoke of the violin, he displayed the most vivid enthusiasm, and now and then quivered involuntarily with emotion. I was enchanted. I no longer thought him ugly. But it was a very different matter when I heard the divine

* Revelations of a Lady of Quality in the years 1830 and 1831, Brussels, Haumann & Co.

sounds of his violin at the Opera. I felt that I was transported to another world and that new sensations were coming to birth within my soul. I knew a moment of ecstasy. In the presence of this magician I was prepared for everything. Had the devil himself appeared, I should not have been surprised."

Fortunately or unfortunately for the ladies of Paris, these revelations and sensations came to an end. The magician was leaving Paris. Soon the provinces were all ablaze.

"Paganini is working miracles in the Northern Department," remarked the *Revue Musicale,* after his departure. "People are off their heads with admiration and enthusiasm. At Dunkirk he has been presented with a gold medal with the inscription: *'From the ladies of Dunkirk.'*

"At Lille. . . ."

(At Valenciennes, a small party of ladies embroidered a pair of presentation gloves for the virtuoso. The design consisted of a laurel branch, a sun, and a magic violin. They enclosed this tribute in an ebony box. On the underside of the box they pasted a newspaper cutting, describing Paganini's triumphs at Valenciennes. They hardly looked up from their engrossing task when their husbands came home from work. Their hearts were following their needles and the threads of gold and softest silk, as they traced an intricate pattern around a name and a date:

Paganini
May 8th, 1831

(In Boulogne the fishing boats came in on the rising tide, which brought with it the tang of the sea. The ladies of Boulogne saved up their journal, the *Annotateur,* for the evening hour of leisure. In its pages they were thrilled to read all that they had vaguely felt but had been unable to express:

"Was it only a dream? What is this being, who has only to

appear to rouse storms of applause? Does he belong to this
earth? Or to the skies? Or to regions unknown to us?"

Only a few days ago, on the occasion of a concert which was
worthy of the Kingdom of Heaven, the theatre seemed illuminated with positively religious fervour and adoration. If only
they were still there in that crowded, brightly lighted, decorated hall, which, as they read, they saw again! They recalled
that almost painful feeling of anticipation, the impressive silence, and finally the ovation which greeted the virtuoso. "No
one dreamed of listening to a single note of the Overture to
Oberon, which was played by the orchestra."

At last "He" stood there on the platform, with the seal of
genius upon his pallid brow. Sometimes his glance was veiled;
sometimes his eyes flashed like fire. His black curls fell on to
his shoulders in such picturesque waves that men of letters who
were present were reminded of the paintings of Guido, Carlo
Dolci, "who had a touch of the supernatural," and even the
"fantastic compositions" of Albrecht Dürer—those cabalistic
scenes of his. . . .

But now the Enchanter (as they called him ever afterwards)
had raised his magic wand, with such grace, such power. Mercy
on us! Could they still honestly speak of a purely sacred love?
It seemed as if those magical sounds released everything in nature that was terrible, everything in love that was ardent—
human love, if the truth must be told, such as they imagined it,
with its impulses, its ecstasies, its cries of despair, its biting
irony. As the neighbours said to each other, aptly quoting
Rousseau's fine phrase, it was *"a fire that burned forever and
was not consumed."*

They could hardly tear themselves away from the journal,
which tortured them voluptuously with delicious details of
those vanished delights.

"But that was not all," the journal continued. "There were
more miracles to come. The magician conjured up exquisite

scenes before our eyes. We were in a sunny glade, where two flutes were performing one of those duets, which remind one of the contests between lyre and human voice in the valleys of Greece. Suddenly the birds hidden in the leaves joined in the pastoral concert. We heard the long, brilliant cadences of the nightingale, those voluptuous roulades, which are like the throbbing of a heart overburdened with love and bliss. But the aspect of the enchanter changed. He increased in stature and stood erect. This was the Giant of the Cap des Tempêtes, described by Camoëns. With his mighty wand he struck the rock he held in his left hand, and released a cataract of sparks. The storm answered the challenge and muffled roars heralded its coming. Hark to the crash of the thunder, and to the piercing voices that mingled with the tumult of the sea and the convulsions of nature!

"Then all was calm. We were wafted away to Italy. Under the balcony of a villa, in the waning light of the moon, intoxicated with the scent of fresh jasmine and flowering lilac, we listened to a mandoline accompanying Paisiello's delightful canzonetta *Nel cor più non mi sento.*

"As in all our great operas, heaven had succeeded to hell.

"Pleasure, *dolce far niente,* sweet idleness, on the banks of the Ischia, on the Gulf of Naples, had banished all pain and trouble. In short it was the most delicious contrast imaginable.

"Was it only a dream? . . ."

Pensively they let the journal fall from their hands. Yonder was the English mail boat, leaving the port and rapidly disappearing into the mist. Who could say? Perhaps, as some believed, he was on board.

The sound of the ship's siren aroused in them a vague feeling of uneasiness. For the first time in their lives, they fell, those ladies of Boulogne, to dreaming of Italy, of the Cap des Tempêtes, of Ischia, Naples, Greece . . . nightingales . . . Camoëns's Giant . . . "voluptuous *arpeggios.*"

For Paganini's last concert on October 17, 1832 ("positively the last," as the English said), Rouen had prepared a demonstration of homage that was characteristically French.

It celebrated the guest in Alexandrines which were showered down from the galleries on to the stage of the Théâtre des Arts, accompanied by wreaths of laurel, roses, and immortelles. But this was not all. An actor of handsome presence and medium talent, Valmore, "*Le beau* Valmore," came forward with a paper in his hand.

"From the people of Rouen to Paganini," he declaimed.

"Enraptured by thy heavenly harmony,
The nation has no incense meet for thee.
And yet, to grace thy fame, this favoured town
May add a leaf from Corneille's * laurel crown."

Other lines aimed even higher:

"From thee, thou 'vital spark of heavenly flame,'
We learn that we have souls and whence they came."

While Paganini, thus deified and sung, was returning to his hotel, Valmore was joined by a woman, who was shivering in her cloak, and together they left the darkened theatre.

This was Marceline Desbordes-Valmore, his wife, a frail, quivering flower of romanticism—Marceline, poetess, who dedicated her lyre to love, who sang to the guitar, songs that had not yet been transcribed; Marceline, tragedian, for whom tears and music were one.

"O Marceline," murmured her husband tenderly, as lost in ecstasy, she continued to rhapsodize:

"What rapture, trepidation and delight,
When through the air thy music wings its flight!

•   •   •   •   •

* Corneille was born in Rouen.

O Paganini, thou belovèd guest,
My heart and mind with thy dear name are blest,
As if an angel's wing had touched my breast."

"And in your music is the kiss of heaven," the astonished
passers-by heard her declare. Still in the grip of inspiration, she
declaimed:

"God made of flame that soul of thine.
He quickened it with breath divine.
Yea, in His love, He built a nest
Of singing love-birds in thy breast." *

Her lips, as they framed the words, seemed parted in a kiss.

(This mystical kiss ended the Marceline-Paganini
episode. Nicolò was leaving Rouen for the north of France
and England. The amorous haze that surrounded him dissi-
pated in a violent storm upon London and Boulogne-sur-mer.
Boulogne! Cross-channel boats were continually calling there
and its pavements were polished by the feet of eloping lovers.
Charlotte Watson, an English girl of seventeen, was to be the
love-struck heroine.

"Here is a story of local interest, which we have on official
authority," said that same journal, the *Annotateur*. "Doubtless
the English Press, with its taste for private scandals, will be
busy with it. Watson, the London impresario, with whom
Paganini signed a contract after his first concert tour in England, now accuses him of having taken advantage of his stay
with him to seduce his daughter, who is a minor, after having
half-ruined the impresario himself.

"This thunderbolt, which is reverberating on the French side
of the Channel, was launched by the publication of a letter
from Charlotte Watson, the girl in question, to whom the
maestro had been giving lessons in singing and acting.

* ". . . *mille oiseaux d'amour murmurent dans ton sein.*"

" 'My dear sir,' ran the letter. 'I am so unhappy at home. My father ill-treats me so shockingly that I am obliged to ask for your protection. If you will be kind enough to take care of me, I promise in return to do everything you ask of me.' "

What exactly did Paganini ask of her? The answer was obvious. What in return could he do for her? A great deal. Before his departure from London, "alone and unaccompanied by his victim," he had given a concert for her benefit. He left her in "floods of tears," preparing to join her Machiavelli in Boulogne. He took with him his confidential valet Urbani. It appeared that all the gold that had filled Paganini's coffers, as a result of his famous contract with Watson, was now to be poured out to gild the new beloved. He spent 9,000 francs on a tiara for her, and another 30,000 francs on other pieces of diamond jewellery. He ordered a "smart turn-out," and promised to marry Charlotte, who was to have as a dowry an annuity of 400,-000 francs, guaranteed by his friend Rothschild. Such was the information he gave his servants, the Urbani, and Charlotte herself. She had been entrusted to the care of a discreet friend, who was a barrister in London. . . .

"Genius has very potent charms for a young Miss of sixteen," was the sarcastic comment in Boulogne. The pale sands of its dunes were to be the setting for the Italian comedy, which, according to the *Sunday Times*,* was shortly to be performed. Its headlines proclaimed:

EXTRAORDINARY ELOPEMENT OF PAGANINI AND MISS WATSON

It was a fact that Charlotte had left the shelter of the paternal roof to go to Paganini. She was ready. . . .

It was a Monday in June. The sun rose, red on the horizon, as glorious as the being who had promised her fame, love, and fortune. Without him, life would be empty, unendurable. He was waiting for her. They were to meet again; they were to be united and to share a wonderful existence. Nothing should stop

* June 29, 1834.

her. Mr. Hughes, who was a London lawyer well known for his services to other eloping couples, was to receive her in his house in Carey Street. He was first to procure for her a change of clothes, which would enable her to escape her father in the first instance. Chaperoned by Mrs. Hughes, the lawyer's wife, she would take ship for Boulogne, would see again those magnetic eyes, those hands that could unloose the storm.

That same Monday, Watson heard his daughter's bedroom door slam. He sprang up and dashed after her. But he was too late. He could find no trace of her either in London or elsewhere in England. There was nothing for it but to cross the Channel without delay. The second act of the burlesque was to follow at once.

"Curtain up," the unfortunate impresario might have said, directing his own tragi-comedy.

On Monday evening, like the statue of the Commander, Mr. Watson appeared as the leading actor on the deck of the English mail boat. Paganini's troop, which had come to meet Charlotte, hurriedly decamped, fleeing from the wrath to come. The outraged father landed and at once went to the British Consulate. He appealed to the Consul, Mr. W. Hamilton, who informed the French authorities and requested their help. This was promised and police were placed at his disposal.

On Tuesday evening the Customs' house was the theatre of further scenes which developed rapidly. The first was the arrival of the youthful runaway herself, escorted by Mrs. Hughes. This was the signal for the contest to begin. On the one side there were Mr. Watson and the police, on the other Paganini's champions, Urbani, the valet of *opera buffa*, and his wife, who were hot on Miss Charlotte's trail.

"What's all this? What's all this? Give me the child."

Bludgeons and muskets, bumps and bruises! Urbani took to his heels.

On Wednesday evening on the jetty, father and daughter, now reconciled, embarked for England, accompanied by the exhortations of the British Consul and the congratulations of "all the English families in Boulogne." Soon afterwards Miss Charlotte left for America, where she knew how to exploit all this publicity.

"It is said that Paganini bore his disappointment philosophically," the French journal concluded. "The brilliant creations of his genius, the celestial houris, whom he can conjure up with one stroke of his bow, may well console him for the loss of one simple mortal."

Nevertheless he proceeded to raise Cain. He had had a somewhat serious difference with the Boulogne orchestra (he had had the temerity to refuse complimentary tickets to the members of the Philharmonic and to dispense with their assistance, and he had actually been hissed by them). And now slander was once more pursuing him. But he would strip off the mask from hypocrisy and reveal the truth about the Watsons' domestic affairs. Mr. Watson was a parasite of the concert halls, a shark who battened on artists; he had left his lawful wife to die of grief in Bath. His young son had left home and gone to the dogs, while his innocent daughter (who, by the way, was eighteen, not sixteen, and a promising lieder singer) had to obey Miss Wells, her father's mistress, as if she were the humblest servant. It was from this stepmother that he had wished to rescue Charlotte, from this "concubine" who trailed after Watson on the quay at Boulogne, wearing a yellow straw hat and a green mantle. And this was his reward!

"The Paris and London newspapers are full of the affair," wrote Paganini in the *Annotateur*. "They talk of Miss Watson's 'penitence,' and say that she followed me because I had promised to marry her in Paris and give her jewels and a rich dowry. Her acts were, therefore, voluntary, and by no means disinterested.

"Let the public draw their own conclusions! As for me, I have said my last word about this tiresome business."

❡ A rich dowry! Jewels! Shades of Faust and Mar-
guerita! Shades of Angelina, Antonia, Carolina, Helena, Charlotte. . . .

"The whole enraptured world's a stage for thee," Marceline
had sung.

> "Lord, guard this man of Thine own choice,
> This living echo of Thy voice,
> Whose hands can rouse the angry deep,
> Or charm the raging storm to sleep.
>
> Keep Thou Thy wandering minstrel's feet
> From paths of pain, for oft the sweet
> And soothing magic of his art
> Has healed the mourner's broken heart." *

* Marceline Desbordes-Valmore, *Echo de Rouen*, October 16, 1832.

PARMA VIOLETS

THE tightrope was stretched taut. To please is to succeed. Once you have pleased, you must continue to please. The obligation applies to both tightrope dancer and virtuoso. If the rope were to sag even a little, the acrobat would be hurled into space. Yet how often he longed to relax the tension and to give forth a tenderer note:

My dear son, my darling Achillino,
  These few days which I have spent away from you have seemed to me like ten years. Heaven knows what it cost me to leave you. But knowing your delicate constitution, I have sacrificed the pleasure of having you with me on this unfortunate journey. Not a day goes by without my thinking of you. I pretend that I am talking to you and embracing you. Tomorrow evening I shall have the joy of clasping you in my arms and of saying to you things which are too fond to be put into a letter. I hope you are being good and getting on well at school. I long to press you to my heart again.
                                    Believe me, with deep devotion,
                                              Your Papa Paganini

These letters, written by Paganini in 1832, in the autumn of his life, were of more interest to Germi than to Achillino, who was too young to understand them.

"I am beginning to long for my own country," he wrote to Germi, "but I do not know when I shall be able to come home to rest. I have no desire to drag myself to London this year. . . . Do not cease to love me. I live only for you and for my son."

When the tone of a fine violin tends to become a little blurred, the instrument-makers suspect a defect in the gluing, or a crack, or even deep-seated damage.

Sated with success, Paganini began to suffer more and more from homesickness, which had greatly increased since December 1831, when he had let Teresa die without seeing her again, without being present to close her eyes—those ecstatic eyes of hers that had dedicated him in a dream to the cruel cult, with its incense and its sacrifices, which had become his mission in life. To have been so far away! He "wept bitterly," clinging only "to the certain hope of seeing her again in Paradise," when his own time came. He now realized the truth. The fire of his art was preying on him; the more he tended it, the more brightly he made it burn, the more surely was it destroying him, day by day.

"I ought to take a rest of a year or two," he wrote to Germi, "in order to cure certain distressing symptoms which depress me. The electric tension of which I am conscious, when I make my tragic music, affects me terribly. If I return home and live near you, I shall prolong my days."

To live! To go on living, even in this world which, in another letter to Germi, he described as "a magic lantern show"! Yet he was still capable of manifestations of youthful exuberance. The nervous tension which was consuming him sometimes had a galvanising effect on the old carnival king. He would preen himself, take up the gauntlet, win a joust. In Paris in the spring of 1832 Rossini gave a farewell party to which all the great artists, critics, and musicians were invited. One of the surprise features of the evening was a competition in which each of the guests had to develop a theme. When it came to Paganini's turn, he improvised a Sonata burlesquing the style of his brother musicians, as Rossini at once realized. Stung by this, Castil-Blaze seized a sheet of music and a pair of scissors, cut off the last note of each line and gave the severed notes to

Paganini. On these Paganini grafted an enchanting *Polachetta*.

"We must drink his health," cried Rossini, brandishing a bottle of champagne. The music which accompanied the toast was the *Champagne March*, improvised by Nicolò on the letters C H A G Z. This was followed by the *Café Adagio*, on the letters C A F E.

"What can we do to stump this fellow? Let's think."

"Take away his bow."

"He could manage with a piece of string."

"Let him try."

The silk cord from Paganini's eye-glass was stretched across a silver bowl, and with the aid of this Paganini played the *Punch Aria*, which was the climax of the supper party. It was dedicated to Rossini, who had it published later.

But in the interval between his two journeys to London, the magic lantern show had changed. Suddenly, towards the end of April 1832, it cast a lurid and tragic light.

"People are leaving Paris in crowds on account of the cholera epidemic. The police have issued more than a hundred and thirty thousand passports. The actual number of deaths from cholera is about ten thousand. Next Friday I am giving a grand concert in the Opera house in aid of the sick. Rossini has fled in panic. But I am not in the least afraid. All I wish is to be of use to humanity."

Pale and terror-stricken, some of them perhaps already bearing marks of the fell disease, people exchanged their dwellings, which reeked of camphor, and their gloomy thoughts, for the lights and flowers of the Opera and for that dark angel, who defied the danger.

"I saw a man, who was stricken with cholera on the threshold of the theatre, faint at the *Prayer of Moses*, played by Paganini," said Jules Janin. "I have never known anything more sublime than the concerts he gave during the plague. People arrived trembling; they listened, they wondered, they were moved to tears. All suffering seemed suspended. Death was forgotten, and the fear that is worse than death."

In the career of Franz Liszt, who arrived as a young virtuoso in Paris in that same year of 1832, the Dark Angel was like the Vision of Damascus. He thought of Michelangelo, who proclaimed himself a painter the first time he set eyes on a masterpiece. Delacroix succeeded in transferring to his canvas the sombre and magnetic figure of the maestro, in that tragic setting.

After he had given nine concerts in this eerie atmosphere (eight at the Opera * and one at the Italian Theatre, all of them packed to overflowing), he left Paris and hastened back to London in September. Before he took his departure he merely remarked: "Last year I helped people to forget the war, this year I took their minds off the cholera epidemic. . . . All the musical world, including the conductors of orchestras, have begged me to publish my works. They are waiting impatiently for my method, so that they may adopt, or at least study, the science of violin playing. When I return to Genoa, I shall set up a printing press to publish my works throughout Europe, and I shall correct the proofs myself. Artists have implored me to settle in Paris, but I want to end my days near you in the country of Columbus." †

He, who had once been compared to the wandering Jew, now suffered from an attack of depression and lassitude more in-

* The *Moniteur* announced: "Once again Monsieur Paganini is devoting his admirable talent to the relief of distress. On Monday, April 30, before his departure he is to give a concert at the Opera in aid of the destitute victims of the present cholera epidemic. He will give a first performance of *Matins at the Convent of St. Bernard*, with an accompaniment of bells, orchestra and full choir. The prices will not be raised." April 1832.

† June 3, 1832.

tense than he had ever before experienced. Such was his listlessness that he confessed that he had touched "neither pen nor bow for two and a half months."

℩ Nevertheless, 1833 and the beginning of 1834 added to his laurels, both in Paris and in London. But he was more preoccupied with two fixed ideas than with his own triumphs. One was his desire to have Achillino legitimised. He had set his heart on this. The little tyrant of the Frankfurt days now responded to his passionate affection. At the age of eight he appointed himself to be his father's nurse.

"Achillino is a great comfort to me," exclaimed his father. "At night when I am seized with a violent fit of coughing, the child wakes up, and comes to my aid, and ministers to me with a thoughtfulness which I cannot describe. . . . Yes, his legitimation is now my chief object in life."

His other scheme concerned the purchase of an estate in Italy, preferably in Tuscany, "where he could breathe the air of Dante and Petrarch."

Before long this wish was partly fulfilled. Germi bought, on Paganini's behalf, the Villa Gajona. It was, however, not in Tuscany, but near Parma in the Commune of Vigatto. The Duchy was indicated because he had been officially appointed conductor of the orchestra in Parma and director of the theatre of Her Majesty, the Grand Duchess Marie-Louise, formerly Empress of the French, whom he had known in the old days in Vienna. (He was counting on her influence on behalf of his son.)

"I am engaged to play at the Court on December 12," he wrote. But before that he was to carry out a last concert tour in Belgium and England. The spring of 1834 was occupied by a disastrous visit to Paris and the North, as will be seen later. Genoa, too, put in a claim to her famous son. The occasion

Victor Hugo, Paganini, Rossini, the elder Dumas, George Sand, Liszt, Marie d'Agoult. By Danhauser

Anonymous caricature of Paganini (London)

was the inauguration of the new theatre by the King, on the evening of November 30, 1834.

Genoa! Germi! His country! The sun! Delights which he lived over and over again in anticipation. On a tide of joy he was wafted, weary and worn, into the heart of his childhood.

He made his entrée into the Theatre Carlo-Felice as the equal of the royal pair, Charles Albert and Maria-Theresa. For four hours the esplanade had been thronged with three thousand spectators. The *Gazette* of Genoa summed up two columns of rapturous eulogy in a single phrase: "Paganini has played to us."

The Council of Ten decreed that a coin should be struck with his effigy in the currency of Turin. There were ten of these coins in gold, twenty in silver, forty in copper.

"So he went through the world, coining money," said Janin, "while the densest throngs opened to let him pass."

In Genoa the motley crowd welcomed him rapturously. In the course of 1835 he returned to take part in every festivity that was held in the city. On July 28 the Marchese Di Negro, who had succeeded Paganini's old patron, gave a splendid reception in honour of his fellow-countryman at his country seat of Acquasola. Nobles and poets alike flattered him to his heart's content, while the Marchese Antonio de Brignoles Sales, Sardinian Ambassador to the King of France, made a speech an hour long in his honour. This was followed by a dissertation by Di Negro on the part played by music in the control of the passions and a panegyric on its dictators, Rossini, Bellini, and Paganini. . . .

In the garden of Acquasola, surrounded by murmuring fountains and warbling birds, not far from the drawing-rooms where, as an infant prodigy, he played for the first time, stands a bust of Paganini. Perpetuated in marble, gazing at the horizon shimmering in the heat, his ravaged features look towards

America. In his will, he bequeathed to the city of Genoa, besides a diamond, his violin, his *Guarnerio del Gesù*, on condition that after him no one should play on it. (The name del Gesù was given to Giuseppe Guarnieri, to distinguish him from an earlier, less eminent, Giuseppe. "The term was taken from the initials I. H. S. which were added to his name on his labels." * His instruments were second only to those of Stradivarius.) The city of Balbus, Columbus, and Doria was now to be endowed with the lyre of Orpheus.

Parma. December 1834 *to* July 1836.

Once more he found himself back at an Italian Court with its multitude of chamberlains. This was the court that was once frequented by Sanseverina, the "Chartreuse of Parma." Like one of Stendhal's heroes, he renewed his youth with his Napoleonic memories. In the old days he had served Napoleon's sister. Today it was Napoleon's consort who summoned him to her court, paid him attentions, honoured him with her favour. He was ready to "give his life" for Marie-Louise, that august sovereign, whose graciousness he "appreciated more than anything in the world."

Fétis wrote disapprovingly in his *Revue Musicale*: "We cannot witness without regret the King of musicians sinking to the level of a courtier."

But Fétis was far from being a fairy prince himself, while Nicolò took a childish delight in all court functions. "Suppose a reigning sovereign were to invite a certain friend of yours to dinner," he wrote mysteriously to Germi. "Suppose that, at this dinner, he were to be invested with the Imperial Order of St. George,† what would you say to such an honour?"

Three weeks later he wrote: "The other evening I was at a

* Grove's *Dictionary of Music and Musicians*.
† Order of Constantine, December 23, 1835.

Court Ball, wearing my sword and all my decorations, including the Order of Constantine (*Antinien de Saint Georges*), in diamonds, which is worn on the coat—an interesting innovation."

The second Court Ball, which was to have taken place on February 9, 1836, had unfortunately to be postponed on account of the death of the Queen of Naples.

"What a pity!" exclaimed Nicolò. "Now I shall not be able to dance the gavotte."

But life was not all amusement. He was a "pillar" of both Orchestra and Theatre Committees, the musical delegate, charged by the Princess with the task of restoring concerts and plays to their former glory. He was invested with plenary powers.

Paganini was in his element. The mornings were devoted to rehearsals, and to training the refractory orchestra, which he conducted himself. Pale and self-possessed he showed them the way to success through hard work. He selected his musicians; disciplined them; taught them; rewarded them, and sometimes dismissed them in the midst of complete pandemonium.

The international music centres of Vienna, Berlin, Munich, and London were all under leaders who were at once superb musicians, composers, and organizers. Paganini was determined to become such a leader. He would abolish the somewhat provincial authority of the "master of the clavecin," or the solo violinist, while giving more importance to the violoncello soloist, in the person of maestro Orlando, who was himself a composer. Paganini paid special attention to the disposition of the instruments: the adaptability of the orchestra in accompanying singing, in blending with the voice and producing appropriate effects of light and shade, and the forcefulness with which it interpreted the works of the great masters. All this could be perfectly well achieved without the introduction of foreign elements. The Parma orchestra could become a model orchestra and take its place in the first rank. It had only to accept his guidance.

While his left hand turned the pages of the score, his right arm beat an inflexible rhythm and his eyes looked deep into the world of sound.

"The orchestra is wildly enthusiastic," he said, "and I am happy to have obtained everything I could possibly wish for. The only drawback is that I am terribly busy."

As musical director he was able to produce all his favourite composers: Rossini, Beethoven, Bellini, and their respective operas: *William Tell, Fidelio, I Puritani.*

He was continually harping on his cherished "plenary powers." * When differences arose between himself and the Grand Chamberlain, Count Sanvitale, he favoured the Count with a volley of obscene epithets, worthy of the little gutter-snipe of the old days in the harbour of Genoa. He referred to the Count as *la carogna,* "that carrion." When Rome refused to accept a protégé of his, he abused it as "the filthiest of cities" (*fottutissima*), with an ignorant and imbecile aristocracy. It did not deserve so benevolent a sovereign (the Pope).

Still vituperating, the maestro, wrapped in his furs, stepped into the coach which had been built for him in London, and set out for his villa, Gajona, which was some little distance from the court. Here Germi was to give him the "pleasure of his company" at dinner. What a long time he had had to wait for this happy meeting. Surely his patience deserved to be rewarded.

But, to his disappointment, Germi was not there. He wrote off at once to him: "Without you I am a body without a soul. If you do not intend to come, I shall return to Parma at once."

* "Nothing will be done without my approval. After I had given the orchestra three lessons and had changed the accent of the wind instruments I obtained an excellent effect in *I Puritani.* I made several of the violin teachers pass a test and dismissed seven individuals from the ducal orchestra and that of the theatre because they had no ear." (December 23, 1835.)

His professional enthusiasm and his enjoyment of social gaieties had left him. It was cold. He was alone. Night was closing in. It would soon be autumn. How swiftly the years were passing! "Come as soon as you can," he begged Germi. "Come post haste. I am in need of your comfort."

To pass the time, he wandered restlessly all over the villa: loggia, staircase, drawing-room, veranda.

In his curious head-dress, he looked like Ali Baba as he took stock of his treasures. There were his decorations, his gold medals, his tie-pins, his heavy silver-plate, his diamond rings, his precious manuscripts, his Cremona violins, his Florentine mosaics, and the antique frescoes that adorned the walls of the villa. Finally, there were gifts from all the crowned heads of Europe.* But more precious than all his spoils was his Art. Was it still at his command, that magic formula which opened and closed the doors of the future?

"My courage is greater than my strength," he confessed.

The old familiar, hostile phantoms began to haunt the lake at Gajona: restlessness, ill health, perpetual desire for change.

---

* The collection at Gajona included a locket containing hair of Napoleon I, the Empress Marie-Louise, and the Duke of Reichstadt, gift of H.M. Marie-Louise of Austria.

Tie-pin set with brilliants, gift of Marie-Louise of Austria.

Medal of the Saviour, set with brilliants, gift of Marie-Louise of Austria.

Tie-pin set with brilliants, gift of the Queen of Bavaria.

Tie-pin set with rubies and diamonds, gift of George IV, King of England.

Gold ring set with brilliants, gift of the Czar Nicholas I of Russia.

Eight large gold medals, presented by the Municipality of Genoa.

Large gold medal, presented by the Municipality of Vienna.

Large gold medal, presented by the Ladies of Dunkirk.

Large gold medal, presented by the City of Paris.

Gold snuff-box, with monogram and brilliants, a gift of King Louis-Philippe.

Gold snuff-box, gift of the Emperor Franz I of Austria.

"I have to take medicine every day," he wrote to his dilatory friend. "I was unable to go to Turin yesterday [June 20, 1836]. We can talk things over at our ease on Thursday evening, when I am to have the joy of embracing you."

Concerts that had been arranged at Turin, Genoa, and Nice had to be cancelled. His exhaustion held him in a paralysing grip. "My violin is not too well pleased with me," he said.

Like a true neurasthenic, he burdened the future with the obligations he could not fulfil in the present, and committed himself to vast undertakings. "I have had letters from New York and London, which have given me great pleasure. If my health permits, I shall go to New York and I hope I shall be well enough to spend the winter in Russia and then rush off to America. The prospect of seeing new cities, of earning another million crowns or so, and of securing a sympathetic little girl as fiancée, is not to be despised. . . ."

He referred again to that other scheme, which was even dearer to his heart. "If only I could secure the legitimation of my son! But I hope that that business will soon be off my mind."

Then there was the printing press to be established at Genoa for the publication of his works, and a conservatoire for teaching his famous "secret method." There were two Grand Sonatas to be completed and the Concerto *Della Campana* to be orchestrated. There were, besides, all those palaces which he longed to possess, among them *Il Paradiso*, which was delightfully situated in the neighbourhood of Genoa. He begged Germi to buy it for him: "It would be a sin to let such a treasure be snapped up by a foreigner."

In addition to all this there was a scheme for floating a company to open in Paris, in the autumn of 1837, a Casino of the Arts, which should bear Paganini's name.

"I wish you would take an interest in the shares," he wrote to Germi, on the advice of his cousin Rebizzo, who for his part was eager to restore his fallen fortunes. "I am anxious to add as much as possible to the little patrimony I own in Parma."

❡ A "Casino Paganini"! And a ship called after him, which was to convey him to America for a three months' tour, and afterwards to land him at Brighton with two million dollars in his pocket! Such was the latest proposal made to him by Mr. Watson, who had nearly become his father-in-law. The two had decided to make peace on December 23 in the year of grace 1835. He blessed the post which brought him three important letters. One was from London, from the impresario, the second, which was posted in New York, was from Charlotte, the heroine of the Boulogne elopement, while the third contained proposals for a tour in Russia.

Once again he was defeated by the elements he had challenged. Yet he was determined to carry out his plans, in spite of Germi's sarcasms: "You wish to be warm, and so you propose to spend the winter in Russia. But first you must dash off to France, pay a flying visit to Holland, and tread on German soil again!" . . .

And what of Charlotte, his fair-haired, innocent victim? Blackmail, imprecations, all was forgotten at the thought of that "sympathetic little girl" whom he would perhaps bring home as his fiancée. He would charter that ship, seek her out, give her a dowry, marry her, and convert her to his own religion (for the Sardinian State was not to be trifled with). Charlotte, who embodied his dreams of a one and only love! Charlotte, who was surrounded by the New World's aureole of sunshine and gold—that thrilling new world which his clutching fingers longed to grasp—that new world strung with violin strings like quivering meridians! That new world where autumn violets were flowering!

THE CASINO PAGANINI

*The company's object is to found an artistic and literary
establishment, which shall be called a Casino. This establishment will provide the public, including the foreigners who
flock to Paris, with every kind of entertainment: music, dancing, art, conversation, literature, promenades; and place at
their disposal the most varied means of relaxation and
amusement.*

— PROSPECTUS ISSUED TO THE PUBLIC

W HAT induced Paganini, who was usually so
suspicious, to agree off-hand, not only to bestow his name on
the Casino, but also to direct the inaugural ceremonies, to give
recitals, and to take sixty shares at a thousand francs each? He
was more zealous than his cousin Rebizzo himself. The explanation was to be found in his last visit to Paris, which had
not passed off too smoothly. The trouble began with the Rhône
floods, a catastrophe which had followed upon the cholera epidemic in 1834. Paganini quarrelled with Jules Janin, who was
all-powerful on the *Journal des Débats*. Janin, who was a native
of St. Etienne, was organizing with much publicity a gala performance at the Opera, in aid of his unfortunate fellow-towns-
men, and was counting on Paganini's assistance.

"Would you believe it? He refuses to scrape that eternal G
string of his for one little quarter of an hour with his wonder-
working bow?" he wrote in his *Journal*. "Perhaps some of our
honest, working people in the mountains have heard the story
of a musician called Amphion, who raised cities by playing the
guitar. They did not believe the tale, but now it might come

216

true. If Paganini would work this miracle, he would become the most famous musician in the world. His name would be greater than Mozart's. He would be a household word with the miners of St. Etienne. . . ."

But little did the old sorcerer, the old wizard, care for the sufferings of the St. Etienne miners. His humanitarian instincts had been satisfied by his work for the victims of the cholera epidemic. These victims of the floods were trying to impose on him.

"For the last three months and more," he replied through the medium of the press, "I have not given a single recital in France. My health has not permitted it. I am in need of a complete rest and am returning to Genoa, my home. I have given two charity concerts in Paris. Why should it be supposed that I am anxious to give a third?"

He had refused to be coerced into playing by Jules Janin. Yet he was vaguely uneasy at the storm of imprecations which Janin called down upon his head.

"There is a limit to everything," thundered the *Journal des Débats.* "What right has this man to take such vast sums of money out of France when there is such terrible distress to be relieved? Charcoal-burners and iron-workers, my unfortunate brethren, whose homes have been destroyed by the floods, pardon me, I beseech you, for having appealed on your behalf to Monsieur Paganini. May our imprecations be fulfilled! Let him leave this country burdened with the people's scorn! Let everyone assist him on his journey, so that he may not be robbed of his precious gold! Let innkeepers reduce their charges for his benefit! Let post-chaises take him half price, like a child under seven! May the postillions have the sense to refrain from asking him for a tip! May his journey be all that he could wish! But let no one, on his travels, seek to see him or hear him! May his violin, which never sounds except when it is filled with gold, be accursed and condemned to silence! May he go on his way unnoticed, like the meanest pedlar of adulterated wine or tattered books! Such be his penance!"

But in spite of those maledictions, the following year, 1835, saw society following the lead of charity in endeavouring to enlist the aid of the alchemist Paganini. The idea for the new scheme was suggested by the popular musical entertainments then in vogue in Paris, which had been inaugurated by Père Musard, an orchestral conductor. He took the square of the Ambassadeurs in the Champs-Elysées for his open-air theatre. It had a stage in the centre and a spacious promenade and was surrounded by a light railing. The Parisians took a fancy to these musical promenades. The Saturday evenings became a fashionable institution, which was patronized by the Dukes of Orléans and Nemours, and all Paris society. Instead of supping at the cabarets, they would say: "Let's go to Musard's to-night."

Among the spectators there were two men, Tardiff de Petitville and Rousseau-Desmelotries, who borrowed Musard's idea and developed it into a plan for a Casino on the grand scale. It was to be accommodated in a mansion in the rue de la Chaussée d'Antin (formerly No. 9 or 11 rue Mont-Blanc) which they had bought. It had once been the property of La Guimard, and had subsequently been sold, first to Perregaux, the financier, then to the Duke of Padua, and finally to Laffitte's Bank. The building was next door to the Belgian Embassy, which was frequented by all Paris society. Its imposing façade overlooked well-kept gardens, which stretched as far as the rue des Mathurins and contained a graceful rotunda. Nothing was lacking for carrying out the work of adaptation, except funds. At present it was being done on credit. But it might be possible to extract the necessary capital from the pockets of the public, if the scheme were under distinguished patronage. In 1836 every nerve was strained to obtain Paganini's support. The help of Pacini, his publisher, and of Lazzaro and

Bianca Rebizzo, his cousins, was enlisted. The following letter was addressed to them:

"Strike while the iron is hot. If we can secure Paganini for a partner, success is assured. Use all your influence. If he will not come in for the sake of his own interest, let him do so out of friendship for you. If you should be successful, send me an authorization to sign shares for him on the copies of our contracts. Let your battle-cry be: Paganini! Paganini!! Paganini!!!"

After two years of negotiations, in the autumn of 1837 workmen could be seen setting up the magic name in huge letters on the front of the new Casino. In the summer of 1836, Paganini set out in his carriage on his return journey to Paris, via Turin, Alessandria, Marseilles, and Nice. It was a painful progress, checked at every stage by attacks of fever and rheumatism.

In Marseilles, chance again brought him into contact with the "American" doctor, who saved his life at Pavia, and whose real name was Spitzer. Once more the learned German attempted to cure him. He tried introducing metal *bougies* of graded thicknesses into the patient's bladder. "I am now at number 3," said Nicolò uneasily. "When I get to number 6. . . ."

He was obliged to cancel all but two of his twelve concerts, and to spend most of his time in bed. There he brooded over his plans, which included the Casino Paganini and his voyage to America. He had been persuaded that his career, his interests, his popularity with the people of Paris, were bound up with the success of the Casino. As for the voyage to America, he was dazzled by its possibilities, and his own private hopes. A Swedish three-master was expected to put in at Marseilles between the 25th and 30th of the month, but this was too soon. He had a better idea. Spitzer had assured him that he would be able to return to Paris and to proceed to Le Havre in the winter of 1837. In his reply to Watson's letter, he instructed him to book two passages, one for himself and one for his cousin Rebizzo, on the mail steamer sailing from Le Havre for New York at the end of March. Whatever happened, he had decided to ask for Charlotte's hand in marriage when he arrived in America. But his recovery was painfully slow. Would he never be ready for the sixth *bougie?* Alas! it was all a dream. On March 16 Watson had to cancel the passages booked for Paganini, on grounds of ill health. Perhaps in June. . . . But by the end of June he had recovered just sufficiently to travel to Paris. He was thankful to have been able to leave the coast. As soon as he had arrived in Paris and taken over the directorship of the Casino, he confided to Germi his plans for avenging himself for the incidents of 1834, in spite of his lassitude and the progress of his malady.

"For the last month I have been suffering from an ulcerated throat which has affected my voice. I have been obliged to reply in writing to the thousand and one questions that have been hurled at me, since I made myself responsible for the success of the Casino. I am determined that it shall be opened *next Thursday*."

❡ Paganini, that sinister genius who had got the better of the English! It appeared that, after all, he had not died of cholera in Genoa, as had been reported in the newspapers.* Or could it be his ghost that the ribald gamblers observed from their seat at the tables? In the meantime, in spite of the vast sums that had been lavished on it, the enterprise did not have a good send-off. There were rumours abroad.

---

* "Did you read this laconic announcement: *Paganini has died of cholera?* Such is fame. Nothing more. It is as if one said: Monsieur So-and-So the grocer has died of cholera. O the vanity of sounds that are dispersed on the air. Vanity of the artist, who leaves behind nothing but a violin, which is sold by auction. *Paganini has died of cholera!*"— *Revue de Paris*, October 1835.

It was whispered that the Casino, to take the most favourable view of it, was only a gambling hall in disguise. The directors were said to be swindling the contractors and workmen.

After all, the opening ceremony had to be postponed till November 20, 1837, "on account of Monsieur Paganini's health," said the *Gazette Musicale*. The newspapers made sarcastic comments.

"As for the famous violinist's share in the department of music," Berlioz prophesied, "it will amount to this. On certain days, Paganini will walk three times round the gardens—provided the weather is fine."

The rumours were well founded. Three weeks later the Casino had failed and was shut down. A storm of abuse burst on the heads of the dishonest directors. The cat was out of the bag—there were debts, shady transactions, misappropriation of shares, and the like. Paganini washed his hands of the whole affair and the public followed his example. But the two villains, who were responsible, had no intention of allowing their figurehead to escape scot-free. From being the defendants, they made themselves plaintiffs in the case, and in March 1838 Paganini found himself obliged by order of the court, to play in the concert hall of the Casino twice a week, or pay a fine of six thousand francs a time. The injunction would be enforced, if necessary, by arrest for debt.

Six thousand francs! Twice a week! This to him, Paganini! Well, he would sell his skin dearly. A whole posse of lawyers was mobilized. In his defence he belched forth fire and gold against "the directors of the Casino, who are a band of rogues and assassins. But the newspapers will soon be tired of talking about the matter." *

* The abandoned Casino was used only for some subscription balls and unimportant concerts. It was then taken by a Monsieur Julien and used as a dance hall; then by the aristocratic Committee of a Charity organization; next it became a popular tea garden; then it was taken

Little did he know. It was too good an opportunity for taking revenge on this captious and eccentric foreigner. He was said to be worth millions, and his enormous earnings wounded the vanity of the French, as it had that of the English. Another false step on his part provided the newspapers with further copy.

❦ Pierre Hédouin, one of his most devoted friends in the north, gave several instances of Paganini's increasing mania for economy—his sordid avarice, as people called it—which, Hédouin said jokingly, might "well assist in the study of the maladies of the human mind." The day after one of his concerts at Boulogne, Paganini expressed a desire to buy a black cashmere waistcoat. Hédouin offered to take him to his own tailor.

"No, no, my dear fellow," replied Paganini, "take me to an old clothes shop."

He spent three-quarters of an hour bargaining heatedly to obtain a reduction of a franc on a waistcoat priced at ten francs. Another day Hédouin chaffed him about an ancient flannel vest, which he had patched and darned with his own hand and wore next to his skin.

"You don't understand, my dear fellow. To me an old garment is an old friend. I am fond of it and cannot bear to part with it."

Along with these almost pathologic economies, Paganini had fallen into the habit of consulting everyone he met about his health. A friend of his had the bad taste to take advantage of this practice. A certain lawyer of English origin, Douglas Loveday by name, lived at No. 14 Place d'Orléans, rue St. Lazare, Paris. Paganini was in the habit of calling on him on business

by outside brokers on the Stock Exchange, and finally it was bought by the Board of the Orléans Railways for offices. Eventually the site of the Casino became the present rue Halévy.

connected with the Casino. Loveday was a doctor as well as a lawyer, and Paganini's visits to him sometimes coincided with those of an Italian homoeopathic doctor of the name of Croserio, who attended the Sardinian Ambassador in Paris. Gradually the business relations between the three men developed into friendship. Paganini spoke of adopting Croserio as his doctor, and Loveday suggested that both men should stay with him as paying guests on reasonable terms. The maestro was accompanied by Achillino, then a boy of twelve. The child received piano lessons from Loveday's daughter, who herself profited by advice and auditions from Paganini. At the end of three months, the homoeopathic doctor was exasperated by the consultations, direct and indirect, which Paganini exacted at every meal, and decided to charge a fee. Loveday backed him up and fixed an extortionate rate of payment.

"You were so cunning," wrote Paganini, bursting into a tirade against Loveday, "that a purely formal question, such as 'How do you do?' addressed to me by your hydropathic [sic] friend when he met me at your house, was twisted into a consultation at ten francs a time."

By the way of reprisal he tacked on to his letter a bill for lessons he had given to Mademoiselle Loveday.

Loveday at once seized his pen and wrote a facetious reply. The Baron, he declared, had been lucky to find in Loveday a lawyer whose advice on the Casino case was, he considered, worth more than a hundred and forty thousand francs. The same applied to his plans for visiting St. Petersburg and New York.

"Besides," he continued, enumerating all the benefits he had conferred on Paganini, "I dissuaded you from taking a remedy recommended by a fair somnambulist. Had you taken it, it would have burned up your whole inside, belly, spine, guts and all. There would not have been enough left to make an E string for your famous Guarnerius."

Incomparable artist that he was, the Baron might have shown his appreciation of the admirable régime, which had done him so much good during his sojourn of ninety-nine days in Loveday's house, by giving at least one short performance. But he had pleaded a corn on one of his illustrious feet. Loveday had refrained from pointing out that it was his fingers, not his toes, that he had wished to listen to.

"As for your son," Loveday continued, "when did I ask even a penny for the instruction I lavished upon him daily: the alphabet, French grammar, etc. etc.?

"But as regards the piano lessons my daughter gave to that precious scion of the race of Paganini, that is another matter. I reckon that each of these lessons, which were given to the heir to the wealth, name, and genius of Paganini, was worth two hundred francs, since they were the practical application, the rare fruit, of the excellent advice she had received from you, Paganini, the boy's father. . . ."

Loveday accordingly ventured to support Croserio's claims and to add his own, namely, a demand for thirty-seven thousand eight hundred francs, a sum which hardly sufficed to compensate Mademoiselle Clara and himself. Finally, he had the honour to be, "not Nicolò Paganini, but only his humble servant, Douglas Loveday." *

The cup was full. Paganini was so ill advised as to make this ridiculous quarrel public. He had recourse again to the *Gazette Musicale*,† where he published the correspondence in full.

"My answer," he replied to Loveday, "was to send you a bill for eighty thousand francs for lessons and auditions, etc., given to your daughter. It was tit for tat. But you were alarmed. Perhaps you had visions of bailiffs and their clutches. So you hurriedly safeguarded yourself by giving my letter to the news-

* Letters found in the National Archives, in a bundle of petitions addressed to Louis-Philippe, and published by the *Esprit Médical*, September 17, 1937.
† July 14, 1838.

papers, making it appear a try on, on my part, a masterpiece of extreme rapacity. It was a neat trick. But what proved to me that you meant it seriously and not merely as an attempt to amuse the public at your expense and mine was the fact that, when you sent my letter to the newspapers, you refrained from adding your reply, in which you made a demand for 37,800 francs, in payment of an account which you hastily concocted, to counter-balance my own claims.

"Here are your arguments in justification of your demands:

'Sir,

You state that you lodged with me for ninety-nine days. During that time you consulted me about your health and your affairs. As a doctor and a lawyer, I have a right to a fee for these consultations. I will waive my claims for my services as a doctor but I must insist on being paid as your legal adviser.

'Sir,' your letter continues, 'I am a mine of learning. These are my qualifications: I know, 1. The alphabet (I quote verbatim). 2. French, English and Italian Grammar. 3. Natural History. 4. The History of the Universe. 5. Geography. 6. Homoeopathic Medicine (*risum teneatis amici?* I pander to your weakness for quotations).* 10. Social usages. 11. Manners (*O tempora, O mores* . . . there's more Latin for you). For ninety-nine days, you continue, 'I have lavished all this wealth of learning on your son. I have made no charge for this. But . . . my daughter has given your son piano lessons. I cannot put them at less than two hundred francs each, as the lessons (again I quote your own words) were an inducement to her to work hard. . . . Poor girl. . . . To sum up:

For legal advice	18,000	francs
For 99 piano lessons from		
my daughter	19,800	"
Total	37,800	"

which is the sum you owe me.'

* . . . and apparently to his own weakness for a joke, for he omits items 7 to 9.

"Such is your letter, written under the influence of the summer solstice, at the approach of the dog days. Everyone will sympathize with a man who is suffering from the effects of those baleful influences.

"I have no reply to make. I will merely add the following observations:

"1. With reference to your claim to know French, there are certain slips which you have made; e.g. you put *vous aviez pu,* instead of *vous auriez pu; abstenir de suivre* instead of *s'abstenir de suivre,* etc. etc.

"2. Apropos of your literary style, I do not care for your definition of truth at the beginning of your letter: 'Truth is an essence, whose nature nothing can change.' It is like a perfumer's puff.

"3. Nor do I consider that logic is your strong point. To prove that medicine is a speciality of yours, you say that you are fond of music. It is a curious way of arguing. You might as well say that you were fond of drinking, which proved that you were a lawyer.

"4. Finally I deny that Mademoiselle's lessons were worth 200 francs each. In spite of the pains this estimable young lady has taken in the past, and may take in the future, to improve her touch on the piano, she will never succeed in touching the heart. My advice to her is to go in for pantomime for which, from what I have seen of her playing, she has great aptitude. . . ." *

The readers of the *Gazette* held their sides with laughing at the duel of these two misers. The personality of the musician was merged in a kind of legendary being, a Harpagon without a voice, who could be seen wandering about the Néo-Thermes in the rue de la Victoire, where he was undergoing yet another cure. He was well known to all the little street Arabs. There was no longer any question of concerts. On cold days, he would sit

* July 14, 1838.

by a miserable fire, take his guitar and solace himself with old familiar melodies and sunny memories of the south. His eyes, which had been affected by the glare of the footlights, were soothed by the twilight which was peopled with his dreams. He saw himself, his strength renewed, setting out for London to play yet once again, in this world, to his friends across the Channel, to dedicate to them "the last sounds of his violin." But as for Russia and New York . . . alas! alas!

There was a knock at the door. Another stamped document! That wretched Casino again!

"As regards the new machinations of those despicable robbers," he scribbled immediately, "I hope to send at least one or two of them to jail."

But he seemed to be the one who was heading in that direction. Writs were served on him. He was the subject of lampoons, which covered him with ridicule. One of them represented him standing in the bow of a ship (perhaps the Swedish three-master that had called at Marseilles) setting off in pursuit of Miss Watson, only to find that she was already married. He returned home with his tail between his legs, to the delight of the American newspapers. A copy of the *Revue de Paris* came into his hands. He turned its pages. It contained a bitter satire on himself, which was signed by Castil-Blaze. Everyone, it seemed, was against him, friend and foe alike. The treacherous earth was slipping from under him. He would make one more attempt to regain his footing.

❡ On December 16, 1838, Berlioz, who was still smarting under the recent failure of his *Benvenuto Cellini* at the Opera, sought to re-establish himself by a performance of *Harold in Italy* at the Conservatoire. *Harold* had been written to Paganini's order. Besides his guitar, Paganini possessed a cherished viola. ("I do not know if I told you that I bought a famous and most beautiful viola by Stradivarius when I was

in London," he wrote soon afterwards.) Berlioz's Symphony *
centred magnificently around this instrument, whose timbre
is so often underrated.

But the hisses, with which *Benvenuto* had been received
at the Opera, still rankled. The irascible Berlioz could see the
demons of the *Loge infernale*, with their insufferable arrogance, waiting to riddle this new work of his with their poisoned
darts. Nowadays his friends, the "old guard," served only to
deepen the despair that filled his heart.

When he had finished conducting the Symphony, he returned to the green-room. A tall, phantomlike form detached
itself from a group of musicians and flung itself at his feet, murmuring almost inaudibly: "It is a masterpiece!"

It was Paganini.

"But that was not all," Berlioz wrote to his father. "Not five
minutes ago, his son Achillino, a charming boy of twelve,
brought me the following letter and a present of 20,000 francs.

My Dear Friend [ran the letter],
    Beethoven is dead and only Berlioz could bring him back. I,
who have heard your divine Symphony, which is worthy of your
genius, deem it my duty to beg you to accept as a mark of my
homage, 20,000 francs, which will be paid to you by Baron Rothschild on presentation of the enclosed.
            Believe me your very affectionate friend,
                                            Nicolò Paganini

"I give you the bare facts," wrote Berlioz.

In a letter to his sister he described his visit to the Néo-

* It was referred to in the *Gazette* of December 16, 1833: "Paganini,
whose health is improving daily, has invited Berlioz to write for him
a new composition, in the style of the *Symphonie Fantastique*, for him
to play on his return from England. The work will be entitled: *The last
moments of Mary Stuart*. It will be a dramatic fantasy, with orchestra
and choir, and the viola as solo instrument." But Paganini was not
pleased with the work, and asked for it to be rewritten.

Thermes, where Paganini, who had lost his voice, received him
and talked to him through the intermediary of Achillino.

"When he saw me," wrote Berlioz, "tears came into his
eyes—and I admit that my own tears were not far off. He wept,
this ferocious man-eater, this woman-killer, this escaped galley-
bird, as he has been called a hundred times. He embraced me
with scalding tears.

" 'Not another word,' he said. 'I take no credit for it. It gave
me the greatest joy, the most complete satisfaction, I have
experienced in all my life. You roused in me emotions I had
never suspected. You have carried on the great tradition of
Beethoven.' "

It was like a stone flung into a pool. Of those who were aware
of it, some did justice to the princely gesture, which had rescued
Berlioz from distress. Jules Janin, Paganini's sworn enemy, now
exchanged his former diatribes for passionate eulogies. But
soon other explanations were forthcoming.

"Paganini," said Liszt, "merely wanted to curry favour with
the public, whose disapproval he had earned by refusing to
take part in a benefit concert for Miss Smithson, Berlioz's mistress."

It was suggested that Paganini had merely lent his name to
some munificent and distinguished donor. Bertin was mentioned, the most powerful man in Paris and the proprietor of
the *Journal des Débats*, whose daughter took an interest in
Berlioz. The note to Rothschild's cashier was, like the letter,
dated December 18. It was an order to "pay bearer, Monsieur
Hector Berlioz, the sum of twenty thousand francs, which I
deposited with you yesterday."

And on December 17, the day after the concert and the day
before the presentation, was it not a fact that Bertin, Paganini,
and Janin, of the *Journal des Débats*, had met and arranged
this sensational act of homage to Berlioz. Tongues were wagging faster than ever.

⁋ Since there was nothing he could do, since he could neither play, nor speak, nor defend himself, he decided to leave Paris. He would take with him that "most beautiful Stradivarius viola," and would make music for its own sake— chamber music.

I am thinking of going to Genoa at the beginning of September, to try to shake off my intolerable worries [he wrote to Germi]. What do you say to this plan? I have invoked God's help to improve my wretched health. I hope to live many more years and to have the happiness of embracing you again—a consolation which may almost be compared to the bliss of lovely and genuine music.

Addio,
Yours,
PAGANINI

But the courts did not acquiesce in this delightful plan. Each day the case was becoming more and more complicated and a new coil was added to the snake that was trying to destroy the charmer. Grotesque and ridiculous charges were preferred against him. His neighbour, a business man, who was excited by the general atmosphere of hostility, accused him of plotting to have him assassinated by four moustachioed cutthroats, who were armed to the teeth. As for Rebizzo, his cousin, who had dragged him into the affair, he was lying low.

At last, in January 1839, Paganini left for Marseilles, nursing again the hope that he might be restored to health.* With time at his disposal, in a favourable climate, in a region that was as full of surprises as Paganini's own mind, he was soon seized with a new passion, a last absorbing interest. He was

* "I am hoping for fine weather, so that I can take walks. In the meantime I commend my soul to God. Excuse this brief note.
Your PAGANINI
"PS.—Close your letters more carefully. Rebizzo spies on me, like the Indian in the aria. Feb. 3d, 1839."

capable of anything, even of this strange combination of music and speculation, generosity and rapacity. But who could have guessed that Stradivarius would supply the motive for the new enterprise?

In the old days, when his friendship with Germi first began, quartet-playing, which is one of the purest forms of art, had been the delight of his youth. It doubled the joy to share it with Germi, who had already become the "adorable friend." They had arranged a quartet and had interpreted Haydn and Boccherini. Even now, Nicolò had only to hear a few bars of one of those themes to feel his heart fill with the old emotion and to see, before his failing eyes, Genoa shining in the shadows. In the night which was beginning to gather around him, he was still to find that exquisite essence, which was like the message of a rose, blooming on All Souls' Day. It was worth every effort, since it was to interpret Beethoven, who was now his god. Upon this altar the maestro would offer his tyrannical ego and his Guarnerius del Gesù. He would select players from among a thousand candidates. For once, fortune was to favour him.

In Marseilles he lodged with a lawyer, who had a passion for music.* "He is the sort of man we both like. I wish you could make his acquaintance," he wrote to Germi. "I have given him all Beethoven's quartets and quintets. I promised a long time ago to have a Stradivarius 'cello sent to him. Will you despatch it from Genoa care of my friend Brun in Marseilles? I should like it as soon as possible."

Scarcely had the 'cello arrived when he wrote to Germi again: "My friend Brun would like you to come to Marseilles for a fortnight to play in the Mozart Quintet. We will play you Beethoven's last Quartet. You shall have lodgings near me. . . ."

The home of this "amateur 'cellist who had a remarkable

* Treasurer of the Philharmonic Society.

knowledge of music" and musical instruments, was No. 1 rue de Coq.* It had a garden, and a terrace with a balustrade around it. Arriving there after ten days of travelling, Paganini was delighted with it. Camille Brun did the honours with the help of his chief clerk, Louise Bondil, who happened to be also his cook. These evenings, when every possible subject was discussed—friendship, music, travels, business—were Paganini's first relaxation for months. Everyone talked except the maestro, who had almost completely lost his voice. But Achillino was his interpreter. He exhibited the Stradivarius viola and asked about other violas of the same make. The violoncello which Germi had despatched from Genoa arrived in perfect condition. Brun was delighted with it and set to work to study the 'cello part of the last Beethoven quartets. Being a collector himself, he asked, casually, what the market value of the 'cello might be.

"In Paris," replied Achillino, "the violins of Guarnerius del Gesù are fetching 2,800 francs, those of Stradivarius about 5,000, his violoncellos between 6,000 and 7,000. The instrument you are playing on is a very rare and beautiful specimen. It is worth anything between 10,000 and 30,000 francs. It depends on the purchaser."

"And on the salesman," suggested Brun.

He thought the Baron should profit by his vacation to make his millions "work." There were many rich dilettanti in Marseilles who would be tempted by an authentic instrument which had been played on by Paganini.

This kindled a spark in Paganini's mind.

The next day he wrote to Germi: "You had better send me your Guarnerius violoncello. I intend to sell mine as well. I am certain to find a purchaser in Marseilles."

On February 3 he wrote: "I have just bought from Professor

* According to the researches of B. de Miramon Fitz-James: *Paganini in Marseilles*, Fuéri, in Marseilles.

Merighi of Milan a Stradivarius violin and violoncello and a second Amati violin. Instruct L. B. Mignone to send 385 louis d'or at once to Merighi. The instruments must be carefully packed and sent to you at Genoa, where you will examine them before despatching them to Marseilles."

The fever of speculation was rising sharply as will be seen by the temperature chart:

Feb. 17th. You had better come to Marseilles at the end of March. . . . The tone of your Guarnerius is not as good as it ought to be. It is partly due to the sounding board and the bridge. We must see if we can change them. Messrs. Carli have my Amati viola. I wish you would send it to me, together with the Guarnerius violoncello which Milzetti gave me at Bologna. Collect my Amati violoncello from Parma and ship it off to Marseilles, together with my Stradivarius and my André Guarnerius.

March 19th. The six instruments arrived in perfect condition.

March 20th [to Merighi]. I have completed my set of four Stradivarius. Look out for violoncellos, violins, and violas at prices which will enable me to sell them at a profit. I shall give you a percentage of the proceeds. Be careful not to say that Paganini is the purchaser, as that would send the prices up.

April 16th. Examine the violins by Filippono that are offered for sale, and see if there are any violins by Guarnerius del Gesù and Stradivarius and ask the price.

June 10th. In Marseilles there are at least thirty amateurs ready to buy my instruments.

And now the house in the rue de Coq was adorned with Amati, Guarneri, and Stradivari. As formerly in his villa Gajona, Nicolò gloated over his treasures. Brown, yellow, or reddish-gold, they were made of different kinds of wood, under a glossy veneer of precious varnish.

"For heaven's sake, don't tell me of instruments that are in poor condition or have been repaired."

Through those veins that were once swollen with sap, the ichor of music should pour anew, restoring them to life.

When he could sleep again, he selected a viola player and a second violin of the name of Pascal. With himself at the first desk and Brun at that of the 'cello, the Paganini Ouartet had come into being. And they were actually playing on four authentic Stradivari—"my quartet of Stradivari," as the maestro jealously called it.

It was a memorable moment, as in astronomy, when stars cross each other's path in the Zodiac—an auspicious moment in the world of music. It had taken many generations for human endeavour to culminate in a Stradivarius, a Beethoven, a Paganini.

"You will be charmed, I hope, with the last four quartets of Beethoven," he wrote to Germi, whose opinion he had always sought.

Alluding to Germi's expected visit, he added, "My heart is in need of comfort."

This meeting with Germi was to be a memorable occasion. An event had taken place which concerned the deepest love of Paganini's life. Germi was married, and Paganini had not yet met his wife. He had written from Paris to congratulate him. Now he was to see the ravishing Camiglietta. He had once written to Germi: "Seal your letters more carefully. I cannot bear to have them profaned by other eyes."

But since the wife of his friend loved that friend with all her heart, his friend's friend must needs include her in his devotion. Nicolò was looking forward to their visit, but though he was disappointed not to see them in March, he wrote to Germi: "It will be as well for you to wait for the fine weather. Come whenever it suits you. How are you?"

When he was feeling better he said jokingly: "The celebrated professor of music and dancing, Monsieur Achillino, sends greetings to you."

For the sake of the boy's education he was thinking of entrusting him first to the Jesuits in Marseilles, and later to those in Genoa. He forbade him to enter into correspondence with Bianchi, who had married a certain Felice Brunati. He was eager to go on living, and fortified himself with admirable sentiments: "More than ever it behoves us to store up happiness for the years to come. We must be of good cheer for the sake of the future. Let us not lose courage."

But a single post sufficed to crush this spirit of optimism, and to break the truce. He received a letter from Paris informing him that 20,000 francs damages had been awarded against him for his refusal to play at the Casino.

"I have two and a half months in which to appeal against this iniquitous sentence," he wrote at once to Germi. "You must prepare my defence immediately. O Rebizzo! Rebizzo!"

Panic seized him. Beethoven and Stradivarius were silent. Germi could and must save him. Was he not the Paganini of lawyers? "*Amico pregiatissimo, Amico carissimo, Amico amatissimo,* I beseech you to love me."

With such litanies of friendship he sought to exorcise his evil fate. In the meantime, the law was quietly and mechanically taking its course. The verdict was given against him. Paganini lost his appeal and his advocate, Monsieur Double, sent him the information as a New Year's greeting in 1840.

"Would you advise me to go bankrupt?" he asked Germi. "I enclose a copy of my lawyer's letter."

"It is with profound regret," wrote Monsieur Double, "that I write to inform you that your case against the Casino has unhappily resulted in a monstrous judgment, pronounced by the Court. I am so utterly overwhelmed, so deeply distressed, that I hardly know how to tell you what has happened.

"Not content with confirming the sentence, against which you were appealing, the Court, on the petition of the plaintiffs, has raised the amount of damages to the exorbitant figure of

50,000 francs. As you are aware, there was no lack of zeal and devotion on my part, no lack of ability and devotion on the part of your other advocate Monsieur Chaix d'Est-Ange. We did and said on your behalf and in your interests all that was humanly possible. But the plaintiffs, very skilfully linking facts together, perverted the truth and posed as innocent victims. Thanks to the impression produced on the Court by their lies, they succeeded in securing this unjust, this scandalous verdict against you. In short the Court was led to believe that you were generally considered a man of *capricious and eccentric character* and they jumped at the chance of striking a blow at one who was said to be a multi-millionaire.

"Such, frankly, was the impression made on myself, your other advocate and all who were present in court." *

"The final verdict," the Court declared. But there was worse to come. The consequences were unbelievably terrible: his instruments were to be distrained as a guarantee. Such was the punishment that "Harpagon" was called upon to endure. A certain Monsieur Sergent had been despatched to the vice-consul for France at Nice, Monsieur Borg, with instructions to enforce these orders.

"It would cause me infinite pain," groaned the victim, who was still incredulous, "if Monsieur Sergent were to sequester my instruments in Nice. . . ."

But on Good Friday, April 17, the mills of human and divine justice worked together.

"Yesterday," wrote Nicolò, "Signor Borg, the vice-consul for France, and Monsieur Adolphe Sergent, the Casino's agent, came to execute the sentence of the French court of law. I told them that I was not well enough to deal with the matter myself and referred them to you."

* Nice, January 4, 1840.

❦ His instruments! The very rhythm of his heart! The gallows-bird, Monsieur Sergent, had left Brun's house empty-handed. But what would happen in Nice? This time the monster with the iron claws would clutch his prey.

My brain has ceased to function [Paganini said repeatedly]. My most beloved Germi, I would have replied to your letter, but I have been tortured by my anxieties day and night. I am waiting for the doctor's report on the catarrhal affection which is getting rapidly worse.

I am losing strength.

Addio, mio caro, addio.

YOUR PAGANINI

TRAGIC MUSIC

"The tension I feel when making my tragic music exhausts me terribly. If I lived near you, my days would be prolonged."

— *Manchester, January* 1832

HE was caught by his own wonder-working machine, crushed like an insect between his fortune and his fame. His body was now too frail for those flights of his, whether of angel or of demon. All that remained was the human element. But he was putting up a gallant fight.

"All the doctors in Paris and Germany have given me up," he wrote in the winter of 1838, "but I am going to try a clever physician, who was recommended to me by the Marchese Gianluccio Durazzo. He is Dr. Benneck of 'Bordo' and has done some wonderful cures."

Dr. Benneck succeeded the famous Magendie, President of the Academy of Medicine in Paris.

During his treatment there was suddenly a tiny ray of hope. "After three days he paid me another visit," Nicolò continued. "When he had felt my pulse several times he decided that there was an improvement. 'I have saved you,' he said. 'I shall cure all your ailments. *It isn't the case that your lungs are affected or that the intestine is strangulated. I undertake to restore you to Europe, fit as a fiddle, plump and robust, with all your organs functioning normally.*'

"I am not to pay him by the visit," Harpagon concluded, "I am to pay him when he has cured me. If all his promises come true, I may give him my violin into the bargain."

238

But after a deceptive improvement in his health, there were almost daily fluctuations between hope and despair. His body, which was specially adapted for music, seemed to vibrate even more sensitively to his malady. What dissonances, what strange heartbreaking harmonies were the result of the doctor's prescriptions! Everything was worth a trial; he would try everything: doctors, savants, surgeons, healers, bone-setters, quacks. They examined his throat, from which no sounds now issued, and his ruined digestive organs. By their orders he spent the summer of 1839 in the Pyrenees.

"I am leaving for Balaruc on Wednesday or Thursday to try the mud baths. I hope they will do me good."

But the mud baths proved to be bad for his nerves. He decided to go to Montpellier and consult the medical faculty for which it was famous. Then he was tempted to try yet another cure. "I am anxious to hear what the renowned (*rinomatissime*) Dr. Lallemand, who is at Vernet-les-Bains, has to say," he wrote. But when he had consulted him, he demanded yet another opinion.

"There is a Dr. Guillaume, who is famous, although he does not practice. He is a philosopher, a savant of genius, with the highest reputation in Montpellier."

It was left for Dr. Guillaume to dot the "i"s.

"As I never lose an opportunity for acquiring knowledge," Dr. Guillaume wrote to his colleague Lallemand, "I hasten to submit to you my own theory concerning the malady from which the famous maestro is suffering. It can be summed up in a few words:

"*Paganini is a fiery soul, imprisoned in a violin.* The soul is intact, but the walls of the instrument are frail in the extreme. The chords are there, but are not vibrating as they should. There is excessive nervous tension affecting the lumbar region of the spinal marrow. The soft palate and the roof of the mouth seem both to be attacked by a syphilitic virus. Before prescribing any treatment I shall wait to hear what you have already ordered."

Suddenly, Dr. Guillaume, of whom he had such a high opinion that he was thinking of confiding his son to him as a pupil, fell out of favour. Paganini described him as a "regular humbug." In the end the maestro decided to be his own physician. He returned to his old quack remedy, the *Elixir le Roy*, which was like liquid fire. It put the patient into a violent fever, which either killed or cured him. He made up his mind that doctors were useless, and embarked on a course of powders, balms, wines, herb teas, injections, and the like. He had a whole outfit of *bougies*, and tried every kind of régime, from strict dieting to "heavy meals of rich food, washed down with Bordeaux," although he had no appetite.

He spent another month at Vernet-les-Bains, taking a final cure.

"Paganini is reduced to a shadow," someone wrote from Vernet. "He has lost his voice and can express himself only by means of his fiery eyes and his angular gestures. His glorious violin, which has made him famous, was lifted out of the carriage at the same time as its master. The invalid is to take baths from the Elisa spring, at a temperature of 22 degrees [centigrade] of heat."

Such was his condition when he returned to Marseilles. Taking with him all his instruments, he embarked on the S.S. *Marseilles* for Genoa, at the end of September 1839.

℄ All his friends gathered around him in consternation. Rebizzo, arriving from Turin, met the "Paganini of advocates" as he emerged from the hotel where Nicolò was staying.

"I shall never forget what Germi said to me, when Paganini, exhausted by unspeakable sufferings, returned for one last week to his native town," wrote Rebizzo, the cousin who was responsible for so many of Paganini's troubles. "The expression on Germi's face will always haunt me. The sound of his voice will always echo in my heart. He said to me bitterly: 'I have just left him. . . . Courage! we must have courage. Alas, it is a case of Napoleon on St. Helena!'"

The winter climate of Genoa was too cold for the invalid, and in November he left for Nice. When he arrived there, he had to be carried from his carriage to his bed. He was a mere skeleton, a dying man. His bony forehead was covered with a silk cap. He fingered a hundred different phials. He never went out. But he was still struggling, old wizard that he was, against the witches, who had now turned against their master.

"I had had no sleep for twelve days. I am tormented for at least twenty hours out of the twenty-four by a nervous catarrhal cough, fever, or rheumatic pains. By the mercy of heaven, however, I managed to get four hours' sleep this morning, and I am taking advantage of this to write to my dear friend Germi. . . ."

Another time he wrote: "I still have that diabolical feeling of suffocation. Because of this I cannot keep my promise to orchestrate my compositions for London. I hope I shall be better in the spring."

He intended to spend the spring in Genoa. Was it to be his last?

"I may meet him in Paradise sooner than we think," he said of a friend, Giordano by name, who had recently died.

Chastened by suffering, the great man's egotism was disappearing. His thoughts turned anxiously to others: his sister's children, his son, the "adorable friend," whom he endeavoured to comfort.

"On the threshold of the New Year [1840], I wish you every possible happiness. . . . How are you?" he repeated more than once. "If only you would take the *Elixir le Roy*, you would live to be a hundred."

Achillino had recently left the Jesuit College in Marseilles.*
The son of the man who was "in league with the devil" had just
made his first communion with "ten charming youngsters," belonging to the first families in Marseilles. His legitimation,
which had been obtained from the Sardinian Government,
was made valid for the Duchy of Parma. Nicolò could die in
peace.

"I am overjoyed at this favour granted by our most gracious
sovereign. As might have been expected, it has had a beneficial
effect on my health."

Although Achillino had a gift for music, he preferred classical studies. He was never to know the ecstasies and agonies of
"tragic music," under whose rigorous laws the maestro was now
suffering so severely.

"My malady is due to general exhaustion of the nerves. It
is my own fault," he admitted. "I have overstrained and over-
worked them."

But each new attack drew from him lamentations. "My
weakness is increasing," he scrawled. "*Addio.*"

Once again he set out on his travels. He had set his heart on
hearing Beethoven's Mass performed in one of the churches in
Marseilles. When he came out of the church, he was helped,
tottering, to his hotel. If his last wish was to be fulfilled, if he
was to hear once more the organ of his childhood and the bells
of San Lorenzo, he would have to make haste. He knew it, and
once more he set out in his Berlin. Genoa was not far off and
the carriage travelled swiftly. But at Nice he collapsed. He
could go no farther. After this terrible drive, he had to be car-

---

* "I removed my son from the college," he wrote in sudden anger
against the Jesuits, "because the director, who is a venal and extrava-
gant man, imposed on him fasts that were not enjoined by the church,
and did not teach him the principles of literature."—Marseilles, September 7, 1839.

ried as quickly as possible to the house of his friend, Count de Cessoles. "It is a charming spot," he said, "but with too much of a northern aspect."

He was already chilled to the bone.

April.

I can digest no food. I have no appetite. My weakness is increasing. The swelling in the leg has mounted to the back of the knee. Because of this I have to crawl like a snail.

Germi's letters were his only ray of light. For the sake of his replies, he forced himself to write to him.

Never stop loving me [he pleaded]. I cannot tell you what a comfort your letter was. I am waiting to hear about the card which you must have received by now. I embrace you tenderly.

Your friend PAGANINI

While Germi could trace, almost day by day, his friend's path through the gloomy maze he had to tread, the dying maestro was still clinging to life and refusing obstinately to see the priests. Was he really so desperately ill? He would make his own peace with God.

"*Santo Iddio!*" he exclaimed at the end of an ominous week, "*Santo Iddio*, my strength is at an end."

In the month of May, when Nice was a bower of flowers and perfumes, Paganini, speechless, convulsed, and icy-cold, was gradually becoming incapable of moving. As a child he had been subject to attacks of catalepsy, which resembled death.

"According to my patient's account," wrote Dr. Bennati, "when he was a child, his grief-stricken family thought that he was dead. He was already wrapped in his shroud and was about to be placed in the coffin, when a slight movement revealed to those present that he was still alive."

Swimming up from those mysterious deeps, like a diver who still bore on his person the traces of the phosphorescent waters, he had brought light to dark nights of war, plague, and misery. But now, in the fragrant springtime, there was none to pluck him from his shroud.

During the night of the 27th, after the servants had left him, Achillino was watching by his father's bedside, nursing him as he had done in childhood. A light streamed into the room which was so penetrating that the eyes of the dying man half opened. Through the open window, the brilliant full moon was flooding the room with radiance, which enveloped the maestro and his son.

So intense was this stream of pearly, dead-white light, that Achillino, who, to his joy, had just succeeded in pouring a little liquid down his patient's throat, had the illusion that his father had suddenly recovered the use of his limbs and that they were carrying him to a land where the river banks were discoveries, the forests memories.

The trees in the garden quivered, all silver in the moonlight. They whispered to him all his past life. But there were also rocks in that place, rocks with faces that killed, and a crazy architecture: illuminated palaces with demons clustering on the balconies, bidding defiance to the cathedrals.

Was it San Lorenzo? The images on the church began to fade. Slender hands, or, rather, long, hairy paws, stretched out and tried to climb up the bars of light that fell through the window like so many cords. They would seize him by the throat at last.

Who was this dreamer who cried out in his sleep with the death-rattle in his throat? He was seized with a fit of coughing, a final spasm. It was as if an iron hand were clutching him and strangling him. Then, as in those distant days in the cathedral in Genoa, when the boy, overcome by the cataract of sound that poured from the organ, gradually lost consciousness, he rolled his eyes upwards. At that moment a ray of moonlight glided across the violin which was hanging on the wall above the bed. Achillino saw the Guarnerius del Gesù looming in the shadow, bridge, finger-board, and strings, while two dying hands tried in vain to reach it.

CHARON'S BARQUE

> At his own request, I make no mention here of my old friend Germi. I beg my son to follow his counsels. I wish all ceremonies to be dispensed with at my funeral, and I desire that no musician shall write a Requiem for me. A hundred masses are to be said for me at the Capuchins. I bequeath my violin to the city of Genoa to be preserved there forever. I commit my soul to the infinite mercy of my Creator.
> This is my last will and testament.
>
> Genoa, April 27, 1837

SUCH were his dying wishes. Achillino was his sole heir, and the Marquess Lorenzo Pareto was appointed to be his guardian. According to the *Gazette du Midi*, Paganini left between £120,000 and £160,000, but actually the amount was about £80,000, sterling.* It consisted partly in real estate, partly in French, English, and Sicilian Government bonds. There were two legacies to be paid out of the estate, one of £3,000 and one of £2,000, to his sisters. An annuity of £48 was settled on La Bianchi, another of £248 on "a lady in Lucca." Lazzaro Rebizzo, his cousin, and his friends Giordano and Pietro Torregiani, were appointed executors. His famous Guarnerius del Gesù was bequeathed to the city of Genoa. No mention was made of his other instruments.

When the news of Paganini's death had spread abroad, dense crowds invaded Count de Cessoles's house, which the maestro had never left again. Chattering in the accents of the South, they filed past the bier, on which the body of Paganini, embalmed, swathed in linen, and wearing all his decorations, was lying in state. Already it was bearing the weight of a new

* Grove's *Dictionary of Music and Musicians*.

246

anathema. In view of his record and the fact that he had died without receiving the sacraments, the Archbishop of Nice, Monsignor Galvano, had formally forbidden any religious form of burial. The bells, which had already begun to toll his knell, were silenced by his order.

The news was like a trail of gunpowder. The whole matter was passionately debated by partisans on either side. As they gazed on that face, with its diabolical sneer, and the waxen cheeks with their deep furrows, the common people were carried away once more by superstitious horror. The dead man wore on his head a turban of Madras muslin with curiously shaped corners, which in the flickering light of the candles threw strange and terrifying shadows. Women shrieked as they filed past, while even some of the men were seen to faint. All demanded that the coffin should be provided with a glass lid, which would enable them to gaze at their ease at this musician, who had been the devil incarnate.

While the clergy persisted in their refusal to allow him Christian burial, the friends of Paganini mustered around Achillino and Germi, who were supported by Count de Cessoles, President of the Royal Senate at Nice, and Count de Maistre, Governor of the Province. They decided to carry the war into the proper quarter, in order to obtain a few square feet of consecrated ground.

The task was a difficult one. This last case that Germi was to conduct for his friend, which concerned the salvation of his soul and his final absolution, was the hardest he had ever fought for him. The Archbishop, it was said, had already been approached when the legendary figure of the dying maestro had arrived in Nice. Appalled at his scandalous past, Monsignor Galvano had instructed Father Pietro Caffarelli, canon and confessor and theologian of St. Réparatrice, the parish in which the sinner was residing, to undertake this formidable conversion. The canon's report was horrifying in the extreme.

"Paganini was a good Catholic," his advocates maintained, in an appeal which they addressed to the Archbishop. His last will and testament, the education he gave his son, that son's first communion, proved it. And there was the testimony of one of his servants, Francesca Gigli, "La Gigli," as he called her. This maid had for a long time been in the habit of serving the sick man with fish on Fridays, and she had heard him say to Achillino and a friend, who had just come back from Mass: "Bravo, my children."

"I said the *De Profundis* with him and his son," Francesca continued, "and he was overjoyed when the boy translated the Psalms to him."

The other servant, Teresa Repetto, however, who had been won over by Caffarelli, the confessor, expatiated on Paganini's dislike for that priest. As soon as the Canon entered the room he had facetiously begun the conversation with the words:

"*Ah! Ah! Moussu Paganini, a hura, es plus l'oura de sonna lo zon-zon!* (It's no time now to be fiddling.)"

Paganini withered him with a glance and drove him out. But he returned to the attack again and again, until finally the door was slammed in his face by the master's order. She herself was beaten and turned out of the house by Paganini when she tried to introduce the Father to Achillino. But all the witnesses agreed that at their last meeting, Paganini, in exasperation, promised by a gesture, since he could not speak, to write his confession on a slate, which he asked one of his intimate friends, Tito Rubaudo, the advocate, to bring to him.

"With an expressive gesture of the hand," said Rubaudo, "he gave me to understand that when his confessor had learned all there was to know about his sins, he would quickly rub the slate clean and proceed to do his part."

But Rubaudo had not realized that the matter was urgent, and the slate was never brought to Paganini, because of the alternate phases of somnolence and nervous irritability that had possessed him, until the final crisis had suddenly supervened.

For his part, Caffarelli had rested on his laurels after this partial victory. He added that on the occasion of his last visit, Paganini had fixed him with a sidelong and disdainful glance and had ended by telling him bluntly and repeatedly to "clear out," as he had bored him long enough.

"How could Paganini, who had no voice and no strength whatever, utter threats and beat a servant?" the opposite side objected.

Caffarelli remarked that he had never been able to observe in the sick man any "sentiment or word becoming a Christian," nor had he ever seen in his possession any religious emblem. On the contrary, in the ante-chamber he had noticed "four indecent pictures, one of them a Venus in the most indelicate attitude." These obscene pictures proved to be copies of masterpieces, which were in the Farnese Museum and in the Vatican. Moreover, when the executors removed the seals, they found no less than "two crucifixes, three madonnas," etc.

"In an access of diabolical fanaticism," Count de Cessoles, who had taken Achillino into his house, protested pathetically, "his persecutors talk of depositing Paganini's remains at dead of night in the bed of a torrent. The hearts of all good men must bleed at the idea of Paganini's mortal remains having the Paglione * for a tomb."

"It behoves his own country," the petition ended, "to offer a resting place in consecrated earth to her famous son, whose last act was to dedicate to her, as a tribute of love, that instrument of his glory, his wonderful violin, which has roused the admiration and enthusiasm of all Europe. In days to come the world will ask: Where is Paganini's tomb?"

To make it possible to wait for a solution, it was decided to carry out a more thorough embalming of the maestro's body.

* A torrent in the neighbourhood of Nice.

It was proposed to appeal, simultaneously, to the Metropolitan of Genoa and King Charles-Albert, to allow the body to be brought to Genoa and interred there.

This filial appeal to Genoa the Superb touched the King, who sought to reconcile his religious sentiments and respect for the Church with his desire to render homage to Genoa's illustrious son. While lending his support to the petition addressed to the Archbishop of Genoa, Monsignor Tadini, he suggested that the maestro's remains should be secretly deposited in some non-Catholic burial ground, such as the Protestant cemetery, to await the Bishop's reply, according to which he could be either buried with proper funeral rites or be transferred secretly to the villa Gajona near Parma.

In the meantime the executors, who had collected fresh evidence, appealed from the judgment of Monsignor Galvano to the Royal Senate at Nice. Families were divided by passionate debates concerning the salvation of this man who had been possessed of the devil and still troubled the world of the living. Monsignor Tadini's reply was debated before it was received. But it was not long delayed. The Archbishop of Genoa categorically upheld the decision of the Archbishop of Nice.

There was no unconsecrated burial ground in Genoa, and the Protestants refused to accept the body of the magician. Besides the notoriously dissolute life of the dead man, his refusal of the sacraments was a "public scandal, which was all the more serious and more flagrant because of his celebrity. The pernicious effect that it was bound to have on religion, should funeral rites be accorded to this unbeliever, seemed more than sufficient justification for the course that had been adopted."

The canons, therefore, refused *ipso jure*. They were adamant.

In October 1841, after both petitions had been rejected, Achillino, accompanied by the Marchese Pareto, his guardian, and Castellini, his lawyer, arrived in Rome. This time he intended to refer the matter to the "capital of the Catholic world." Pope Gregory XVI quashed the judgment of the two prelates and appointed a new commission to make searching inquiries into the religious convictions of the deceased. All the witnesses, including Paganini's chemist and confessor, were summoned again in an attempt to clear up this case, which had been conducted in such a "Machiavellian manner." More and more evidence was piled up, but nothing came of it, and one by one the winter months slipped away.

One day in April a certain barque hoisted sail off the coast of Nice, and without attracting attention, put out to sea. Paganini had once visualized himself as a second Leander, crossing the Atlantic to meet another Hero. The fancy had seemed reality, but now the reality had a legendary air.

We bear witness that, in this port of Nice, the remains of the late Baron Paganini, duly embalmed according to the correct formula, have been placed on board the sailing barque *Maria-Maddalena* of Sardinia (Master: Gio-Baptista Rasteu), which is bound for Genoa. The remains were deposited in a zinc case, which was hermetically sealed and enclosed in a second case of walnut, which in its turn was placed in a coffin of white wood, in the form of a parallelepiped, marked on the outside with the letters M.D.S. (Magistrats de la Santé, Public Health Department). The barque has left Nice for Genoa, where the coffin will be immediately transferred to the Villa Paganini at Polcevera. We call upon all magistrates, sanitary inspectors and other officers of the Health Department, not to offer any let or hindrance to this transaction.

Following the example of the civil authorities in Nice, the officials in Genoa carried out the customs formalities with the utmost despatch and secrecy, so that the people should have no inkling of what was going on. They were already asking, indeed, noisily demanding to know, where Paganini's body had been hidden between May 1840, the time of his death, and April 17,

1844, the date of the sailing certificate of the barque *Maria-Maddalena*. Shelterless, driven from its last refuge, what had become of it?

According to the recollections of old inhabitants of Nice, in May 1840, after the crowds had at last departed from the house of Count de Cessoles, a leaden silence enveloped it. No one cared to venture near it after nightfall, and there were certain manifestations which sorely tried the nerves of the occupants. There were lights that came and went suddenly, dazzling the beholder. Groans were heard. Snatches of music escaped beyond the walls. At last, one moonless night, the measured, soldierlike tread of men carrying a heavy burden echoed through the house.

It was thought that the remains had been hidden in the dark cellars of the Hospital, which night after night were the scene of a Witches' Sabbath that terrified the passers-by. Here an unsuccessful search for the body had been made. Next, it was said, to avert ill luck, it had been flung into one of the huge vats into which the débris of the olives is thrown after the oil has been extracted. From this hiding-place, Count de Cessoles himself was believed to have removed it, and to have transferred it either to his own estate at Cap St. Jean, or to the Hospital at Villefranche, or to the park of the Count de Pierlas at St. Jean-Cap-Ferrat. No one could be positive, because he had employed four taciturn peasants,* who kept their own counsel. While they were carrying out their task, there had been a raging storm, which had smothered every sound. The site was close

---

* Actually the Count of Pierlas, the Count of Cocconato, the sculptor Alexis de Saint-Marc, and the painter Felix Ziem. Ziem was at that time twenty. Three years before, when Paganini was passing through Dijon, on his way from Turin to Paris, he had seen and heard him at a private reception. "With his violin," he said, "he filled my head with Scenes of Venice." (Maurice Barrès, *Du sang, de la volupté et de la mort.* Appendix.)

to the sea, which deluged the workers with blinding spray, so that they could never find the exact spot again.

Others believed that the body of the accursed Genoese had found a refuge on one of the Lérin Isles in the Mediterranean. It had been placed on board a ship, but when the captain was refused admission to the Port of Genoa, he had disembarked the coffin and hastily buried it on the little island of St. Ferréol. Later, another mysterious vessel had removed it from this purple crag. Where the body rested there still remains a yawning chasm, known locally as Paganini's Hole. Literature, too, has endorsed it:

"As we draw near the Ile St. Honorat," wrote Maupassant,* "we pass close by a naked red rock, bristling like a porcupine, so uneven, so armed with teeth and spikes and claws as to render walking on it almost impossible. You have to pick your way between these defences and advance with caution. It is called St. Ferréol. A little soil, come from no one knows where, has accumulated in the holes and crannies of the rock, and out of it have sprung varieties of lily and a charming blue iris of a tint that seems to be derived direct from heaven.

"It is on this curious reef, lying in the open sea, that the body of Paganini was buried and remained concealed for five years. So strange a fate was worthy of that weird genius, so grotesque in his gestures, frame and physiognomy, that he was believed to be possessed of the devil. His super-human talent and excessive emaciation made of him a legendary being."

❡ In the meantime, on April 22, 1844, after touching, in all probability, at Bordighera, San Remo, Port Maurice, Savone, etc., the *Maria-Maddalena*, with all her lights extinguished, tied up at the same quay where formerly Antonio Paganini corded bales for America. Thanks to the precautions that were taken, no one suspected that, beneath the conven-

* *Sur l'eau. Études.*

tional wrappings, the dead Orpheus was returning home. That same evening he was deposited in the family villa at Polcevera. If he might not lie in hallowed ground, he would at least find rest in his own domain.

Then the trouble began again. His own countrymen were terrified to hear strange and mournful sounds haunting the little house. It was impossible to keep him there. Soon afterwards Marie-Louise gave permission for his return to the Duchy of Parma, where he found a more hospitable refuge in the Villa Gajona. It was said that the body had been interred in one of the most private corners of the park. Achillino lived on in the villa. At first he was surrounded by sympathetic friends. Gradually, however, these fell away and he was left alone, with only his dead father for company. But Paganini had been a Chevalier of the Order of St. George. Thanks to this distinction, in 1853, after eight years of this mournful *tête-à-tête*, Achillino obtained permission for a preliminary religious service to be held at the Steccata of Parma, a church belonging to that Order of Chivalry.

❨ 1875. Years had passed. At the age of fifty, Achillino was still hoping for a pardon for the soul of his father. In spite of a happy marriage and a carefree existence, he was a melancholy man. He paced the alleys of the Villa Gajona, reflecting that of all who had struggled to obtain that pardon, none survived; neither Lazzaro Rebizzo, nor Count de Cessoles, nor Germi, "the adorable friend." Only he and his eldest son, Attila Paganini, were there to receive in the following year the decree from Rome, reversing the verdict. At last Paganini was to be allowed to repose in consecrated earth. They arranged the funeral procession, which they hoped would be the final one, to the cemetery of Parma. Torches preceded it and the whole population followed the bier along the steep banks of the Baganza.

1893. One last rival of Paganini's, the violinist Ondriceck of Prague, crossed the Alps, eager to render homage to the maestro, who had been the supreme virtuoso of the century. The old Baron received his guest with due solemnity. Together they went to the cemetery and Achillino had the coffin opened. They gazed, fascinated, upon the body of the magician, which had crumbled away in its mouldering dress of ceremony. The enigmatical features were still intact. On his breast were his innumerable, many-coloured decorations. Would they never suffice to pay Charon's toll?

1896. Twenty years after his tumultuous homecoming, it seemed that Paganini was once more to be condemned to wander before he could attain the grace of eternal repose. It was officially announced that, after long debate, the Municipality of Parma had decided to transfer the cemetery from its present position to a new site. Contractors and stone masons had already been engaged.

It was spring, and the transfer was facilitated by the softness of the earth. The young leaves were out; a warm wind wafted the perfume of violets and narcissi, which were crowded together to make room for the new arrivals. The flowers were on good terms with the dead. Their mauve and white symbolized secret prayers and secret solaces. Some day the stone that imprisoned the dead would have to release its victims.

Here in the new *Campo-Santo* of Palermo, in a landscape enveloped in a bluish haze, stands a monument of geometrical design, which is built of granite from Lake Maggiore. It is clearly visible from afar and towers haughtily above the tombs, as if in protest against the excessive sweetness of that smiling prospect. The following inscription is deeply engraved in the granite:

HIS SON ACHILLINO OF PALERMO
'RAISED THIS MONUMENT
TO HIS IMPERISHABLE MEMORY

Above it his armorial bearings and eulogistic phrases are recorded.

At one side is carved the legend:

NICOLÒ PAGANINI WHO DREW FROM THE VIOLIN
DIVINE MUSIC

Around the tomb, light as the tiny waves that ripple over the surface of the water, delicate grasses sway in the breeze, cradling at last the body of one who was believed by many to have been possessed of the devil.

APPENDIX

Op. 1 *Twenty-four Caprices* for solo violin. Published by Ricordi. Milan. 1820.

Op. 2 *Six Sonatas* for violin and guitar, or violin and piano. Published by Ricordi.

Op. 3 *Six Sonatas* for violin and guitar, or violin and piano. (Dedicated to Maître Dellepiane.) Published by Ricordi and by Breitkopf and Haertel. Paris. 1851.

Op. 4 *Three Quartets* (VII, VIII, IX) for violin, viola, violoncello, and guitar. (Dedicated to Catherine Raggi Pallavicini, Filippo Carrega, Luigi-Guglielmo Germi.) Published by Ricordi.

Op. 5 *Three Quartets* for violin, viola, guitar, and violoncello. Published by Ricordi.

Op. 6 *First Concerto*, in E flat, for violin and orchestra. (First posthumous work.) Published by Schott and Co. Paris. 1851.

Op. 7 *Second Concerto*, in B minor, for violin and orchestra. Published by Schoenenberger.

Op. 8 *Le Streghe* (The Witches' Dance), for violin and orchestra. Published by Schoenenberger.

Op. 9 *Variations on "God save the King."* Composed in Vienna in 1828. Published by Schoenenberger.

Op. 10 *Variations on the Air "Oh mamma, mamma cara,"* from the *Carnaval de Venise.* Published by Schoenenberger.

Op. 11 *Sonata Mouvement Perpétuel,* better known as *Moto perpetuo.* Published by Schoenenberger.

Op. 12 Introduction and Variations on the Air *Non più mesta accanto al fuoco,* from *La Cenerentola,* by Rossini.

* According to the classification established by A. Codignola (*Paganini intimo*). Published by the Municipality of Genoa, 1935.

Op. 13 *I Palpiti* for violin and orchestra. Introduction and variations on the air *Di tanti Palpiti*, from *Tancredi*, by Rossini.

Op. 14 Variations on *Baruccaba* for violin and guitar. Dedicated to Luigi-Guglielmo Germi. Published by Schoenenberger.

Compositions for solo violin, or with a bass

Op. 15 *Three Ritournelles* for violin and double bass.
Op. 16 *Three Duets* for violin and violoncello. Dedicated to Paganini's admirers.
Op. 17 *Cantabile* for violin and piano.
Op. 18 *Nicolò Paganini to Monsieur Henri Bonaventura.* (Larghetto, Allegro, Più Mosso.)
Op. 19 *Cantabile Valzo.* Dedicated to Camillo Sivori.
Op. 20 *Sonata for solo violin.* (Adagio, Allegro.) Dedicated to the Princess Elisa Bacciochi. *Duo Merveille* or *Une Merveille de Paganini*, for solo violin.

Violin and Orchestra

Op. 21 *Pot-pourri.* (Introduction, Maestoso, Andantino with variations and Finale.)
Op. 22 *Sonate Militaire.* (Introduction, [Allegro] Moderato, [Largamente], Maestoso, Andante con Variazioni, Finale.)
Op. 23 *St. Patrick's Day.*
Op. 24 *Sonate à Preghiera.* Composed in 1828.
Op. 25 *Sonate amoureuse et galante.* (Allegro giusto, Adagio cantabile, with Recitativo assoluto and Più Mosso.)
Op. 26 *Sonata and Polonaise*, with variations. Accompaniment of two violins, two clarinets, violoncello, double bass, and viola in the "*canzonetta.*" Composed in Milan, in 1827.
Op. 27 *Noble Sonate Sentimentale.* (Introduction, Allegro agitato, Hymn and Variations.) The theme is that of the Austrian national anthem, by Joseph Haydn. Composed in Vienna in 1828.

Op. 28 *Polonaise* with Variations.

Op. 29 *Sonata* with five Variations. Composed in Naples in 1826.

Op. 30 *The Spring.* (Introduction, Larghetto cantabile amoroso, Recitativo, Andante con variazioni.)

Op. 31 *Napoleon.* First Sonata for violin and orchestra on the 4th string. (Introduction, Larghetto, Andante giocoso, Three Variations, Finale.) Composed at the Court of Lucca, in 1805.

Op. 65 *Marie-Louise.* Sonata with variations on the G string. Note on the violin part by the composer: "With accompaniment of two violins, viola, violoncello, double bass, two oboes, and two horns, composed by N. P. on one string."

Op. 32 *Warsaw Sonata.* (Allegro vivo, Dolente, Sostenuto Allegro, Thème Polonais en Andantino, Seven Variations, Finale presto.)

Op. 33 *Tarantelle* for violin and orchestra.

Op. 34 *Ballet champêtre* for violin and orchestra.

Op. 35 *Sonata for viola.* (Introduction, Larghetto with Recitative with viola solo, Presto, Andante sostenuto and Cantabile, Theme and Variations.) Composed in London in 1834.

Op. 36 *The Tempest* for violin and orchestra. (Prélude en ouragan, Primo tempo, beginning of the tempest; the stormy sea, prayer, the hurricane, the height of the storm, calm, Finale brillant.) Composed in Vienna in 1828.

Op. 37 *The Convent of St. Bernard, Pendule* for violin and orchestra. (Sonnette [introduction], Andante Sonnolento [*pendule*], Minuetto [Moderato], Dawn [lento], Larghetto, Maestoso con variazioni, Rondo.)

Op. 38 *Sonate Appasionata* for violin and orchestra. (Introduction, Larghetto appasionato, Allegro vivace, Variazioni, Finale presto and prestissimo.)
Nel car più non mi sento for violin and orchestra.

Compositions for solo guitar

Op. 39 *Grand Sonata.* (Allegro risoluto, Romance, Amorosamente, Andantino variato, Scherzando.)

Op. 40. *Minuet*. Dedicated to "Signora Dida."

Op. 41 *Guitare Martiale*.

Op. 42 *Compositions variées pour guitare*. (Andantino, Minuetto, Allegro, Andantino, Minuetto, Andantino, Finale for French guitar.)

Op. 43 *Two Minuets* for guitar. Dedicated to Emilia di Negri.

Op. 44 *Caprice* for guitar.

Op. 45 *Sonata* for guitar.

Op. 46 *Minuets*. Dedicated to Marina Banti.

Op. 47 *Sonatina*.

Op. 48 *Minuets*.

Op. 49⎫
Op. 50⎬ *Miscellaneous Compositions*.
Op. 51⎭

Op. 52 *Minuet*. Dedicated to "Signora Dida."

Op. 53 *Miscellaneous Compositions*. (Valzo, Andantino, Rondocino.)

Op. 55 *Two Minuets* for guitar, violin and viola.

Op. 56 *Three Minuets and a Waltz* for guitar.

Op. 57 *Sonatina and Minuets* for guitar.

Op. 58 *Sinfonia ludovisia* for guitar.

Op. 59 *Short pieces* for guitar. (Minuet, Valzo, Cantabile quasi Allegro and Valzo andantino.)

Duets for Violin and Guitar

Op. 60 *Six Duets* for violin and guitar. Probably written for Camillo Sivori.

Op. 61 *Sonate Concertante* for guitar and violin. Dedicated to Emilia di Negri.

Op. 62 *Canzonetta*.

Op. 63 *Duetto Amoroso*. (Beginning, Entreaty, Timidity, Content, Quarrel, Peace, Pledge of love, Warning of departure.) Dedicated "to a lady of high lineage."

Op. 64 *Cento of Sonatas* for violin and guitar (18 pieces).

Trios for instruments played with the bow, and the guitar

Op. 66   *Trio* for violin, violoncello, and guitar.
Op. 67   *Two Trios* for two violins and guitar.
Op. 68   *Trio* for viola, guitar, and violoncello.
Op. 69   *Serenade* for viola, violoncello, and guitar. Dedicated to Domenica Paganini.

Quartets for instruments played with the bow, and the guitar

Op. 70   *Second Quartet* for violin, viola, guitar, and violoncello. In four time. Dedicated to Luigi-Guglielmo Germi.
Op. 71   *Seventh Quartet* for violin, viola, guitar, and violoncello. In four time. Dedicated to the Marquise Catherine Raggi Pallavicini.
Op. 72   *Eighth Quartet* for violin, viola, guitar, and violoncello. In four time. Dedicated to the Marquis Philippe Carrega.
Op. 73   *Ninth Quartet* for violin, viola, guitar, and violoncello. Dedicated to Luigi-Guglielmo Germi.
Op. 74 ⎤
Op. 75 ⎥ *Four Quartets* (10th, 12th, 13th, 14th). In four time. Dedicated to Luigi-Guglielmo Germi.
Op. 76 ⎥
Op. 77 ⎦

String Quartets

Op. 78   *Three Quartets* for two violins, viola, and violoncello. Dedicated to the King of Sardinia.

Vocal Music

Op. 79   *Caprice Vocal.* Written in 1823.

BIBLIOGRAPHY

Antologia (Nuova) (139). *La vita e l'arte di Nicolò Paganini,* (Manassero.)

E. ANDERS. *Nicolò Paganini, sa vie, sa personne et quelques mots sur son secret.* (Delaunay, Paris, 1831.)

A. ARNYVELDE. *La Question de l'Opéra en 1831.*

BELGRANO. *Imbreviatura,* 1822. Genoa, Tipografia del 1st. Sordomuti.

O. BRUNI. *Nicolò Paganini.* (Firenze, 1904.)

BERLIOZ. *Correspondance inédite. Mémoires.* (Paris.)

BONAVENTURA. *Paganini.* (Modena Formiggini, 1911.)

R. DE BEAUVOIR. *L'Opéra.* (G. Havard, Paris.)

A. BACHMANN. *Les Grands violonistes du passé.* (Paris, Fischbacher, 1913.)

M. BARRÈS. *Du sang, de la volupté et de la mort.* (Plon, Paris.)

G. CONESTABILE. *Vita di Nicolò Paganini.* (Perugia, 1851.)

A. CODIGNOLA. *Paganini intimo.* (Genoa, 1935.)

E. R. CURTIUS. *Balzac.* (Paris, Grasset.)

LISZT À LA MARA. *Lettres.* (Breitkopf und Härtel, Leipzig.)

P. HEDOUIN. *La Mosaïque.* (Boulogne-sur-Mer, 1856.)

B. DE MIRAMON FITZ-JAMES. *Paganini à Marseille.* (1941, Fuéria, Marseille.)

METTERNICH. *Mémoires.* (Plon, Paris, 1881.)

A. NIGGLI. *Nicolò Paganini.* (Leipzig, 1892.)

G. NICOLAI. *Arabesken für Musikfreunde.* (Leipzig, 1835.)

J. G. PRODHOMME. *Paganini.* (Laurens, Paris, 1927.)

EL. POLKO. *Paganini und die Geigenbauer.* (Leipzig, 1875.)

M. REUSCHEL. *Un violoniste en voyage.*

STENDHAL. *Vie de Rossini.* (Paris, Michel-Lévy, 1854.)

SPOHR. *Selbstbiographie.* (Cassel, Wigand, 1860.)

J. M. Schottky. *Paganini's Leben und Treiben als Künstler und als Mensch.* (Prag. J. G. Calve, 1830.)

H. Vieuxtemps. *Gesammelte Schriften.*

Dr. Véron. *Mémoires d'un Bourgeois de Paris.* (Paris, Librairie Nouvelle, 1856.)

J. Wasielewski. *Die Violine und ihre Meister.* (1893.)

S. Zweig. *Marceline Desbordes-Valmore.* (Nouvelle Revue Critique.)

Gazette Musicale de Leipzig. 1830. No. 20.

La Farfalla. Bologne, 1840.

Mémoires. (Manuscrit anonyme.) Musée du Thêâtre de Trieste cité par Codignola: *Paganini Intimo.*

Lord Derwent. *Rossini.* (N.R.F., 1937.)

L. Day. *Nicolò Paganini, of Genoa.* (New York, Macaulay, 1929.)

L. Escudier. *Mes souvenirs. Les virtuoses.* (Paris, Dentu, 1868.) *Vie et aventures des cantatrices célèbres suivies de la vie anecdotique de Paganini.* (1856.)

F. Fayolle. *Paganini et de Bériot.* (Paris, 1831. Legouest.)

F. J. Fétis. *Notice biographique sur Nicolò Paganini.* (Paris, Schœnenberger, 1851.)

Grove. *Musical Dictionary.*

Goethe und Zelter (*Briefwechsel zwischen*). (Berlin, Duncker und Humblot, 1833–1834.)

Gentil. (Manuscrit.) *Mémoires d'une habilleuse.*

Guhr. *L'Art de jouer du violon de Paganini.* (Paris, Schott, 1831.)

G. Harrys. *Paganini in seinem Reisewagen und Zimmer.* (Braunschweig Viewig, 1830.)

R. D'Harcourt. *Goethe et l'art de vivre.*

H. Heine. *Nuits florentines.* (Paris, Mercure de France.)

G. Imbert de Laphalèque. *Notice sur le célèbre violoniste, Nicolò Paganini.* (Paris, Guyot, 1830.)

Ed. Istel. *The secret of Paganini's technique.*

J. Kapp. *Paganini.* (Schuster und Loeffer, 1913, Berlin et Leipzig.)

Lamothe-Langon (Comtesse de). *Révélations d'une femme de qualité sur les années 1830 et 1831.* (Bruxelles, Haumann & Co.)

Revue et Gazette Musicale. (Années de 1829 à 1835.)

264   BIBLIOGRAPHY

Revue de Paris. (Années 1831–1832.)

Autographes. Analysés par la Maison Chavaray, 3, rue de Fursten-
berg, Paris.

INDEX

ABOUT THE AUTHOR

Renée de Saussine was born at Boisclaireau, her grand-mother's château in the west of France and spent her summers there as a girl. Her parents' home in Paris was a gathering place for many of the writers and musicians of the day—Marcel Proust, Gabriel Fauré, Darius Milhaud, Francis Poulenc, Maurice Ravel, and many others. Thus Miss de Saussine came naturally by her love of music. She studied violin with Eugène Ysaye, Jacques Thibaud, and Sergei Prokofiev, and appeared in concerts in Europe and South America. In addition to her biography of Paganini, Miss de Saussine has also written several novels. She lives in Paris and spends her summers in a villa near Dieppe.